The
Series

Derek Tidball (Bible Themes)

The Message of
the Holy Spirit

The Bible Speaks Today: Bible Themes series

The Message of the Holy Spirit

The Spirit of encounter

Keith Warrington

Vice-Principal and Director of Doctoral Studies,
Regents Theological College, West Malvern, Worcestershire

Inter-Varsity Press

INTER-VARSITY PRESS
Norton Street, Nottingham NG7 3HR, England
Email: ivp@ivpbooks.com
Website: www.ivpbooks.com

First published 2009

British Library Cataloguing in Publication Data
A catalogue record for this book is available from the British Library.

ISBN 978-1-84474-397–1

Set in Stempel Garamond
Typeset in Great Britain by Servis Filmsetting Ltd, Stockport, Cheshire
Printed and bound in Great Britain by Ashford Colour Press Ltd, Gosport, Hampshire

Inter-Varsity Press publishes Christian books that are true to the Bible and that communicate the gospel, develop discipleship and strengthen the church for its mission in the world.

Inter-Varsity Press is closely linked with the Universities and Colleges Christian Fellowship, a student movement connecting Christian Unions in universities and colleges throughout Great Britain, and a member movement of the International Fellowship of Evangelical Students. Website: www.uccf.org.uk

Contents

BST | The Bible Speaks Today

GENERAL PREFACE

THE BIBLE SPEAKS TODAY describes three series of expositions, based on the books of the Old and New Testaments, and on Bible themes that run through the whole of Scripture. Each series is characterized by a threefold ideal:

- to expound the biblical text with accuracy
- to relate it to contemporary life, and
- to be readable.

These books are, therefore, not 'commentaries', for the commentary seeks rather to elucidate the text than to apply it, and tends to be a work rather of reference than of literature. Nor, on the other hand, do they contain the kinds of 'sermons' that attempt to be contemporary and readable without taking Scripture seriously enough. The contributors to *The Bible Speaks Today* series are all united in their convictions that God still speaks through what he has spoken, and that nothing is more necessary for the life, health and growth of Christians than that they should hear what the Spirit is saying to them through his ancient – yet ever modern – Word.

ALEC MOTYER
JOHN STOTT
DEREK TIDBALL
Series editors

Author's preface

The omniscient Spirit is available to guide believers as they gaze at God. He beckons them to come ever closer to him. He encourages them to take pleasure in the benefits of the remarkable salvation provided by Jesus. He is the one who takes the inexplicable gift of eternal life and makes it theirs to enjoy. Without him, we would have little. With him, we have more than we need. He is the smiling face of God to us who chooses to live in the centre of our lives. He blesses us with his presence and graces us with his gifts.

I hope that this book will be an enjoyable and rewarding journey in partnership with the Bible and the Spirit. It is my prayer that you will be more closely drawn to him as the Spirit's closeness to you becomes more apparent as he is explored through these pages. I dedicate it to all those who are on a journey with the Spirit and who wish to relate to him at deeper levels of experience. May your encounters with the Spirit be a constant cause for wonder and worship.

I am grateful to all who have helped me in my adventure with the Spirit. To my undergraduate and postgraduate students at Regents Theological College, England, including my students who have, with reference to the Spirit, begun to tread where few others have gone before. In all our studies together, as we have gazed at the Spirit, we have found fresh delights. I am also grateful to my Research Assistant, Dr Timothy Walsh, Dr Philip Duce (Theological Books Editor, IVP) and Dr Derek Tidball (BST Themes Series Editor) who have checked for errors and improved my style. My wife, Judy, who is my constant friend and guide, is a gift of the Spirit to me and an integral support to my mission in life. Even though she has a busy life of her own, she has read the text and contributed to the discussion throughout. Finally, I am grateful most of all to the Spirit who has allowed us with our fragile minds to explore him and has been prepared to help us as we do. We will continue the quest in eternity but I am grateful for the opportunity to commence it now.

Chief abbreviations

ESV	English Standard Version
KJV	King James Version
LXX	Septuagint
M.	Mishnah
NASB	New American Standard Bible
NIV	New International Version
NT	New Testament
OT	Old Testament
RSV	Revised Standard Version

Bibliography

T. G. Brown, *Spirit in the Writings of John* (T. & T. Clark, 2003).

G. D. Fee, *God's Empowering Presence* (Hendrickson, 1994).

G. D. Fee, *Listening to the Spirit in the Text* (Eerdmans, 2000).

S. Ferguson, *The Holy Spirit* (IVP, 1996).

A. Heron, *The Holy Spirit* (Marshall, Morgan and Scott, 1983).

C. S. Keener, *The Spirit in the Gospels and Acts* (Hendrickson, 1997).

R. P. Menzies, *The Development of Early Christian Pneumatology* (Sheffield Academic Press, 1991).

M. W. Mittelstadt, *The Spirit and Suffering in Luke-Acts* (Sheffield Academic Press, 2004).

C. H. Pinnock, *Flame of Love. A Theology of the Holy Spirit* (InterVarsity Press, 1996).

J. B. Shelton, *Mighty in Word and Deed. The Role of the Holy Spirit in Luke-Acts* (Hendrickson, 1991).

T. Smail, *The Giving Gift. The Holy Spirit in Person* (Darton, Longman and Todd, 1994).

R. Stronstad, *The Charismatic Theology of St. Luke* (Hendrickson, 1984).

M. M. B. Turner, *The Holy Spirit and Spiritual Gifts Then and Now* (Paternoster Press, 1996).

K. Warrington, *Discovering the Spirit in the New Testament* (Hendrickson, 2005).

K. Warrington, *Pentecostal Theology: A Theology of Encounter* (T. & T. Clark, 2008).

Introduction

The Holy Spirit has, to a large degree, received limited comment in comparison to the published material exploring the Father and Jesus. This can be attributed to a number of reasons. There is not a great deal of specific information concerning the Spirit in the OT where the Spirit and God are often viewed synonymously (Job 27:3; Ps. 33:6; 104:29–30). Furthermore, it is sometimes difficult to determine if the Hebrew word *rûaḥ* refers to the Spirit or the wind, for it can be translated as both. The fact that when the Spirit is mentioned in the OT it is in connection with his influencing only a small number of people also undermines his significance in the minds of many believers today. As a result, they have not realised his full potential for them.

This restriction in the OT is emphasized, in that the Spirit mainly inspires important leaders (including judges and kings) or those with special tasks rather than ordinary folk. It is generally men who are chosen and empowered by him. Likewise, only the covenant people of God are anticipated as being able to benefit from his resources. This limitation has led some to believe that he functions similarly today with regard to believers. However, this is not the case. Furthermore, in the OT era, personal empowering by the Spirit was intended only to be for a temporary period until the prescribed task had been completed; and the intended commissions were somewhat limited, mainly relating to prophecy or leadership or both. Although enduements of power were anticipated in the future, these were assumed to be for God's people. Finally, there was no Jewish expectation that Messiah would impart the Spirit though they did anticipate that he would be anointed with the Spirit (Isa. 61:1–3). Thus, most Israelites were not expecting a personal infusion of the Spirit into their lives, even when Messiah came. Many believers today have assumed the same or have not anticipated a life-changing encounter with the Spirit.

It is in the NT that the Spirit is presented more clearly, and

11

identified as being available to all believers from salvation. From thereon, the NT writers catalogue a library of information concerning the Spirit. In this, they explore his character, identify his resources, stress the importance of his partnership with believers and categorise the potential he offers to each one.

His desire is to empower believers and also to affirm them, enabling them to serve God and each other more successfully, but also to help them to realise more accurately their status, in relationship to God. Thus, he is not simply to be intellectually acknowledged but also to be personally encountered and experienced. He is not merely to be studied but also to be enjoyed as the source of inspiration and creativity in life. He is not only a powerful force but also a personal mentor. He brings about change as well as empowering believers in the process of change. He gives liberty, inspiring joy, wisdom, faith, truth and revelation, amongst other gifts, and believers must ensure that such a fountain of good gifts is never quenched.

A number of characteristics will become clearer as we move through this exploration of the Spirit. Most significantly is the recognition that he is inexplicable but, at the same time, invites us to explore him. Furthermore, because he seeks personal encounters with us, such encounters with him should be expected as we better appreciate who he is. Another central characteristic related to the Spirit is that he is more interested in what he can do for us than what he can achieve through us. His agenda is to affirm our status more than it is to empower us to help him. Although he is pleased to do the latter, it must not be forgotten that his desire is to do us good as well as to do good through us, to the benefit of others.

Despite this treasure house of information, many believers still lack an appreciation of the remarkable nature of the Spirit. Compounding the problem is that he has sometimes been valued more for the gifts that he bestows than for who he is. Too often, he is viewed as simply 'the third person of the Godhead', generally mentioned after the Father and Jesus, rarely prayed to (many are even uncertain as to how to address him), some believers being uncertain as to whether he should be worshipped. Unlike Jesus, he has no body and is therefore often confused with the Father or simply becomes a synonym for 'God'.[1]

His description as the 'Holy Ghost' has been another hindrance to better appreciating him as a personal mentor to believers. However, although we may not be able to see his smile, we can know his joy;

---

[1] On some occasions, it is difficult to differentiate between Jesus and the Spirit (Rom. 8:9–11; 1 Cor. 15:45) and often they function in partnership (Eph. 3:14–17).

we may not be able to see his tears, but we can know that he feels sadness; he may have no ears, but he hears our softest cry; he may have no eyes, but he sees us even in a crowd and also sees how we feel when nobody else does; he may have no personal name, but he is not anonymous. He may be a force but he is also our friend.[2]

Very often, believers assume that Jesus walks with them and the Father guides them but the Spirit has little practical relevance. The Spirit, however, is important and central to, and immanently involved in, his creation, the church, and individual believers—more often and more regularly, more intentionally and strategically, than most believers realise.

The primary focus of this book is not the development of a dogmatic theology of the Spirit which comprehensively explores his relationship and inter-dependency with the Father and Jesus. Thus, scholarly discussions that explore the mystery and complexity of the Trinity and the place of the Spirit are not offered. Not all aspects of the Spirit's character have been probed; nor have all issues relating to the Spirit's mission been addressed. Thus, the identity of the baptism in the Holy Spirit and its implications in the life of believers has not been covered in depth. This is not because the concept is not important but, as with other aspects, it has been the subject of much discussion elsewhere.[3]

---

[2] Throughout this book, the Spirit will be referred to with the masculine pronoun. The Hebrew for 'spirit' (*rûaḥ*) is often, though not always, feminine while the Greek for 'spirit' (*pneuma*) is neuter and personal pronouns for the Spirit in Greek in the NT are thus also neuter. When the term *paraklētos* is used in the Gospel of John with reference to the Spirit, masculine personal pronouns are used in association with it, because it is a masculine noun. English translations have traditionally used the masculine pronoun with reference to the Spirit because the Latin for 'spirit' (*spiritus*) is masculine. Some authors prefer to use the neuter pronoun 'it', as A. Heron, *The Holy Spirit* (Marshall, Morgan and Scott, 1983), *passim*. C. H. Pinnock, in *Flame of Love: A Theology of the Holy Spirit* (InterVarsity Press, 1996), pp. 16–17, makes a case for the use of the feminine pronoun, noting that it honours the feminine-like characteristics of the Spirit, but ultimately he rejects it because the Spirit also has non-feminine characteristics and the church 'is the feminine counterpart to God'.

[3] For discussion from an evangelical perspective, see M. A. Eaton, *Baptism in the Spirit: The Teaching of Martyn Lloyd-Jones* (IVP, 1989), J. D. G. Dunn, *Baptism in the Holy Spirit*, (SCM, 1970), M. Green, *I Believe in the Holy Spirit* (Hodder and Stoughton, 1975), pp. 123–147; from a classical Pentecostal perspective, see W. W. and R. P. Menzies, *Spirit and Power. Foundations of Pentecostal Experience* (Zondervan, 2000), pp. 189–208, D. Petts, 'The Baptism in the Holy Spirit' in K. Warrington, *Pentecostal Perspectives* (Paternoster, 1998), pp. 98–119; from an alternative Pentecostal perspective, see K. Warrington, *Pentecostal Theology: A Theology of Encounter* (T. & T. Clark, 2008), pp. 95–130; from a Charismatic perspective, see H. I. Lederle, *Treasures Old and New: Interpretations of 'Spirit-baptism' in the Charismatic Renewal Movement* (Hendricksen,1988), J. Rodman

This book is fundamentally a theological exploration, practical and biblically based, of the person of the Spirit. He is a friend to be enjoyed more than a force to be accessed, a partner with whom we are to become better acquainted not the subject of a doctoral thesis on which we are to be examined. He is the Spirit who seeks to encounter us and desires that we encounter him; he is fundamentally inexplicable but he desires that we explore him and enjoy the journey. The anticipated consequence of this relationally-based and experiential encounter is that transformation should take place on the part of those who have been privileged to be touched by his presence.

When Jesus left his disciples and went to heaven, he gave the best gift he could, the Spirit. He is more remarkable than many believers know and has much more to give than they may anticipate. At the commencement of this journey, we acknowledge that we are standing at the edge of an impressive, unfathomable sea of truth relating to the Spirit, and we walk into it knowing that he will be our guide and partner in the process.

It may be appropriate to read the book a chapter at a time in order to digest the contents; each chapter is a separate exploration of an issue relating to the topic. In the Study Guide at the conclusion of the book, I have offered a number of questions and suggestions that I hope will provide an opportunity for some of the characteristics of the Spirit to be teased out and applied.

Williams, *Renewal Theology*, vol. 2, *Salvation, the Holy Spirit, and Christian Living* (Zondervan, (1990), pp. 137–409, M. Turner, *The Holy Spirit and Spiritual Gifts Then and Now* (Paternoster, 1996), pp. 150–168; from a Catholic perspective, see K. McDonnell and G. T. Montague, *Christian Initiation and Baptism in the Holy Spirit: Evidence from the First Eight Centuries* (Liturgical Press,1994); from an ecumenical perspective, see K. D. Yun, *Baptism in the Holy Spirit: An Ecumenical Theology of Spirit Baptism* (University of America Press, 2003).

1 Samuel 16:11–13; Matthew 3:11–16; Acts 2:2
1. Who is the Holy Spirit and what is he like?

1. Introduction

Have you ever been in a situation where you can't remember some-one's name? It happens to me all the time. It's considerably more confusing if you are trying to meet someone and you don't know what she or he looks like. This has also happened to me. Some years ago, I was speaking at a conference in Boston, Massachusetts and I was running late for the session. I arrived just in time and saw the leader from the back of the lecture hall. Because he did not know what I looked like, however, he did not realize that I had arrived. He knew my name but not my face.

There's someone we know whose name we know, but I suspect our knowledge about who he is and what he does for us may be limited. We know his name but we're not so sure about what he looks like. He's the Spirit, the Holy Spirit. I want to introduce him to you more intimately for he does much more for us than we can imagine.

The Holy Spirit is difficult to define. As soon as we attempt to explain him, our language becomes less helpful than we may have hoped. It is important to remember that not only is our intellect too small to encompass him but also our language is too limited to explain him. At best, it provides metaphors that help us to tiptoe our way into an exploration of his character. Much time has been spent on deciding how best to refer to the Spirit. To describe him as an 'entity' or a 'force' sounds too impersonal; to refer to him as a 'person' suggests he's human and circumscribed; to define him as a 'member of the Godhead' begs the question 'what kind of member?' To address him as an 'individual' sounds as if there are three gods. Even referring to the Spirit with a masculine pronoun is not necessarily the best. The Greek word (*pneuma*), often translated as 'Spirit' in the NT, is neuter while the Hebrew noun, often used to refer to the Spirit (*rûaḥ*), is feminine. Theologians have struggled to make sense of the Trinity and also to present it in language that is understandable to believers.[1] Creeds have been devised that have sought to exclude error and have resulted in succinct expressions of propositional truth, though often needing the mind of a lawyer to understand the facts expressed therein. Defining the members of the Godhead as persons, modes, separate beings have all served to confuse as much as they have helped to explain the Trinity. In it all, the discovery of the personal nature of the Spirit has all too often been lost. It is sufficient to say that the Spirit, the Father and Jesus are each independent and interdependent, separate but inseparable, distinctive but constantly engaged in reciprocal relationships with each other.

The Holy Spirit is a distinct person in the Godhead (Matt. 28:19; Luke 1:35; 1 Cor. 3:16; 1 Thess. 4:8). As such, he is involved in a number of significant events, including creation (Gen. 1:2; Ps. 104:30; Isa. 32:15–20), the regeneration and transformation of believers (Titus 3:5), and eschatological[2] renewal (Isa. 44:3–5). Although a variety of descriptions are offered for the Spirit – 'Spirit of God' (1 Cor. 2:11), 'Holy Spirit' (Acts 16:6), 'Spirit of Jesus' (Acts 16:7) – only one person is being referred to.

Although often referred to as 'the third member of the Trinity', this is not a helpful description as it could imply a divine hierarchy. The Spirit is not subservient to the Father or Jesus. He is not their divine servant nor is he less deserving of our worship, service and honour. He is God. Indeed, Fee identifies the Spirit as being central to Trinitarian thought for 'it is through the Spirit's indwelling that we know God and Christ relationally, and through the same Spirit's indwelling that we are being transformed into God's own likeness'.[3]

All our words are inadequate to do justice to the one who pre-dated languages; he cannot be contained by any or all of them. He, like his name 'Spirit', is a mystery. The marvel is that he has invited

---

[1] For a readable and thus helpful exposure to the main issues, see T. Smail, *The Giving Gift. The Holy Spirit in Person* (Darton, Longman and Todd, 1994), pp. 32–54.

[2] Eschatology is a study of events related to the end of time, deriving from the Greek *eschatos* (last).

[3] G. D. Fee, *To What End Exegesis? Essays Textual, Exegetical, and Theological* (Eerdmans, 2001), p. 350.

us to explore him, to commence a journey that is to be our eternal destiny – the endless discovery of the Spirit.

The Holy Spirit is, by definition, set apart, the term 'holy' (Greek *hagios*) best being translated as a reference to his uniqueness rather than merely his sinlessness. He is different in a number of respects. His character identifies his uniqueness but also does his willingness to benefit those who walk with him. Indeed, it is a marked characteristic of the Spirit that he chooses to partner believers and to develop them as they grow, endeavouring to ensure that they are more and more like Jesus in their lifestyles. He is a personal, dynamic and perfect guide. He speaks and so must be listened to. This demands developing a personal relationship with him, walking with him, learning to recognize his voice and responding to the guidance he gives. The Spirit is actively involved in the process of salvation (1 Cor. 6:11; 12:3, 13; Heb. 2:4; 6:4; 9:8, 14; 10:29). He is committed to setting believers apart (Rom. 1:4; 1 Pet. 1:2), affirming them (1 John 3:24; 4:13), pro-actively transforming them ethically and spiritually (2 Cor. 3:16–18; 6:6–7; 2 Thess. 2:13; Titus 3:5–6), inspiring and empowering them.[4] However, the Spirit also expects believers to be active in improving their lifestyles (Eph. 5:18–19). If they are controlled by him, they will benefit from his influential presence. His fruit will be personally and corporately experienced, and their lifestyles will increasingly become reflective of his character (Gal. 5:22 – 6:1).

The Spirit is a limitless resource for believers with regard to their spirituality. He is the one who makes it possible for people to enter the kingdom of God (John 3:5–6). He reveals to believers that they are adopted (Rom. 8.15–16), with all the privileges and responsibilities of that fact, and that they can relate to God as their Father, experiencing eternal life from the start of that relationship. His presence in their lives is the evidence that believers are authentic children of God (Rom. 8:9).

The Spirit provides resources for all believers and expects them to be used, and used sensitively for every task he sets. Thus, he diversely distributes gifts (Rom. 1:11; 12:6–8; 1 Cor. 1:7; 12:4–11, 27–31; 14:1, 12) for the benefit of all, inspiring and initiating evangelism (Acts 1:8; 4:8, 31; 6:10; 7:55; 9:31; 11:24; 13:9, 52; 1 Pet. 1:12), preaching (Luke 1:15–17; 2:29–32; 4:14–15, 18–19), prophecy[5] and

---

[4] Acts 6:3, 5; 8:39; 10:38; 13:2; 20:28; Rom. 14:17; 15:13, 16, 18–19; 1 Cor. 2:4; Eph. 3:16; 2 Tim. 1:6–7.

[5] Luke 1:41–45, 67–79; 2:25–32; Acts 2:17–18; 11:28; 19:6; 21:4, 11; 1 Tim. 4:1; Heb. 3:7–8; 10:15; 1 Pet. 1:11; Rev. 1:10; 4:2; 17:3; 21:10.

THE MESSAGE OF THE HOLY SPIRIT

other charismata.[6] He establishes the church as a body (1 Cor. 3:16–17), and is committed to unity (Phil. 1:27; 2:1–2), welcoming folk from all people-groups and backgrounds (2 Cor. 13:14; Eph. 4:3). Believers are therefore to realize the importance of maintaining unity, protecting it as a priceless treasure. They are to recognize that the aim of the Spirit is to welcome folk from all people-groups and backgrounds and to shed the love of God through each believer. The Spirit is committed to relationship with believers and to ensure that that relationship is inclusive of the Father and the Son. The Spirit is to be experienced and his presence to be enjoyed though such closeness has serious consequences including the possibility that believers may hurt him.

Since the Spirit indwells believers and is God (Rom. 8:27), he relationally bonds the believer to God (Eph. 2:18), functioning (with Jesus) as a mediator (1 Tim. 2:4–5) between the believer and God. As Pinnock aptly writes, the Spirit 'choreographs the dance of God' and enables believers to join in, teaching them as they go.[7] Thus, he inspires and fills, empowers and encourages, supports and affirms all believers in an immanent and ongoing interchange. In coming to earth, he did not leave the Father and Jesus behind, for in his presence, they also are present. Although he is supra-spatial and supratemporal, he is also intimately present with every believer. He is the gift of Jesus to the church but insofar as the Spirit is God, he is also his own gift to the church.

He is centrally presented by the biblical authors as being dynamic and desirous of encounters with believers. The Spirit is encountered in a variety of ways, often determined by one's personality, temperament or the current situation of the believer concerned. It is important that any particular event, where the Spirit may have manifested himself, should not be viewed as necessarily normative for all, since the dynamic and creative Spirit has the capacity to interact with believers in ways that are most appropriate to them. Some encounter God in the presence of loud worship, others in silence; some in the cacophony of the city, others in the stillness of the countryside; some in the depths of their emotions, others in their intellect; some in prayer, others in the reading of the Bible; some often, others infrequently. The central imperative is to develop a personal relationship with him, allowing him to be the initiator of

[6] Examples of charismatic endowments by the Spirit are also located in the OT: strength (Judg. 14:6, 19; 15:14); leadership (Gen. 41:38; Isa. 11:1–3); military authority (Judg. 6:34; 11:29–33); skill (Exod. 31:3–4; 35:31); wisdom (Dan. 5:14); prophecy (Num. 11:25, 29; 24:2; 1 Sam. 10:10; 19:19–24; Mic. 3:8).
[7] C. H. Pinnock, *Flame of Love. A Theology of the Holy Spirit* (InterVarsity Press, 1996), p. 37.

any experiences, enjoying them when they occur and enjoying him in their absence.

The Bible helpfully provides a number of metaphors associated with the Spirit that illustrate aspects of his being and mission. Caution is needed however in determining the meaning behind the metaphors because different characteristics may sometimes be intended by the same metaphor when it is used elsewhere. Thus, while fire (often associated with the Spirit) may be identified with judgment, as will be demonstrated, it can also be linked with protection (Exod. 13:21) and affirmation (Acts 2:3). Similarly, the images of wind (Isa. 40:24; 41:16; Jer. 4:11–13) and water (Gen. 6:17; 2 Sam. 22:16; Hos. 5:10) are also associated with judgment, as well as other characteristics. All are used with reference to the Spirit. The most likely reasons for the use of varying metaphors in their respective contexts will determine their specific meaning there.[8]

It is no surprise that the Bible often uses metaphors to express characteristics of the Spirit for he is fundamentally inexplicable. Word pictures make it possible to explore the Spirit by comparing him with features in our experience. This will not result in a conclusive theology of the Spirit but will facilitate a greater appreciation of his being. Rather than attempt to completely understand or circumscribe the Spirit with definitions, it is more helpful to recognise that though he welcomes us to explore him, he does not anticipate that we will fully understand him.

He is like the universe – an endless resource for investigation and wonder. The universe delights us, fires our imagination, leaves us speechless, reminds us of our smallness and motivates us to explore it. So also the Spirit is our infinite source of enquiry, intrigue, exploration and discovery. The Spirit desires us to encounter him endlessly, not in order to completely understand or explain him but so that we may partner him more intimately.

In fact, although a theology of the Spirit may be developed from the Bible, which would result in us gaining a better appreciation of his character and relationship within the Godhead, that is not the reason for his being referenced throughout its pages. The issues of importance to the biblical authors (and their readers) relate much more to the practical significance of the Spirit to them. They wanted to discover how they could walk with the Spirit and what practical difference it would make in their lives. Questions relating to

---

[8] For example, see the metaphor of the wind as symbolic of or related to notions of emptiness, enmity, instability, judgment and supremacy in 'Wind', in L. Ryken, J. C. Wilhoit, T. Longman III, (eds.), *Dictionary of Biblical Imagery* (InterVarsity Press, 1998), pp. 951–952.

his identity were introduced and then largely passed over but were closely followed by a desire to know how that information could help influence an appropriate response to him. Whether there is a divine hierarchy in the Godhead, how the Spirit differs from the Father and the Son and what relationship Jesus had with the Spirit were issues discussed by later theologians. The authors of the Bible were much more interested in the practical, dynamic consequences of encounters with the Spirit.

The Spirit is to be encountered and experienced. Fee underscores this by concluding that the Spirit is more than a creedal belief and is better recognised as 'God's empowering presence'.[9] It is an exploration of his activity rather than a comprehensive survey of his actuality, his roles rather than his reality that are concentrated on by the biblical authors. They readily affirm his existence but concentrate on identifying how he can change them, not on how they can understand him. They recognise that he is inexplicable but they desire to experience him; they acknowledge he is incomprehensible but they aspire to encounter him; they cannot comprehend him but they long to touch him, to be transformed by him, to be people of the Spirit.

2. Oil (1 Sam. 16:13)

Oil is often associated with the Spirit in the Bible. On occasions in the OT, the process of anointing someone with oil was associated with their receiving the Spirit. After he was anointed by the prophet Samuel, the Spirit 'rushed upon' David (1 Sam. 16:13, ESV). Thus, the concept of 'anointing' was related to an infusion of the Spirit (Isa. 61:1) leading to people being enabled, by the Spirit, to undertake a commission or complete an action, as evidenced in the ministry of Jesus (Acts 10:38) and the lives of believers (2 Cor. 1:21–22). Similarly, the term 'anointed' is used in association with the Spirit as when Jesus preached his first sermon in Nazareth (Luke 4:18).

A fundamental use of oil in the ancient world was as a medicine (2 Chr. 28:15; Isa. 1:6; Jer. 8:22). Josephus[10] records that doctors recommended that Herod, in his final illness, bathe in oil and Philo[11] praises the medicinal properties of oil, especially in the toning of muscles. It was also regarded as being a medicinal agent outside Judaism, Seneca referring to the benefit of anointing for

---

[9] G. D. Fee, *Listening to the Spirit in the Text* (Eerdmans, 2000), p. 29.
[10] Josephus, *Wars*, 1.657.
[11] Philo, *De Somn.*, 2.58.

sea-sickness.[12] Similarly, Pliny[13] and Galen[14] recommend the medicinal application of oil while Celsus[15] states that oil was used to treat many diseases. Therefore, because of the well-known therapeutic properties of oil in Jewish and non-Jewish societies, it is possible that this is reflected in the anointing procedure. The Spirit, who was associated with anointing and oil, similarly comes to offer wholeness, a sense of completeness and well-being in the fullest sense.

At the same time, oil was regarded by the Israelites as symbolizing a number of characteristics that would encourage the one who was being anointed. In particular, it identified the presence of the Spirit who was participating in their missions, enabling them to fulfil them successfully. The practice of anointing was a very common feature of Jewish life and its history and, therefore, it is not surprising that the use of the verb 'anoint' should be incorporated in association with the Spirit in biblical and modern Christian literature. Fundamentally, those who were anointed with oil were identified as people who had been entrusted by God with important responsibilities. The anointing procedure affirmed them in their new roles and also indicated that from then on, superior power would be made available to them to enable them to complete their tasks. Thus, kings (1 Sam. 10:1; 16:1) and priests (Lev. 8:12) were anointed and appointed to their positions, often by prophets. The anointing procedure was also used to signify an infusion of God's strength (Ps. 89:20–25) or wisdom (Isa. 11:2). Anointing with oil was also linked with friendship and love (Pss 23:5; 133:2) as well as being understood as being a gift of God (Jer. 31:12). It was also associated with the bestowal of honour and affirmation (Matt. 26:7; Luke 7:46) and, since it was regarded as being precious, the one who was anointed was also deemed to be special. Not only does this imply the importance to God of those anointed, but it also suggests the idea that God will support them as they complete their commissions (Ps. 84:9).

Thus, the association of the Spirit with oil and anointing provided for the ancient readers a wide range of positive images that might help elucidate aspects of the Spirit's involvement in the lives of believers. The Spirit, who was associated with the anointing process especially in the OT, is similarly identified in the NT (Luke 4:18; Acts 10:38). As such, he still provides opportunities for new life and fresh commissions for believers. Furthermore, he enables them to fulfil objectives that he sets for them, gifting them and facilitating

[12] Seneca, *Ep.*, 53.5.
[13] Pliny, *Nat. Hist.*, 15.4.7.
[14] Galen, *De Simpl. Med. Temp.*, 2.10–13.
[15] Celsus, *Treatise de Medicina*, 2.4.4.

their involvement in the expansion of the kingdom of God (Acts 8:39; 13:2; Rom. 12:6–8; 2 Tim. 1:6–7). The Spirit still affirms those whom he anoints (Rom. 8:14–17; Gal. 4:6) and provides the framework for a life in which joy of an eternal nature is central (1 Thess. 1:6). As with OT prophets, he inspires believers to be the mouthpieces of God (Acts 2:18; 11:28), providing guidance for others (Acts 8:29; 11:12). The authoritative Spirit anoints, commissions and enables believers to fulfil divinely-inspired objectives. What is sensational is that although, in the OT, this was limited to a few, now it is universally applied to all believers.

3. Fire (Matt. 3:11)

As preparation for the coming of Messiah, John the Baptist stated that Jesus was to provide a different baptism from his. Whereas he baptized in water, Jesus was to baptize *with the Holy Spirit and with fire* (Matt. 3:11; Luke 3:16). The word 'with' (*en*) is capable of a number of translations (in, by) but they do not greatly affect the meaning of the phrase. The parallel use of this word with regard to John's baptism in water helps provide an understanding of his meaning when he refers to Jesus' baptism with the Holy Spirit. As a person is baptized – in (association with) water, so the believer is to be baptized – in (association with) the Spirit. While water baptism functions symbolically, affirming a difference in lifestyle and commitment, the Spirit functions similarly but also resides with the believer to effect the change. While the baptismal water evaporates from the believer, the Spirit remains and energizes the believer.

What also appears in Jesus' baptism, however, is the association of fire with the Spirit. To the modern reader, fire may be identified with an image of a roaring blaze on a winter's night, providing warmth, light and protection from the cold. The image conjures up an inviting atmosphere where those 'in front of the fire' benefit from the cosy ambience it generates. However, John does not speak about being 'in front of the fire' but being 'baptized with fire'. The latter picture is of being overtaken and engulfed by a forest fire, feeling its heat increasing until one is absorbed by it. Likewise, when the readers of the Gospels read of the baptism with the Spirit and fire, they would have thought of its devastating force.

The ancient world was fearful of fire that could completely destroy a house, street or part of a city in minutes. Since people lived in close proximity to one another and built their homes with combustible materials, any fire would easily engulf one's neighbour's property also. Access to large supplies of water or fire-extinguishing tools was limited; often, when a fire was discovered, the best they could do was ensure that the inhabitants were saved. When the great fire of Rome occurred in AD 64, it devastated the city and lasted for six days. Of the fourteen districts in Rome, four were completely destroyed and seven were severely damaged. Nero's palace and the eight-hundred-year-old temple to Jupiter were also destroyed while countless numbers of people were burned. Five years later another major fire burned much of Rome down, while in the reign of Titus it happened again (AD 80). Fire was a fearful phenomenon to the people of the ancient world. One can only imagine the consterna-tion caused when John, known for his own fierce style of preach-ing, informed his readers that the one following him was going to baptise people with fire.

a. Fire is associated with judgment to come

The most immediate association that a Jew would have had with fire would have been of the holiness of God (Exod. 3:2), with attendant issues, including the motifs of consecration (2 Chr. 7:1–3), destruction (Gen. 19:24), the anger of God (Jer. 15:14; Hos. 5:10; 8:5), the refining properties associated with the cleansing of sin (Isa. 4:4) and judgment (Exod. 9:24; Isa. 11:4; 30:28) in which the fire removes the dross whilst purifying the metal (Zech. 13:9; Mal. 3:2–3). Even the protective pillar of fire for the Hebrews acted as the source for judgment for the Egyptians (Exod. 14:24). In the presence of the burning bush, Moses realised that he was in the presence of a holy God and thus removed his shoes as an act of humility before God (Exod. 3:2–5). God is rep-resented by fire and, as such, is to be feared (Exod. 3:6). The ancient prophets spoke of fire in conjunction with the judgment of God (Mal. 3:1–4; 4:1–2). It is little wonder that the writer to the Hebrews takes advantage of this association between fire and judgment when he writes of 'a fearful expectation of judgment and of raging fire' (Heb. 10:27), identifying God as 'a consuming fire' (12:29). Because of these associations of fire with judgment, it is therefore likely that these are the features intended by John the Baptist for his Jewish hearers with reference to the Spirit (see also Matt. 3:12). This is not a picture of lying in front of a fire enjoying its friendly flames, but of a baptism of fire that engulfs the one who experiences it. The fastest forest fires travel at over six kilometres per hour. To be baptised with fire was anticipated as an experience that would have consequences related to holiness and judgment; it was not to be played with.

The aspect of judgment in association with the Spirit in John's preaching may refer to the capacity of the Spirit to purify believers from sin and to facilitate a life of practical holiness. However, it is

23

more likely that it refers to his role in judging unbelievers who reject the witness of Jesus and are destined to be burnt with unquenchable fire as chaff, as amplified in the following verses (Matt. 3:12; Luke 3:16).[16] The community of Qumran, which was established to the north of the Dead Sea and thus close to the traditional location of John's baptising ministry, similarly used the metaphor of fire. The people who lived there sought to prepare themselves for the coming of Messiah and lived relatively isolated lives that focussed on prayer, copying and reading the ancient Scriptures and other religious documents. Theirs was a disciplined lifestyle that included religious and agricultural activities. In many of their hymns, they refer to a fiery river of judgment that would engulf unbelievers.[17]

It is in this respect that the metaphor of fire is appropriately associated with harvest elsewhere (Matt. 13:39, 40) and eschatological judgment (2 Thess. 1:7, 8; 2 Pet. 3:7). The fire that is associated with the Spirit is eternal (Matt. 3:12; Luke 3:17); this is not a temporary refining of believers but a devastating, frightening prospect of judgment awaiting those who choose not to believe. John the Baptist's message is clear; the one who is to follow him has the authority to deliver the most terrifying judgment. He is to operate in the power of and in association with the Spirit of fire; fire is not intended as an image of warmth and light but of devastation and ruin. Many Israelites anticipated that judgment would be associated with the coming of Messiah though the expectation was that it would be unleashed on the wicked, mainly constituting the Gentiles. John's challenging message is that judgment would be directed to any Jews or Gentiles who were not prepared to accept Jesus as their Saviour.

Paul will write of the role of the Spirit to wash and renew (Titus 3:5) but there it relates to the gracious work of the Spirit in the lives of believers. The sobering ministry of the Spirit, reflected in the preaching of John the Baptist, is one that must not be forgotten by believers and should spur them on to follow in John's footsteps – pointing people to Jesus, who alone can protect them from the pronouncement of judgment against them. The message of John is clear – the Spirit burns (see also Isa. 4:4).

b. Fire is associated with judgment that has passed

The reference to fire in Acts 2:3, in the context of the believers receiving the Spirit whilst in Jerusalem, identifies the presence of the

---

[16] R. H. Gundry, *Matthew. A Commentary on His Handbook for a Mixed Church under Persecution* (Eerdmans, 1982, 1994), p. 49.
[17] *1QH.* 3:28–29.

God of judgment and fire. It is probable that the fire that descended on Mount Sinai (Exod. 19:18), in order to identify the descent of the Lord and described as a 'devouring fire' (Exod. 24:17, ESV), forms the backdrop to its reference in Acts 2:3. Those in the Upper Room, who were filled with the Spirit, were in the presence of none other than God himself, the fire (and the wind) representing that fact. Luke records the prophecy concerning the coming of the Spirit in association with fire (3:16) and it seems likely that his mention of fire in describing the Upper Room experience must have also been to draw the memories of the readers back to that prophecy. The fact that they have not been 'devoured' by the fire indicates that the Judge, manifested in the Spirit, has acquitted them.

c. Fire is associated with transformation

Fire is potentially lethal. However, after fire, new life often occurs. The process of transformation, though at times painful and costly, can be redemptive. On August 13, 2003, the largest forest fire in the recent history of Switzerland destroyed 200,000 trees. One year after the blaze, there appeared to be hardly any growth. However, on closer examination, it was discovered that just as many plant species were growing as there had been before the fire had started. Thereafter, the biodiversity exploded and, within two years, there was an even greater diversity in vegetation than before the fire had ravaged the territory, resulting in a remarkable colonisation. Indeed, one strawberry plant was discovered which had been absent prior to the blaze. The fire had caused growth. As forest fires generate growth, the fire of the Spirit facilitates the possibility of spiritual growth. The Spirit of fire is the greatest catalyst for character transformation; his role is to fan into flame whatever he has deposited in believers, causing new growth and the removal of all which would restrict it from becoming a reality. He is the 'living flame'.[18]

4. Dove (Matt. 3:16)

The main purpose of the Gospel writers in presenting the information concerning the dove at the baptism of Jesus[19] is not to identify which type of bird landed on Jesus' head or even to cause us to enquire why it was a dove and not another bird. The significance of the narrative is to establish that the Spirit descended on Jesus. This

[18] Pinnock, *Flame of Love*, p. 9.
[19] Matt. 3:16; Mark 1:10; Luke 3:22; John 1:32.

was visually affirmed in that a bird, which incidentally was a dove, a common bird in Israel,[20] landed on Jesus, Luke referring to it as 'in bodily form'. It is not evident that anyone saw the dove except John the Baptist (John 1:32–33). The type of bird was less important than what it represented. The dove was a Messianic marker for John (and, potentially, for the readers of the Gospels), demonstrating that Jesus was the Son of God and the one who was to baptise others with the Holy Spirit (John 1:34).

Having established a major reason for the association of the Spirit with Jesus, it is now appropriate to explore reasons why the bird was identified as a dove. It is possible that the reference to a dove relates to the creation of the world in which the Spirit hovered, as a bird, over the waters (Gen. 1:2) though a dove is not actually mentioned there.[21] The dove sent out by Noah (Gen. 8:8–12) however supports this feature of new life and this may provide the most likely relevance of the metaphor, especially given the initiatory aspect of the baptism of Jesus to his forthcoming mission.[22] Reminiscent of the return of the dove to Noah's ark to indicate that a new world was being presented to the survivors, the presence of the Spirit with Jesus encourages the readers to believe that a new world is to be offered to people whose world is crumbling and whose lives lack hope.

Others derive meanings from associated aspects of a dove, including its being a symbol of peace, its beauty (Song 1:15), innocence (Matt. 10:16), association with sacrifices (Lev. 1:14; 5:7, 11), use as an affectionate term for a loved one (Song 2:14) or its occasional identification with the nation of Israel (Hos. 7:11; 11:11; b. Ber. 53b; Shab. 49a).[23] However, the association between a dove and the Spirit is rare in Jewish literature and it is therefore unlikely that the readers would have automatically linked the two.

Given that the Gospel writers associated the dove with the

[20] Before it became extinct, the Passenger Pigeon (a type of dove), was reputed to be the most common bird in the world.

[21] A Jewish association between a dove and Gen. 1:2 occurs at about the end of the first century AD (b. Hag, 15a).

[22] W. D. Davies, D. C. Allison, The Gospel According to Saint Matthew, vol. 1, (T. & T. Clark, 1988), p. 334; J. Nolland, in Luke 1 – 9:20 (Word, 1989), p. 161, draws a contrast between the Spirit of fire and judgment associated with the baptism of John the Baptist, and the dove-like Spirit associated with Jesus' restorative ministry. Similarly, D. L. Bock, in Luke 1:1 – 9:50, vol. 1 (Baker, 1996), p. 339, notes that although Noah's dove 'symbolizes the end of judgement and the beginning of grace', the baptism of Jesus includes judgment (Luke 3:16–17). However, the mission of Jesus was both restorative and judgmental, depending on whether he and his message were accepted.

[23] It is not clear why NT writers would have associated a dove with Israel, especially when Ephraim is described as a 'silly dove' (Hos. 7:11).

Spirit and not the mission or person of Jesus, it is possible that any meaning arising from its presence relates to the qualities associated with doves that help describe the kind of Spirit who descends on Jesus. Thus, it may indicate that 'The Spirit descended on Jesus with the grace of a dove',[24] or gently or swiftly (Ps. 55:6; Hos. 11:11) becoming part of the mission of Jesus. Other characteristics associated with a dove that are also related to the Spirit include the importance of purity; doves prefer to live in clean environments and are sensitive to smoke and unclean water. It is no coincidence to note that John twice records that the Spirit remained with Jesus (John 1:32, 33), indicating a purity that merits the presence of the Spirit.[25] It is not necessary to assume that the dove actually remained with Jesus and thus again the metaphor is to be understood as being of considerably less importance than the reality of the Spirit, who did remain with Jesus in contrast to his previous manifestations. The challenge to the readers is to determine whether they will also recognize the dove-like presence of the Spirit as did John the Baptist as he manifests himself to them, and respond to his leading.

5. Wind (Acts 2:2)

In Acts 2:2, the Spirit is described in association with a powerful wind, reminiscent of occasions in the OT when God revealed himself to people (2 Sam. 22:16; Job. 37:10). When the Spirit is associated with the wind in Acts 2:2, the message, especially to Jewish readers, is clear – the presence of God is being anticipated. In John 3:8, Jesus provides a parallel between the Spirit and the wind[26] and, in particular, in the context of the relationship with the Spirit that may be enjoyed by believers. As one may hear the sound of the wind, so also believers are identified as hearing the voice of the Spirit. As neither the wind can be controlled, nor can the Spirit. As it is not possible to accurately determine where, when or in what direction the wind may blow (especially in the first century when metereology was much more primitive than today), so also the Spirit is sovereignly in control of his own agenda. He is supremely in charge. In

---

[24] Bock, *Luke 1:1 – 9:50*, p. 339.

[25] On the first occasion, the Greek aorist is used, probably indicating a definite association of the Spirit with Jesus, while on the second occasion the present tense is used, probably to indicate a permanent and ongoing relationship.

[26] In the OT, the Hebrew word translated 'Spirit' is *rûah* (Gen. 8:1; Exod. 10:13; 1 Kgs 19:11; Ps. 1:4; Ezek. 37:9) while in the NT, the Greek equivalent is *pneuma* (John 3:8; Rom. 8:26; Eph. 6:18), both of which may also be translated elsewhere as 'wind' or 'breath'.

the presence of the active Spirit, lives are changed. Sometimes, people's journeys to faith are preceded by powerful events that would indicate that a superior force has used a strategy to bring them to a particular point in their lives whereupon they have placed their trust in Jesus. For others, the journey has been more natural and the Spirit, as a gentle breeze, has carried them to the Saviour.

Valuable lessons concerning the Spirit may be learned as a result of the association that is presented between him and the wind. Wind produces energy; air doesn't. It is only when air moves, as wind, that energy is generated, and the faster the wind blows, the greater the energy that is produced. The picture offered by Ezekiel of dead bones being vitalised identifies the Spirit as the energising force that achieves the miracle (Ezek. 37:9–14). In the OT, the Spirit (Hebrew *rûaḥ*) is identified as being powerful (Exod. 14:21; Ezek. 13:13–14), the external power of God (Num. 11:17; 2 Kgs 2:9) or the dynamic presence of God (Ps. 139:1).

The phenomenon of the wind is a common feature in all cultures, past and present. When the Jews, who were present in Jerusalem on the day of Pentecost, heard the sound of a *violent wind* rushing through the room (Acts 2:2), they knew what that indicated – a force greater than them was present. If anyone has experienced an earthquake or even a tremor, they will have recognized their finiteness in the presence of such power. The Jewish sailors among those in Jerusalem on the day of Pentecost were used to the beneficent nature of the breeze that filled the sails of the fishing boats on Lake Galilee. They also knew that the soft zephyrs that gently tugged their sails could, in a moment, strike panic and cause havoc with a sudden and fierce injection of power sweeping down onto the Lake from the Golan Heights.

Although modern technology is increasingly harnessing the huge potential of wind power through wind turbines, it is never to be forgotten that the same wind that can benefit thousands has the capacity to bring destruction and chaos by its devastating force. For example, in August 2005, New Orleans witnessed the sweeping and shattering consequences of Hurricane Katrina that resulted in damage estimated at $75 billion in the worst and costliest natural disaster in the USA, resulting in the deaths of 1,200 people. The wind can be a friend and a foe, can bring a soft touch and also shocking turmoil. Similarly, the awesome power of the Spirit should never be taken for granted, even by believers who are more used to his beneficent breeze in their lives.

The wind is also fundamentally unpredictable. In the Bible, it is gentle (Gen. 3:8; John 20:22) and strong (Exod. 15:8). Meteorologists are able to describe what causes the wind to be created and even to identify certain winds (Sirocco, Mistral, Chinook) and from whence they emanate. They have even discovered the jetstream that flows about twelve kilometres above the earth. They can categorize global wind patterns and differentiate between different levels of wind power, using the Beaufort Scale, devised over two hundred years ago, to do so. However, despite the latest technology, there are still many uncertainties related to the wind. One only has to try to fly a kite to see how often the wind manipulates the direction of the kite in random ways. To predict where the kite will go is beyond our ability to determine. The wind is its own controller.

Similarly, the Spirit is largely a mysterious force. Although he has chosen to reveal something of his character and aspirations, he is still beyond us. Therefore, we explore him sensitively, humbly and in the recognition that he is too complex for our finite minds to comprehend. He is a marvellous mystery whom we have been invited to explore, an awesome being who is beyond eternity and yet he treats us as if we were the most special people in all of history.

Jesus' description of the Spirit as being like the wind in John 3:8 similarly relates to its mystery and unpredictability. However, believers have been let into a great secret for although he is still largely inscrutable, they are able to hear his voice, recognise his presence and hear his guidance. They can identify his presence in their lives by their experience of him and the changes he makes. As the wind can be experienced, so also the Spirit is desirous of encountering believers experientially, impacting them spiritually, emotionally, intellectually and physically. As the wind functions powerfully, so does the Spirit, controlling the lives of the people he directs. He is sovereign, uncontrollable, dynamic but also personal, life-impacting and life-changing. He may be known both intellectually and experientially, making a mark on believers. He develops them as the wind strengthens a young tree, causing it to grow by creating testing opportunities for it to cling on to its roots. He is supremely in control of that development and, in that regard, he can be trusted in his ongoing relationship with the believer.

He is an integral part of life. As weather would stagnate without the wind, so also the Spirit is the one who energises the lives of believers. Sometimes, his force is powerful as was the wind when it was measured at 509 km per hour in Oklahoma, thirty metres above the ground. On other occasions, the Spirit is as gentle as the breeze that lifts a leaf and then lowers it to the ground a few paces away. The Spirit has the capacity to similarly move those in his care. Some years ago, I experienced a difficult time in my life that caused me to wonder about the influential nature of the Spirit in my life. Was he there despite my circumstances? Did he know how I was feeling?

Could he see beyond this storm to a safe harbour – and more importantly, could he ensure that I would arrive there? As a result of that experience, I wrote some words that articulated my feelings and what I perceived was God's response.[27]

> I watched it uncertain – afraid to let go.
> It struggled to hold on, fluttering to and fro.
> The leaf held on with all its might.
> To the tree it held tight
> and all the while the wind softly caressed it and
>   encouraged it . . . to fly
> But it resisted the pull.
> It was safe where it was.
> Who knew where the wind would blow?
> And all the while, the wind warmly caressed it and
>   encouraged it to fly.
>
> One day it did. Tired of holding on, it let go
> and prepared to flutter down
> to the dirt below where it thought it would die.
> But the wind that had gently plucked it from the tree,
>   tucked it under its arm
> and took it high, far higher than ever it had dreamed it
>   could go.
> Once it was tied to the tree
> but now it was free on the breeze.
>
> Lord, I wish I was that leaf. I wish I could trust you that
>   completely,
> to know you hold me – and sense your peace.
> But, I'm afraid Lord, afraid to let go. I fear the future;
> where I might go; what if I fail?
> What will letting go entail?
> Lord?
>
> Son, trust in my Spirit, the Breeze.
> His love for you is what sets you free.
> He says that he'll change you, but love is his mould.
> He promises to hold you, but tight in his fold.
> He promises to use you, but it's all in his love.
> You'll fly – but remember your teacher's a dove.

[27] K. Warrington, *God and Us. A Life-Changing Adventure* (Scripture Union, 2004), pp. 101–102. Used by permission of the publishers.

And together you'll fly in peace on the breeze.
His love for you is what gives you peace.
For my will for you is not a sigh nor a rod;
it's a song . . . to take you high, to me, your God.
My Spirit in you is all you need
to assure you I love you;
for you belong to me.

The Spirit (like the wind) is fundamentally in motion; his desire is to be moving on. The future is the place of exploration, discovery and destiny and he is the one who desires to lead us with an increasing sense of expectation.

Charles Plumb was a pilot who served in Vietnam. His plane was hit by a surface-to-air missile and he parachuted safely to the ground. One day, in a restaurant, a man at another table said, 'I know you. You're Charles Plumb. You flew jets in Vietnam from the aircraft carrier Kitty Hawk. You were shot down but I packed your parachute.' The ace fighter who flew seventy-five combat missions had been preserved by someone whom he didn't know. As a result of the care taken in preparing his parachute, his life had been saved. The Spirit has personally created a safety harness for every believer, carefully ensuring that it fits perfectly to ensure that they are kept safe despite what may happen to them. This protection begins at salvation when we are sheltered from divine judgment, continues throughout our lives and ensures that our commissions and destinies are secured by the Spirit.

Part One
The Holy Spirit in the Old Testament

Genesis 1:1–3
2. The Holy Spirit is the energiser of all creation

1. Introduction

Although it might seem strange now to question whether the Spirit is God, there was a time when many were uncertain about his divine status. As late as AD 380, the Christian writer, Gregory of Nazianzus, noted that many Christians, including theologians, were undecided concerning the identification of the Spirit as God or Creator. In the following year, the Council of Constantinople was held in which a number of doctrines were established. Of significance is the fact that although the Spirit was not identified as being God, he was treated as being equal to the Father and the Son and worthy of being worshipped and glorified with them. In the decades following, the *filioque* debate[1] (or controversy) dominated much of the dialogue between theologians from the East and the West, resulting in ongoing disputes for the next six hundred years. In this period, the complexity of intellectual argumentation concerning the relationship of the Spirit within the Godhead increased while the personal experience of the Spirit became less apparent. However, Genesis 1:1–3 affirms a fundamental and divine feature of the Spirit that also defines the personal, practical and applied nature of his priorities.

---

[1] The issue in question related to whether the Spirit proceeds from the Father (Eastern Church) or the Father and the Son (Western Church). A succession of Church councils addressed the issue (Nicea, Lyons) but the more qualified are their pronouncements, the less practical and applicable (and clear) they become; see A. E. McGrath, *Christian Theology. An Introduction* (Blackwell, 2001), pp. 340–343.

2. The Spirit's creativity is an expression of his sovereign freedom (1:1)

No one suggested the idea of creation to the Spirit nor did it meet a need within him. He chose to do it. His creation of the world was a remarkable act of gracious altruism.[2] He created because he is God and his creation is crafted out of love. Creation reflects him and carries his imprint. The more one considers creation, the more one is drawn to its creator. It acts as divine sermon notes to a congregation of worshippers. It is one of his ways of getting our attention and marvelling at his character. It reminds us of who he is and who we are; it reassures us that the one who created the stars is capable of supervising our destinies also. The details of the creative act are divulged from Genesis 1:3 onwards. However, before they are identified, the author identifies the master-architect – the Spirit. Before introducing the readers to the creation itself, he introduces them to the one who enabled it to be brought into existence. Rather than getting them too caught up with the miraculous act, the Spirit is first announced as the miracle worker.

The Spirit is still involved in his creation and is saddened by everything that would deface it and spoil its beauty. He sustains it from where it was to where it will be. The Spirit who energized creation in its initiation is grieved when he hears it groaning and sees it in bondage. He will not allow it to die in disgrace for he has destined that it should be free to reflect God in all his perfection and beauty (Rom. 8:21–22). Similar references to the role of the Spirit in his capacity to create fresh destinies out of disasters that affect his creation are recorded in the OT (Isa. 32:15; 44:3). Johnson writes of the Spirit as 'the mobile, pure, people-loving Spirit who pervades every wretched corner, wailing at the waste, releasing power that enables fresh starts'.[3] Wholeness is the heartbeat of the Spirit – salvation in its fullest and eschatological sense.

The Spirit ensures that creation as well as the church evolves according to his plan, despite the opposition of sin. Creation has occurred but it is still occurring. It is a past and a present event and the future will manifest a different expression of the Creator Spirit's creativity. The world is not in freefall or rudderless – the Spirit is intimately involved in its history and its destiny, its hidden and revealed areas. It is his creation and he has the authority to go

[2] K. Warrington, *God and Us. A Life-Changing Adventure* (Scripture Union, 2004), pp. 11–19.
[3] E. A Johnson, *She Who is: The Mystery of God in Feminist Theological Discourse* (Crossroads, 1992), p. 213.

wherever he chooses in it and order change. There are not any no-go areas for him, no secular and sacred divides.

He is the author of the climactic and the initiatory, the cataclysmic and the soft nuance, the immense and the sub-atomic, the immediate and the open-ended, the sharp intrusions and the graceful dance of partners in harmonious motion. He is in his world and he surrounds it. He has created it and will conclude it, energizing all he creates to achieve its designed end, watching it from a distance but also intimately involved in its progression. He is its designer and its mechanic, its architect and its structural engineer, its friend and its God. Believers need to realise afresh the very significant commitment of the Spirit to the planet, catch his vision and articulate a practical response to a mission that takes seriously global issues and determine to make a difference. This may be practically demonstrated in reducing waste, utilizing precious resources, spending money, or campaigning on behalf of ecological and global issues that affect the world in which we live.

3. The creative Spirit (1:2)

One of the fundamental characteristics of the Spirit relates to his creativity or, at least, his energising of the process of creation (Job 33:4; Ps. 33:6; Isa. 32:15). It is only one aspect of his being, but it relates to so much that it must not be explored too quickly. The first activity of the Spirit recorded in the Bible centres on his creative activity (Gen. 1:1–2) while the first reference of the Spirit in the NT relates to the creative act of overshadowing the birth of Jesus (Luke 1:35). Such creativity reveals more about the Spirit than may be first imagined. Although God (Gen. 2:7; Job 33:4), Jesus, as the Son of God (Col. 1:16; Heb. 1:2), and the Spirit are identified as being involved in creation, the latter is often overlooked. Pinnock writes, 'Let us stop demoting the Spirit, relegating him to spheres of church and piety. . .The whole creation is home to the Spirit's operations.'[4] The Spirit works everywhere – even in places where believers have not yet gone.

The days of creation have not been completed. The Spirit is still creating opportunities for believers to serve him and each other. The same Spirit who created the universe is actively and intimately involved in our lives. He does not idly sit by and watch the world from a distance; he prefers to move dynamically within us,

[4] C. H. Pinnock, *Flame of Love. A Theology of the Holy Spirit* (InterVarsity Press, 1996) p. 63.

developing fresh experiences, providing unique lessons, innovative opportunities, progressive adventures, imaginative prospects, creating what we will be out of what we are.

4. The Spirit is powerfully active in his creativity (1:2)

The Hebrew term often translated as the Spirit (*rûaḥ*) is sometimes translated 'wind' (Gen. 8:1) or breath (6:17). The divine creative force, referred to by *rûaḥ* in Genesis 1:2, indicates that it is the Spirit who is being referred to. Of course, the readers would not anticipate that the reference to the Spirit is in the context of the Trinity as they were monotheistic. Similarly, one should not assume that verse 1 states that God (the Father) created the world and that the Spirit took over in verse 2. Here, the writer is more interested in exposing the complexity of the task and the sublime creation achieved – such creative authority is owned by the one in whom the readers have placed their trust, the Spirit.

The fact that the Spirit *was hovering over the waters* is worthy of consideration. The term for *hovering* has been variously translated (moving, brooding, sweeping). It is rarely used in the OT (Deut. 32:11, 'hover'; Jer. 23:9, ESV, 'shake'). The meaning is probably that the Spirit 'hovers', watching over the darkness, in the sense of controlling it and keeping it in place. In May 2003, NASA featured an image on its website identifying it as the Astronomy Picture of the Day. It is a photograph of a dying star, beautifully blue in the centre and surrounded by jets of dust that radiate out into the darkness of space, resulting in a blue core in the shape of a circle enclosed by shades of grey to soft brown. It looks like an eye, despite being a trillion miles long and 650 light years away. Some have named it 'the eye of God'. The Spirit views all creation as the heavenly watcher. However, he watches over his handiwork not from a distant galaxy but from within ours, not from heaven but from within the human heart.

At the same time, the active characteristic of the creative force is hinted at in Genesis 1, in that the hovering will soon be followed by an artistic design being implemented. The picture painted by the author is reminiscent of a bird that flutters over its young protectively, but which also flaps them out of the nest to fly on their own. It is not content to allow them to be passive but encourages them to achieve their potential. Similarly, the Spirit 'flies' over creation, encouraging it to aspire to its intended objective.

5. The Spirit brings something out of nothing (1:2)

The writer describes the earth as being *formless and empty*. However, the original Hebrew terms are nouns, not adjectives and 'desert and a wasteland' is a more appropriate translation.[5] It is not that the original creation was chaotic (Isa. 45:18–19) but that in the first instance it was devoid of substance; it was still empty (Job 26:7); the work had not been yet completed. The canvas had been prepared but the picture had yet to be painted in all its vivid beauty. The framework had been formed but the internal features were yet to be filled in. In comparison with what was to come, it was a place of nothingness. The writer is not describing creation as having no shape or form; rather he is introducing us to the timetable of creation which started with creation from nothing, to creation in which there was nothing, to the creative act that completed everything the Spirit desired. The prose presents a picture of sovereign control over the creation of the world that is fundamentally beyond the imagination of the ancient and modern readers. Consequently, when reading it, it is helpful to read it in the knowledge that theological rather than geological reasons undergird its presentation.

Furthermore, the world was covered in darkness. Although this could be assumed to refer to a negative concept (Exod. 10:21; Ps. 88:12; Prov. 2:13), it is to be remembered that God created darkness as well as light (Isa. 45:7). Rather than view these terms scientifically, it is more appropriate to ask what the writer was seeking to portray by such graphic imagery. These ominous descriptions probably refer to the potentially daunting nature of the creative task ahead: it is a dangerous time of *darkness* and *the deep*; no one has walked this way before; no architect's plans are available. Whoever takes this building programme on needs to be prepared for a most incredible and complex construction. Such a massive undertaking needs supernatural power. It is as if the writer is indicating that the creation of the world was a momentous act but that the rest of the process was enormous by comparison. For a start, before anything else can be attempted, something has to be done about the lighting. This is where the Spirit is presented as being the divine architect of the future. The Spirit was involved in the process of taking the potential to its completed form. Creation had yet to receive light

[5] V. P. Hamilton, *The Book of Genesis. Chapters 1–17* (Eerdmans, 1991), p. 108. The translation is complicated by the fact that the second word is only used two times elsewhere in the OT (Isa. 34:11; Jer. 4:23) – the first word is used over twenty times, with a variety of meanings employed (Deut. 32:10 – a desert; Job 12:24 – a wasteland where there are no tracks).

and life, animals, birds, fish and, most importantly, a community of people. The Spirit was in charge from the beginning, energising the planning and delivery of the final product.

The creativity of the Spirit is reflected in people who have been given the capacity to be creative. The same creator who formed the animals gave them to Adam 'to see what he would name them' (Gen. 2:19). God gave Adam the privilege of adding to his divine creative work and to put his mark on it by choosing the names he wanted to give to each animal; and as he did, God was interested to observe him in this enjoyable role.

So also, believers especially have a responsibility to be creative, determining how to develop frameworks for personal change. The responsibility of the believer is to recognise that the Spirit who created in the past also desires to create the future, but this time through believers. Rather than view the future as the incoming tide that comes to us, believers ought to recognise their role as those who move towards the future, preparing themselves for it and creating strategies that will enable them to achieve set targets. The list of possible creative acts is endless – projects to plan and complete, ideas to be realised, networks to be established, or new habits to be formed. Each of the above has one thing in common – the opportunity for creative change. Ask yourself this question – 'Am I living in the present realising that there is a future to be grasped, or living in the present as if the future didn't exist?' Parsons writes, 'God has created us to have dreams,' and aspirations initiated by God are the springboards to help us fulfil the Spirit's plans for us.[6]

In 1975, I finished my undergraduate studies. I was twenty three years old with my life ahead of me. I was beginning to recognise my gifts and allowing myself to dream. I felt that my strength was in the area of teaching and that God was leading me in that direction, so I drew myself into that future potential by preparing myself for it. I started postgraduate studies in order to be better equipped and was thus ready when the invitation came to join the faculty at Regents Theological College, where I am currently the Vice-Principal.

What is God saying to you about your future? Seek to identify God's plan for your life and fulfil it. You have role in creating something out of yourself. Develop a personal framework for change, a structure that provides for individual growth and development. It will not happen overnight; as an old Chinese proverb says, 'Even a journey of one thousand miles starts with a few steps.' However, the Spirit has made it possible for us to make a difference; take advantage of his creative resources. Helen Keller was nineteen months old

[6] R. Parsons, *The Heart of Success* (Hodder and Stoughton, 2002), p. 104.

when she became deaf, dumb and blind. She learned how to speak when she was six years old by pressing her fingers on her teacher's throat to feel the vibrations that were made when she spoke. She eventually learned to read and write, graduated from Radcliffe College, and established the Helen Keller Home for Blind Children, becoming a lecturer and travelling the world in the process. She was asked, 'Is there anything worse than being blind?' She replied, 'Yes, being able to see but having no vision.' May the Spirit grant us the ability to realise the hope to which God has called us and enable us to achieve his aspirations in us. May we know his incomparably sensational power (Eph. 1:18–20), and see what he sees of us and our future.

The prospect of heaven should function as a stimulus to our activity on earth. It will not be a time for limited activity but the chance to engage in life to its fullest with no restraints, but with endless energy and the capacity to excel in all that we do. Life in heaven will provide opportunities to achieve fulfilment in ways that make our best successes now look like half-hearted victories. Therefore, in the light of what is yet to come, the optimistic believer will strain to achieve more, taking a leaf out of the book that belongs to the Spirit and be creative, as he is, in all one does.

Judges 3:7–11; 6:24 – 8:28; 11:1–40; 13:25 – 15:15
3. The Holy Spirit works wonders through weak people

1. Introduction

The Spirit is often referred to in the Bible in association with verbal proclamation, especially prophecy, and ethical renewal. People spoke because the Spirit inspired them and he also inspired them to be people whose lives were increasingly reflective of the character of God. The Spirit enabled people to function effectively and to achieve the objectives he desired for them (Gen. 41:38; Exod. 31:3–4; 35:31–35). The book of Judges contains some of their stories, especially with regard to leadership where the Spirit provided the necessary resources (Num. 11:17; 27:18). However, the author demonstrates that these aspirations were not always achieved.

The presence of the Spirit in our lives is no guarantee of personal victory. Although his power is made available to those he calls, it must not be taken for granted. It is there to enable us to partner him, not to enable us to set the agenda that we think is best. He is always the leader who calls us to follow him, not to stride ahead of him. The saddest consequence occurs when we are granted the resources of the Spirit but fail to access them fully, resulting in our not achieving our potential.

2. The Spirit enables leaders to lead

a. Othniel (3:7–11)

Othniel was granted the ability to function as a judge by the Spirit (Judg. 3:10). Prior to his appointment, evil reigned in Israel and the people were punished by being enslaved to an oppressive conqueror; after Othniel died, the cycle of despair returned. When he was leading the people under the guidance of the Spirit, however, the people prospered. The Spirit brought peace where previously there had been pain, and stability where there had been chaos. It is instructive to note that Othniel was not plucked out of nowhere; he had already proved himself to be a courageous candidate for the Spirit (1:13) with a proven pedigree (the nephew of Caleb, 1:13) of whom nothing negative is written. The Spirit can choose whoever he wishes to work for him but often the most likely candidates are already demonstrating that they are ready for more commissions.

b. Gideon (6:24 – 8:28)

The Spirit demonstrates his flexibility in choosing Gideon who is a less likely candidate in that having been chosen, he initially doubts his calling (6:36–40). Nevertheless, Gideon was inspired by the Spirit not just to lead the Israelites but, in particular, to fight their enemies (6:33–35). As in the experience of Othniel, the Jewish people had repented after another cycle of prosperity, blessing and sin (5:31), leading to a rejection of God (6:1), punishment and oppression (6:2–5), resulting in repentance and deliverance (6:6–7). As a result of the repentance, God sends Gideon to be their deliverer and he is empowered by the Spirit (6:34).

As with Othniel, Gideon had already proved his candidature by destroying an altar to Baal and rebuilding an altar to God, both in response to a divine command. This was a courageous action that not only demanded physical strength but confidence to respond to the inevitable anger of the worshippers of Baal. However, he did not just destroy any altar to Baal; it belonged to his father (6:25). To perform such a presumptuous action against one's father was culturally unacceptable. It wasn't made any easier in that God informed him that he was to sacrifice his father's seven year old bull on the new altar.

It is little wonder that Gideon was so concerned about the fallout from his family and the men of the town that he did it in the secrecy of night in the hope that no-one would know that he had been the perpetrator (6:27). Nevertheless, his fear should not undermine one's estimation of his action, for the consequences of such an act could have been death. If any test needed to be passed before the Spirit decided whether to commission someone, Gideon had passed it with flying colours. He was an ordinary man but one who demonstrated a character appropriate for a manifestation of the presence and power of the Spirit.

Before the Spirit chose to use Gideon to rid the Israelites of the oppressive Midianite armies, Gideon had to get rid of an idol from his own home. The Spirit desires those whom he empowers to be worthy of his presence and commission. It is not surprising to read that after he did this, the Spirit *took possession of Gideon* (RSV, literally, 'clothed' him). As a result, he was enabled to lead those who were prepared to follow him (6:34) and together they defeated the foe. Even with an army that he reduced in number on three occasions to just 300 men, the battle was over before it had begun and the Midianites fled without a fight (7:9–23). Although the task seemed like an insurmountable mountain to climb, it was easily overcome by blowing trumpets and lighting torches. The power of the Spirit was what brought the enemy to its knees – Gideon could relax and watch the miracle.

Sometimes, the Spirit uses believers to achieve great commissions though their actual involvement is little more than to be an observer of his power in their midst. On many occasions, I have presented lectures, preached sermons or led discussions and have been impressed with the Spirit's ability to affect those to whom I have spoken. The fruit has, to a degree, been the result of prayerful preparation but more significantly due to his power. Spiritual fruit has not been due to my presentation skills but to his presence and touch upon the lives of those present.

A story was told of a monk who asked to be used by God throughout his life but when he reached heaven, he expressed to the Lord his disappointment that his prayer had not been answered, as few had been blessed as a result of his life and ministry. It was then that the Lord revealed that when he passed people, his shadow brought blessing to those upon whom it fell. Although a fictitious story, it expresses the truth that often the Spirit blesses others through us even when we have been unaware of it. Words have been spoken, gestures offered, smiles given, deeds done, prayers uttered and unbeknown to those engaging in the action, the Spirit has supernaturally worked a miracle on their behalf for the benefit of others. On occasions, others may even thank us for the words or actions we offered because of the difference these made in their lives; in truth, we may have been oblivious to the part we played in the process but the Spirit picked it up and carried it to the people concerned, depositing it in their lives for their good. Meanwhile, we have been unwitting partners with the Spirit in the process of ministering to others.

Gideon continued to present a worthy pattern of behaviour in that he continued to subdue Israel's enemies and, most importantly, encouraged the people to recognise that God was their ruler, even turning down their request to be their first king (8:22–23). However, the presence of the Spirit did not result in automatic righteousness for Gideon. Indeed, he succumbed to the temptation of prestige and arranged for an ostentatiously decorated garment, called an ephod, to be designed and created for him. Not only this, but also such a garment was normally designated for the high priest only, for when he served in the tabernacle. Unfortunately, now there was an alternative. The new ephod had become an idolatrous substitute.

It may have been that Gideon surmised that he needed another ephod to accompany him as a judge since the high priest at Shiloh was not functioning appropriately as God's representative. Other reasons could be offered that indicate that Gideon's motives may have initially been pure, but the consequences of his decision were devastating. The writer uses language guaranteed to shock the readers. The Spirit-appointed and empowered Gideon had lost his way and created something as a result of which *all Israel prostituted themselves by worshipping it* as well as it becoming *a snare to Gideon and his family* (8:27). The details are passed over by the writer but a question mark hangs over the rest of his life. An empowered life that is preceded by the removal of an idol, closes with its replacement by another that has an even greater negative influence over the lives of others.

Gideon appears to have assumed that since the Spirit had inspired him for one task, he had authority for other roles also. He had forgotten that the Spirit was in charge of handing out the jobs. This tendency to presumption is traced earlier in the narrative also. Although he was commissioned to rid the land of the Midianites, which he did, it appears that he went beyond his orders, for he also killed those that he thought should have helped him (8:17) and others who had previously killed some of his family (8:18–21). It is to be remembered that the same Spirit who grants power also expects fruit reflective of his character to be present in the lives of those he empowers. His involvement in our lives does not guarantee that defects and deep-seated negative character traits will be automatically excised from our lives. The challenge is frightening. Those who see Gideon slide away from a position of Spirit-empowered security will do well to ensure that their victories are not overvalued and become the seedbed for presumption. One must never assume that the same Spirit who affirms us and commissions us to serve him is prepared to allow us to set the agenda thereafter.

c. Jephthah (11:1–40)

Following the familiar cycle of sin, punishment and repentance (10:6–16), God delivers Israel. The Ammonites were to learn the same lesson at the hands of Jephthah as the Midianites did from Gideon. They also were to feel the power of the Spirit against them when Jephthah stalked and harried them after defeating them in battle (11:29). This time, the deliverer chosen by the Spirit was similar to Othniel and Gideon in that he also was a mighty warrior (3:10–11; 6:12), but different from both in that he was an outcast, the son of a prostitute, who had been rejected by his family when natural sons were born to his father and his stepmother. Thereafter, he became a leader of a group of ruthless mercenaries who existed by raiding the properties of those in the vicinity.

Not only is this an insight into the deepening spiral of hope-lessness and despair among God's people, but it also reminds the readers that it is the Spirit who chooses who will be empowered by him to achieve his objectives. As Wilcock writes, 'A more unlikely saviour for the people of Israel we have yet to meet.'[1] Jephthah was an unlikely candidate and yet his response to those who, having rejected and marginalised him, still requested his help may tell a different story – for he decided that he would only accept their commission if God was clearly on his side. The Israelites did not refer to God as their potential saviour nor did they ask him to rescue them; instead, they looked to Jephthah to help them in their perilous plight. It is Jephthah who recognises the importance of the presence of God in any mission (11:9) and it is he who is increasingly being presented as a likely candidate for the Spirit's work. The fact that the Spirit *came upon* him demonstrates, that despite his poor pedigree, he was the right man for the job (11:29).

As with Gideon, however, the presence of the Spirit in Jephthah does not guarantee that he will always make the right decision either, and he makes what appears to be a presumptuous vow that leads to tragedy in that his daughter is taken from him (11:30–31, 34–40). The Spirit who empowered him did not stop him from making mistakes; that was his responsibility (Ps. 141:3).

d. Samson (13:25 – 15:15)

Perhaps of all the judges inspired and empowered by the Spirit, Samson is the most unusual. The Spirit *began to stir him* before he was commissioned by him (13:25). Thereafter, the Spirit empowered him to kill a lion (14:6), thirty men (14:19) and to break rope (15:14), as a consequence of which, he killed one thousand men. In between these strange supernatural endowments is a mixture of events, each of which relates to the Philistines, the enemies of the Israelites. The

[1] M. Wilcock, *The Message of Judges* (IVP, 1992), p. 110.

violent, self-willed Samson judged Israel for twenty years (15:20). He was miraculously supported by God (15:19) and, throughout his life, was a one-man threat to the Philistines who dominated Israel (14:4).

Although his life was filled with what appears to be rather unsavoury elements, his affirmation in Hebrews 11:32 (along with Gideon and Jephthah) cautions us from too hastily delivering a negative character assessment of him. It is true that he portrayed a number of negative characteristics: his desire to marry a Philistine woman, rather than a Jewess (14:1–4), gambling (14:10–18), his bias to vengeance (15:8), his sexual misdemeanours (16:1), his lies (16:6–14), his poor choice of wives (16:18–22), and his tragic ignorance as to the fact that the Lord had left him (16:20). However, the Spirit still chose to use him and, in all his troubled life, there were still glimpses of a man who knew that he had been called by God (13:2–7) to act on his behalf (15:18; 16:28).

Samson's birth had been miraculous in that his mother had previously been unable to have children (13:2) and because it was announced by an angel (13:3). Furthermore, the angel prophesied that he would 'begin the deliverance of Israel from the hands of the Philistines' (13:5). This was a man with a huge potential; the issue to be decided was whether he would fulfil it and achieve the target that God had set for him – as did Othniel, Gideon and Jephthah, in that they had each rid Israel of their oppressors.

Unfortunately, although Samson made some movement in this direction and, at his death, killed more Philistines than in all his previous battles with them, the prophecy was only partially fulfilled. The Philistines maintained their stranglehold over Israel and rather than introduce a time of peace and prosperity, morality in the land plummeted. Micah creates a graven image in consecration to God (17:3) and initiates his own priesthood (17:5), which he establishes throughout Israel (18:20, 30) as a competitor to the authentic house of God at Shiloh (18:31). Sexual abuse of a kind never experienced before in Israel occurs (19:22–30), as does civil war (20:1– 48). Little wonder that the final words of the book record the fact 'everyone did what was right in his own eyes' (21:25, ESV), a statement that is repeated after the demise of Samson is recorded (17:6).

The potential for a great victory was present in the divine choice of Samson before his birth. In many respects, he had more chance of success awaiting him, given the angelic promises concerning him to his parents and the regular references to the Spirit in his life (four times in comparison to one each for Othniel, Gideon and Jephthah). The tragedy of Samson's life is that the aspirations awaiting him were fulfilled only to a very small degree. He may have achieved much but it could have been more. Although he is mentioned in the list of OT heroes (Heb. 11:32), he did not fulfil his potential. His is a life that stands as a warning to the readers to fulfil all that could be fulfilled, to accomplish all one's ambitions, to perform according to one's full potential. The presence of the Spirit in his life is a tragic reminder of all that could have been achieved if he had followed the Spirit more closely and attentively.[2] Instead of ridding the land of Philistines, he marries one of them (14:1) and invites thirty of them to his wedding (14:10, 19). The man, whose life could have provided an appropriate climax to the book of Judges as one who led the people, in the absence of a king (17:6; 21:25), ends his life in a despairing, final act that attempts to make up at least a part of the potential that was present in his life at his birth.

3. Conclusion

All these characters were significantly empowered by the Spirit for specific tasks. The same potential is available for all believers. Therefore, we should live in the realm of possibility rather than pessimism, of opportunity rather than fear of failure. The Spirit empowers people who take time to be prepared. The challenge to us is to live in ways that bring ourselves to the attention of the Spirit for the right reasons. He can use anyone but he prefers to use those who use their lives to serve him even before he commissions them.

The Spirit often chose to use people in ways that reflected their previous lives. Othniel, Gideon and Jephthah were all warriors before being commissioned by the Spirit to defeat the enemies of the Israelites. Their previously developed skills were enhanced by the Spirit but they were not initiated by the Spirit. Often times, the Spirit chooses to take advantage of characteristics, sensibilities and strengths already present in our lives. Sometimes, new gifts are initiated but often, aspects already present are used by the Spirit to achieve his objectives though he chooses to add supernatural power to them.

---

[2] D. Jackman, in *Judges, Ruth* (Word, 1991), notes that he is 'a continual reminder of spiritual potential; but sadly, he is also a reminder of actual failure' (p. 217).

Part Two
The Holy Spirit in the Gospels

Luke 1:41–79; 2:25–35
4. The Holy Spirit is associated with proclamation

1. Introduction

When the Spirit communicates through people in the Bible, he does so in various ways, though it is often through the medium of speech. The experiences of all those who prophesied, in the NT era, demonstrated that the days of God's apparent silence were over. The long awaited prophecy of Joel 2:28 was being fulfilled. As a result, both men and women had the opportunity to hear God speak to them and then pass on the messages. The Spirit was initiating a new era. The opportunity for us today is also to function as mouthpieces of the Spirit who dwells within us.

The association of the Spirit with proclamation and especially prophecy is clear in the OT[1] and the NT.[2] Prophecy refers to the facility of God to speak through people, sometimes with a revelation of the future (Acts 1:16 – see Pss 69:25; 109:8; Acts 11:28; 21:10–11; 1 Pet. 1:10–11), but much more often reflecting a divine message for the present. Prophecies that are inspired by the Spirit are identified as those that encourage, build up and comfort the hearers (1 Cor. 14:3). They are not to destroy but to improve, not to pull down but to pick up, not to identify defeat but to show the way to success, to value the hearer, as the Spirit does, as one who has the potential to grow spiritually.

Luke, in particular, emphasizes the role of the Spirit in enabling

---

[1] Saul (1 Sam. 10:9–12); David (2 Sam. 23:2); Amasai (1 Chron. 12:18); Azariah (2 Chron. 15:1); Jahaziel (2 Chron. 20:14); Ezekiel (Ezek. 11:5); Daniel (Dan. 4:8–9, 18; 5:11, 14); Joel (2:28–29); Micah (Micah 3:8); Zechariah (Zech. 7:12); for all (Num. 11:29); Messiah (Isa. 11:2).

[2] Acts 2:17–18; 11:28; 19:6; 21:4, 11; 1 Tim. 4:1; Heb. 3:7–8; 10:15; 1 Pet. 1:11; 2 Pet. 1:20–21; Rev. 1:10; 4:2; 17:3; 21:10.

believers to speak on his behalf.[3] In Acts 2:17–18, Peter announces the fulfillment of Joel 2:28–32 which declares that as a result of the Spirit being poured out, prophecy will be manifested through many. Not only is the Spirit forecast as being received by all believers but, as a consequence, Peter informs his hearers that they will experience prophecies, visions[4] and dreams. The future event for Joel has become a present event for Luke. It may have been a surprise to many that this was to include Gentiles and servants. Although the original prophecy was addressed to the Judeans (Joel 1:2; 2:23), the Spirit has a wide agenda that will include representatives from the world, not just Israel. Such a broad range of people is prefaced by the description of the Spirit being 'poured out'; he will not be dripped into the lives of the one or two; he will deluge the church.

A torrent of prophecy is anticipated in which believers are to be inundated with opportunities to speak for the Spirit. Such expressive, passionate and extravagant language indicates that the heart of the Spirit is to involve believers in his mission. The age-old dream of Moses – that all God's people would be prophets (Num. 11:29) – finally became a reality as a result of Pentecost. Thereafter, Luke records (Acts 19:6) that Ephesian believers prophesied after the Spirit had come upon them.[5] On two other occasions (Acts 11:28; 21:11), the Spirit inspires prophecy in which the future is foretold. In the first, a famine is predicted, resulting in the believers being able to prepare for the food shortages that would ensue.

2. The Spirit speaks through righteous people (Luke 1:6; 2:25)

Both Elizabeth and Zechariah are described by Luke as *upright in the sight of God, observing all the Lord's commandments and*

---

[3] See also Acts 4:25 (Ps. 2:1–2); 28:25–27 (Isa. 6:9–10).

[4] Rev. 4:2; 16:13; 21:10.

[5] The Ephesian disciples (*mathētai*, Acts 19:1, a term elsewhere used to describe Christians – Acts 16:1; 18:23, 27; 19:9; 20:1, 30; 21:4, 16) were believers (19:2) who had not yet received the Spirit until Paul met them. Some have suggested that their status as believers was in question, or that they needed confirmation that they were believers, or that their baptism by John was inauthentic. Others conclude that the author identifies them as true believers who have not yet received the Spirit. It appears that Luke views their situation as anomalous, which Paul corrects. Having already been baptised in water (Acts 19:3), and re-baptised in the name of Jesus (19:5), the Spirit then 'came on them' and they spoke in tongues and prophesied (19:6). Although Luke chooses not to explain the precise nature of any deficiency in their spirituality, he does indicate that without the Spirit, they would have missed the substantial benefits that come with his presence in their lives.

regulations blamelessly (1:6). Similarly, before mentioning that Simeon was inspired by the Spirit, Luke informs his readers that he was *righteous and devout* (2:25). In Jewish society, righteous people were identified by their moral lifestyles in relationship to God and their community. It was a definition of character and attitude, of personal and corporate responsibility. Such people were portrayed as being worthy of the companionship of the Spirit. Thus, in the OT, the Spirit was associated with prophets and others who similarly were identified as walking closely with God.

It is no surprise therefore that, when writing about Simeon, Luke reveals that *the Holy Spirit was upon him* (2:25), inspiring him to go to the temple, where he saw the baby Jesus. Taking him in his arms, he thanked God for this moment, prophesying that Jesus would be *a light for revelation to the Gentiles and for glory to your people Israel* (2:32). As in the OT, the Spirit often chooses to speak through those who are prepared for such an occasion, through lives that demonstrate a practical commitment to and reliance on God and his values.

Of interest is the fact that John also describes himself as being 'in the Spirit' prior to the revelation he received that was to be given to the seven churches in Asia (Rev. 1:10). Speaking on behalf of the Spirit assumes a prior listening for his voice. Although he is able to interrupt our lives in order to speak through us, his preferred pattern appears to be to speak to those who are already listening and prepared to speak thereafter.

There is no indication in the NT that the Spirit forced anyone to speak on his behalf. He seeks to work in partnership with believers, not pushing them into activity but cooperating with them in anticipation that they will recognize the privilege granted to be his human voice. Thus, when Elizabeth speaks on behalf of the Spirit, Luke writes, *In a loud voice she exclaimed . . .* (1:42), while neither she, Zechariah nor Simeon indicate a reticence to speak for the Spirit.

Though the promise to all believers is that they are to be part of a community in which each may function as a mouthpiece of God (Acts 2:17–18), that does not exclude the need to ensure that their lives are consistent with the Spirit who is to speak though them. Indeed, if believers are to reflect his words, their lives must also reflect his ways. Speaking on behalf of the Spirit demands a determination to live in his shadow, a willingness to develop a righteous lifestyle that best replicates him. In order to achieve this we intentionally need to implement a strategy for holiness.

3. The Spirit inspires the proclamation of good news (Luke 1:41–42)

When Mary visited her, Elizabeth was described as being filled with the Spirit, as a result of which she prophesied concerning Mary and the birth of Jesus. The evidence provided by Luke that she had been filled with the Spirit was that she prophesied. This association of the Spirit with prophecy is common in Jewish literature and it should be no surprise that it is also present in the NT. The reference to the Spirit in relationship with a person thus indicates the possibility of a prophetic utterance on the part of the person concerned. The content of the prophecy was good news about the child who was to be born.

The father of John the Baptist, Zechariah, is also described as being *filled with the Holy Spirit*, an act which is also followed by his prophesying (1:67), which was again concerning good news. The words he spoke concerned redemption to come (1:68) and salvation for the Israelites (1:69). This itself was a fulfilment of OT prophecy (1:70–71) and the promise made by God to Moses (1:72–73) that promised deliverance from their enemies and freedom to serve God without fear (1:74). Furthermore, forgiveness of sins was promised (1:77), as was guidance and peace (1:79). Paul associated the Spirit with joy (1 Thess. 1:6). The Spirit has come to bring hope to those who place their trust in him and his envoys have the privilege of sharing these messages of happiness with others.

The Spirit was associated with good news, including the birth of Messiah and the redemption of both Jews and Gentiles. Given the absence of his speaking to the Jews for centuries prior to this time, many longed for a word of divine consolation or good news from their God, whose active presence was but a distant memory. Many would have assumed that this absence of God would have been their fault. As they had left God and followed their own agendas in the past and been judged accordingly, the silence from heaven may well have left them assuming the worst; if they had chosen to leave God, maybe he had left them. Thus, it is no surprise to hear the first words of the angels to Zechariah (1:13) and the shepherds (2:10) were 'Do not be afraid'. They assumed the worst; to be confronted with an angel of God was a fearful thing. However, Luke introduces the Spirit of God as one associated with joy, salvation and divine redemptive activities relating to the people of God. This is quite a change; in fact, it is a startling development. As believers, this should be reflected in the way that we speak on behalf of the Spirit. A sensitive balance is to be maintained between correction, commendation and congratulation.

4. The Spirit speaks through diverse people (Luke 1:41–45, 67–79)

Elizabeth, as a woman, would have been viewed by many as inferior to men in and outside of Judaism. Nevertheless, the Spirit chose to speak through her. Although the OT includes stories of women who are presented as examples to be emulated and thus valued, by the time of the NT era, many Jews had a patronizing attitude to women. Despite those women who were identified as prophetesses in the OT – Miriam (Exod. 15:20), Deborah (Judg. 4:4), Huldah (2 Kgs 22:14) – few Jews anticipated such re-occurrences in the NT era. It is of interest to note that those who are marginalized are regularly elevated by Luke, including children (18:15–17), shepherds (2:8–14), the poor (4:18), tax collectors (5:27–32; 18:9–14; 19:1–10), Gentiles (7:1–10), non-Jews (8:26–39), Samaritans (10:25–37; 17:11–19) and women (8:40–56; 13:10–17; 18:1–8), including widows (7:11–17; 21:1–4) and 'sinful women' (7:36–50). It is Luke who notes that women accompanied Jesus, providing for him and his disciples out of their money (8:1–3).

It is also of interest to note that the first people to witness the resurrection and to tell the (male) apostles of the empty tomb were Mary Magdalene, Joanna and Mary as well as other unnamed women (23:55–56; 24:10). The evidence of the low esteem in which women were held is observed in the response of the apostles to the testimony of the women in Luke 24:11, 'But they did not believe the women, because their words seemed to them like nonsense.' Women, who were viewed as unreliable witnesses in Jewish courts according to some Rabbis, are the ones who are granted the privilege of witnessing the most remarkable miracle of the resurrection.

Not surprisingly for Luke, therefore, the first occasion the Spirit is mentioned is with reference to Mary (1:35), the first reference to the Spirit enabling prophecy is through Elizabeth (1:41), while Anna is the first person defined as a prophetess (2:36). It is significant that the content of the Spirit-initiated prophecy spoken by Elizabeth relates to none other than Jesus. When the Spirit chooses to reflect on Jesus publicly, he picks a woman as the first honoured herald.

Not only does the Spirit inspire women to speak on his behalf but he also chooses others who are unexpected candidates for such ministry. Although Zechariah was a country priest, and therefore assumed to hold a highly regarded position, such a vocation actually resulted in his being treated with benevolent contempt by some of his urban counterparts, who were much more used to an elaborate lifestyle and cultured context of life and ministry. They served in the Jerusalem temple, one of the wonders of the ancient world and the most important building to the Jews, viewed by many as identifying the centre of the world. He was an outsider, invited in for a few days only before being dispatched back to the rural backwaters. Nevertheless, it was his privilege to burn incense in the temple (Luke 1:9), a once in a lifetime opportunity, that would mark him out thereafter as a person of honour. However, a much greater privilege awaited this rather ordinary priest, one of many hundreds at the time. He would be the first person to speak prophetically to the Jewish community for four hundred years (1:67–79). The Spirit chose to use as his mouthpiece a man who would have been as surprised as many others would at his being chosen for such an honour.

One final defined group who would have been viewed as completely unlikely candidates for the Spirit's inspiration were those who were outside the Jewish constituency. In the past, Gentiles were generally on the receiving end of such prophetic proclamations which typically contained negative contents. Now, the Spirit demonstrates a desire to facilitate Gentiles to function as prophets on his behalf. Some of the names[6] of those who are identified as prophets in Acts 13:1 are non-Jewish, indicating that they may have been Gentiles. This demonstrates that the mantle of prophecy had fallen on those outside the normal racial distinctions of Jewry.

[6] D. L. Bock, *Acts* (Baker, 2007), p. 439.

Luke 1:35, 3:22; 4:1–15
5. The Holy Spirit authenticates Jesus

1. Introduction

In an age of pseudo-messiahs, significant evidence was needed to establish Jesus as the Messiah in the eyes of his Jewish audience. Throughout Jewish history lie the broken dreams scattered by impostors who claimed to be the long awaited Messiah but who left their followers floundering in mists of bewilderment and disappointment. Many of these charlatans claimed miracle-working powers or to have had supernatural visions of the end of the age; some promised material wealth or power, trapping vulnerable and increasingly desperate people in their webs of illusion. But all were doomed to end their dreams, and those of their followers, in despair.

A few years after Jesus had died and risen, Theudas claimed to be the Messiah and raised an army of followers, promising that the Jordan would open, allowing him and his disciples to cross without getting wet. In AD 54, an Egyptian, pretending to be the Messiah, promised thirty thousand Jews who met on the Mount of Olives that the walls of Jerusalem would collapse at his word. Needless to say, neither fulfilled their promises. Even today, there are people who have been identified as being likely candidates for the position of Messiah by their Jewish followers. Probably the most famous was Sabbatai Zevi (1626–1676) who proclaimed himself as Messiah in 1665.[1] At the height of his popularity, it is reckoned that over a million Jews (about a third of all living Jews at the time) acclaimed him as Messiah. News of miracles apparently performed by him spread throughout Europe and prayers were offered to him before

[1] G. Scholem, *Sabbatai Zevi. The Mystical Messiah 1626–1676* (Routledge and Kegan Paul, 1973).

and after his death. Speaking of him, Samuel Pepys, in his diary of 1666, wrote of a Jew in Smyrna who is described as the King of the World and the true Messiah. Although some Rabbis rejected his claims, many Jews accepted him despite the fact that he spoke against the Talmud and engaged in some dubious practices, 'marrying' the Torah as well as a prostitute, to whom he gave the title, 'bride of Messiah'. Although he died in 1676, at the hands of the Sultan of Constantinople, some of his followers were still living in Macedonia in 1943.

In an age of spurious claims, Jesus needed pristine support for his own claim to be the supernatural rescuer of the Jewish people. If he was to be validated as the authentic Messiah, he would need a uniquely authoritative testimonial. The Gospel writers identified John the Baptist as a most important witness to the eligibility of Jesus being afforded this role (Mark 1:2–8; John 1:19–23, 29–34). However, there was an even more important authenticator than John. He was the Spirit.

To have an authoritative affirmation of his claim to be Messiah was vital because of his role. He was expected to usher in the end of time and to initiate the new era in which God would dominate the lives of all, establishing justice throughout the earth, and operating with the wisdom and knowledge that belongs to God, removing sin and its consequences as well as decimating the enemies of the Jews (Isa. 11:1–4). He was to instigate the kingdom of God in which the Jews would be exalted and, as a result, they would exalt God. Although the OT reveals only a little of the role of the Messiah, it is clear that he was an exalted being.[2]

Therefore, if Jesus was to be identified as Messiah, he would need spectacular support. That Jesus would be identified by the Gospel writers as even more significant than was the Messiah, and none other than God himself in human form, demanded the highest evidence imaginable. This was heightened further when it was declared that Jesus was also to dispense the Spirit (Luke 3:16). Such a role was

---

[2] Jewish writers engaged in considerable speculative enquiry concerning his person and mission, many OT verses being inappropriately identified as related to the Messiah. Much of the latter would have significantly advanced the popular expectations concerning him. As such, many Jews believed that the Messiah was pre-existent and lived in God's presence. It was he who would eventually subjugate Satan, ejecting him to Gehenna. Thereafter, he would be enthroned on a heavenly throne, receiving from God comprehensive depths of wisdom. They spoke of him as the Son of God and as infinitely superior to all of God's angels. He was defined as the light of the nations, while his power and glory were delineated as being everlasting. Although they did not equate him with God, he was as close as one gets to being divine. For a modern overview of the topic of Messianic expectation, see N.T. Wright, *Jesus and the Victory of God* (SPCK, 1996), pp. 477–489.

not even expected of Messiah. Isaiah 42:1 (also 11:2; 61:1) notes that the Spirit would be associated with God's servant and the readers would have anticipated that this indicated that he would be successful. However, the Gospel writers established that Jesus would not only be anointed by the Spirit but also that he would give the Spirit to his followers. Such authority is unprecedented. And the Gospel writers relate the fact that none other than the Spirit is the one who offers the stamp of authentication on Jesus.[3]

2. The Spirit authenticates Jesus at his birth (Luke 1:35)

Matthew (1:18, 20) records that Jesus was conceived by the Spirit, the purpose being to inform the readers that Jesus' birth was due to the Spirit's creative power. However, Luke provides more information that helps to establish the sensational nature of the Spirit.

a. The Spirit is holy

In particular, Luke describes the Spirit as holy,[4] as does Matthew (3:11). Although the term 'holy' (*hagios*) can mean 'sinless' or 'perfect', it can also refer to one who has been set apart or identifies someone as being different from others – thus, a holy kiss (1 Cor. 16:20), holy apostles (Eph. 3:5), holy temple (1 Cor. 3:17), holy prophets (Acts 3:21) and holy mountain (2 Pet. 1:18). Luke is not recording that the Spirit is sinless; any Jew would realise that the Spirit of God is, by definition, sinless. However, Luke emphasises that, in a world where people worshipped countless numbers of spirits, the one he refers to is different, set apart, and thus, holy. Generally, when Luke uses the term *pneuma* (spirit) in his Gospel, he is referring to a demon (Luke 9:39).[5] Therefore, when he refers to the Spirit, he describes him as being 'holy, different'.

The Spirit who supervises the birth of Jesus is not just different, however; he is unique. He is not only out of the ordinary but one of a kind.[6] Sinlessness is just part of what makes him different but he is much more significant than that. He is set apart from anything else anyone can imagine, unequalled, incomparable. He's perfect. The one who is thus in his care, in this case Jesus, is guaranteed a perfect start

[3] See also 1 Tim. 3:16; 1 John 4:2–3; 5:7–8.
[4] Luke 1:15, 35, 41, 67; 2:25, 26; 3:16, 22; 4:1; 10:21; 11:13; 12:10, 12..
[5] Also writing of an unclean spirit (6:18) and evil spirit (7:21).
[6] Isa. 40:25.

in life, for the Spirit can only function perfectly. It is rare for people to be satisfied with their workmanship, whether they are composers, authors, painters or musicians. But they are even less prepared to acknowledge that they have achieved the perfect fulfilment of their art when a superior authority examines their work. They may have done the best they could achieve but they will acknowledge that it is not the best that could be achieved. But when the Spirit designs, creates, supervises or achieves anything, it is simply the best that it could be. It is not simply that he has nothing good to compare it with; he does. He compares it with his character, which is perfect, and everything that flows from him is flawless. He's different. He's holy.

Thus, in describing the Spirit as holy, the Gospel writers are making a significant statement about the character of the Spirit. In all aspects of his being, he manifests uniqueness. He is distinctive in a superlative way. It is not simply that he is a little better than all others or that his distinctiveness is subtly different from all others. Rather, he is as different as night is from day, as black is from white, as fire is from ice. He is inimitably matchless.

b. The Spirit is divine

Luke cleverly parallels his reference to the Spirit with a clarification of his identity, referring to him as *the power of the Most High* (1:35). In a world of many spirits, Luke signifies that the Spirit he writes about operates with the power of the Most High God who was revealed to the Israelites in the OT (1:17). He is not indicating that the Spirit is an impersonal force or power. Rather, Luke is desirous of enlightening his readers as to the divine attributes of the Spirit; his power is identical to that of *the Most High*.

c. The Spirit is creative

The ancient, Jewish connection between the Spirit and creation (as explored earlier) may have been in Luke's mind as he referred to the Spirit in association with the birth of Jesus (Gen. 1:2; Job 33:4). Ezekiel 37:14 also associates the Spirit with the creation of life. The Spirit is, by nature, creative, initiating new moves of God, instigating the next chapter in the plan of God for his world. Who better to be involved in this most important and sensational episode in the sovereign act of God than the Spirit, who had also brought the world into being? Furthermore, Isaiah (44:3) had prophesied that the outpouring of the Spirit would result in blessing, described as water on a dry land; if there was a time when a people were in need of refreshment, it was then.

d. The Spirit supervises the birth of Jesus

The presence of the Spirit was neither intended as a medical safe-guard to ensure that the birth of Jesus was successful nor to guar-antee the well-being of Mary. Nor does Luke reveal how the Spirit would initiate the birth of Jesus. Rather, he refers to the Spirit to demonstrate the significance of the birth. Nothing like this had happened before and, given that the child to be born was God in the flesh, it was essential that such an occurrence should be clearly signalled. However unusual the birth of John the Baptist was (Luke 1:5–25), the birth of Jesus was remarkable. However unique the early presence of the Spirit was with John (Luke 1:15), the unique-ness of the presence of the Spirit with Jesus prior to his birth was on a different level. The role of the Spirit was to precede both and thus to authenticate their revelation. As a result of his preceding presence, John was described as having a 'great' mission (Luke 1:15) although Jesus was identified as being *holy* – set apart (Luke 1:35).

e. The Spirit transforms people and situations

The word used to describe the overshadowing (*episkiazō*)[7] or envel-oping (9:34) by the Spirit of the pregnancy of Mary is also used to describe the cloud that rested on the tabernacle (Exod. 40:34, 35), and the protective presence of God (Ps. 91:4) when leading the Hebrews to the Promised Land.[8] The role of the Spirit is to create order and hope, as reflected in the OT (Gen. 1:2; Job 27:3; Ps. 33:6). As such, he welcomes into life the Saviour who will create life out of death and transform darkness into light. The Spirit who is proph-esied as energizing the universe and renewing God's people in the end of time (Isa. 32:15; Ezek. 37:1–14) is the one who supervises the birth of Jesus. The Messiah is present to bring the long awaited renewal and the dynamic Spirit ensures that this will be initiated.

Although the presence of the Spirit was reflected in the lives of some OT people, especially the prophets, it reached a superlative expression in the life of Jesus, who was divinely overshadowed even before his birth and dedicated as being holy at birth. The Spirit did not enter Jesus for the first time at his baptism in the Jordan. According to Luke, the Spirit had been manifesting his presence from the very start, even preparing the abode of the baby before

---

[7] Also Acts 5:15.

[8] Luke may also be drawing from Isaiah 32:15–20, which describes a life of righteousness, peace and justice that was expected after the Spirit was poured out; instead of a wilderness, the Spirit would introduce a fruitful land.

he was conceived (1:31, 35). The presence of the unique Spirit who operates creatively with regard to Jesus, in divine power, authority and protection, indicates the uniqueness of the child even before his birth is recorded. Before he demonstrates his unique person and mission, the involvement of the Spirit has let us into the secret that the child to come must be more special than we could have imagined.

3. The Spirit authenticates Jesus at his baptism (Luke 3:22)

a. The Spirit affirms Jesus

That the Spirit is recorded as descending after the opening of the heavens[9] indicates that he is associated with heaven. The association of the Spirit with Jesus should not be understood as indicating his helplessness without such supernatural aid but to emphasize his unique status. His traveling companion is none other than the Spirit. Luke does not reveal the reason for the presence of the Spirit in this narration of Jesus' baptism nor indicate any change that was effected by the Spirit. However, at the very least and perhaps most importantly, the description is a fulfillment of the Isaianic prophecy (Isa. 11:2; 42:1) that God would place his Spirit upon his servant. This does not mean that this is the first occasion that Jesus was so identified but it does designate to the readers that he was the servant.

It is unlikely that Jesus was divinely designated as Messiah precisely at this moment, especially since Luke has already identified the Davidic pedigree of Jesus in 1:32. It is possible that Jesus' public mission was being inaugurated by the Spirit at this juncture. He was to embark on his mission to preach the good news that the kingdom of God was to be established As such, Jesus was anointed by the Spirit who would be his partner for the duration of the journey. It is also possible that Jesus was being empowered by the Spirit,[10] this being an important element in the activity of the Spirit in the OT; the association of power with the Spirit is evident elsewhere in Luke (24:49) and Acts (1:8). The empowering may have been for the purposes of proclamation or miracles, though the Gospels infrequently record the role of the Spirit in enabling Jesus to perform miracles

---

[9] This is to be understood figuratively as a literary device to indicate the prelude to divine activity, as reflected in the OT (Ezek. 1:1) and the NT (Acts 7:56).

[10] C. H. Pinnock, *Flame of Love. A Theology of the Holy Spirit* (InterVarsity Press, 1996), pp. 85–91.

(though see Acts 10:38); indeed, generally the concept of miraculous power is used with reference to Jesus in the absence of an association with the Spirit (Luke 4:36; 5:17; 6:19; 8:46; 9:1; 10:19; 21:27). Instead, Jesus is presented as functioning in his own authority,[11] and it is his own power that he delegates to his disciples (Luke 9:1). In the temptations by the devil that follow the baptism narrative, Jesus reminds him that he is testing none other than *the Lord your God* (4:8). Thus, Luke does not describe Jesus as a mere man who needed the Spirit, without whom he has little authority or power. Jesus is not a man adopted by the Spirit; rather, he is identified by the Spirit as the one worthy of his presence.

Jesus is thus being revealed to the world, with the backing of heaven, as the legitimate initiator of the kingdom of God, whose worth warrants both his walking with the Spirit and the Spirit walking with him. He was always supreme, but now the evidence is publicly presented, in that the Spirit accompanies him, affirming him to the readers as the divinely designated King of the kingdom. The message is clear. If the Spirit is with Jesus, he must be authentic.[12] The descent of the Spirit upon Jesus affirms him as a worthy vessel for the presence and activity of the Spirit. To his readers Luke reveals the Spirit legitimizing Jesus, validating him as the promised Messiah. He may be empowered by him, but he is primarily endorsed by him. As Bock writes, 'The Spirit leads and confirms more than he empowers Jesus.'[13]

The Spirit descends on Jesus at his baptism not in order to adopt him into the Godhead, but rather to affirm his already-existing status and rightful position (Matt. 1:20). He is the worthy messenger of the gospel; indeed, he is the incarnation of the gospel. The presence of the Spirit validates Jesus as the Messiah (Isa. 11:2; 42:1; 61:1), and as the one authorised to present and represent the good news. Only the Spirit could validate such a person; and that he authorised Jesus was the highest and surest affirmation that could be offered.

Thus, after the affirmation of the Spirit and the Father, Luke records a genealogy of Jesus (3:23–38), the purpose of which is to further identify Jesus as the one who is perfectly qualified to preach good news to the poor (Luke 4:18). His pedigree is certain; his roots go all the way back to 'Adam, the son of God' (Luke 3:38). The message to the reader is certain. Heaven and history affirm Jesus: the

[11] Luke 4:36; 5:12, 17; 6:19; 9:1; 10:19.

[12] In Old Testament literature, the Spirit functioned as a 'marker', identifying leaders (Exod. 33:15–16; Judg. 6:34; 1 Sam. 16:13).

[13] D. L. Bock, in *Luke 1:1 – 9:50*, vol. 1 (Baker, 1996), p. 345; he also states, 'one can speak of the Spirit's anointing not just in terms of wisdom, power, and enablement, but also in terms of endorsement and confirmation' (p. 344).

descent of the Spirit at his baptism and his line of descent in the past demonstrate his unique worth; he is worthy of their attention. The result of the confrontation with the devil that follows is a foregone conclusion. Although the devil may hope for a knockout, he is in for a shock as his opponent stands before him, having received the applause of the Spirit and the affirmation of a dignified ancestry. The battle commences but the odds are unfair, for Jesus is supreme; the Spirit observes the confrontation but has little reason to get involved.

In this fundamental respect, the disciples differ from Jesus. For them, the Spirit provides power but, for Jesus, the references to the Spirit's presence are to enable the hearers (and John the Baptist) to appreciate who he is. Jesus may look just like a man but his association with the Spirit tells a different story. No ordinary man could ever enjoy the unique relationship of the Spirit as that he experienced. He truly was Heaven's ambassador and in this narrative, Heaven reveals its pleasure in accompanying him, in the person of the Spirit, on the journey to save the world.

b. The Spirit affirms Jesus' mission

The uniqueness of his endowment of the Spirit indicates Jesus' unique mission; the uniqueness of his mission presupposes a unique endowment. In the pedagogical or instructive framework of the Gospels, it is inappropriate to stress the influence of the Spirit on Jesus at the expense of a recognition of his unique status. Jesus was not a mere man who had devised a plan to save the world. His was a God-inspired mission, and the affirmatory role of the Spirit on this occasion was intended to emphasise this feature. Jesus demonstrated that he was the Messiah and Saviour, and revealed himself as the Son of God, the fullest expression of God imaginable. For such a unique mission, it was important that the Spirit be recognised as present in an affirming role. This was to be a joint mission by the Godhead, undertaken by Jesus with the Spirit and prefaced by the words of the Father concerning his beloved son.

The Spirit is seen to function in the lives of John the Baptist and Jesus in ways that have not been repeated in anyone else. This fact demonstrates the uniqueness of Jesus and of the one who prepared for his coming. Later, in 7:28, Luke will record that the least in the kingdom of God is greater than John. Jesus however is inimitable. He had been the only one on whom the Spirit had descended and remained (John 1:32). This is a feature of such importance that it is included in the words of God to John the Baptist, to help him recognise the Son of God (John 1:33). This exaltation of Jesus is important for the readers in order to ensure that they recognize the privileges and responsibilities that come with such an assessment. The one on whom the Spirit was prophesied as resting (Isa. 11:2) is none other than the man from Galilee. Such a person with whom the Spirit chooses to remain is the one with whom readers should also choose to remain.

c. The Spirit affirms believers

Jesus is the authoritative messenger from God; the presence of the Spirit demonstrates this fact by focussing his divine spotlight on him. This motif is continued throughout the NT (John 15:26; 16:14); the Spirit is constantly pointing believers to Jesus. Similarly, he vindicates Jesus throughout his life on earth (1 Tim. 3:16), in his miraculous ministry (Matt. 12:28), and in his resurrection (Rom. 8:11; 1 Pet. 3:18), designating him as the Son of God (Rom. 1:4). He is still engaged in the same affirmatory role today (1 John 4:2; 5:7–8). Therefore, as the authentic one, Jesus is to be obeyed; as the validated one, he can be trusted safely; as the endorsed one, he is worthy of our devotion.

Remarkably, the Spirit who supported him in his unique service is also made available to all believers to ensure that their God-given commissions are similarly completed. The individual missions of believers are clearly different from the mission of Jesus as they are also different from other believers. However, the Spirit not only commissions them but facilitates them in order to ensure that they have the potential to fulfil their objectives. The Spirit is associated with the creation and completion of commissions, with powerful proclamations, and with being a constant presence for those he chooses to partner. Such provision is also available to believers who need supernatural support to achieve the agenda that God has set for them. They cannot do it on their own; seeing the Spirit in partnership with Jesus provides confidence that he will similarly walk with them.

One of the most powerful roles of the Spirit today is to affirm us and thereby encourage us in our lives. As believers, it is important that we take a leaf out of the agenda of the Spirit and affirm others by encouraging them. John Wesley remarked,

> Do all the good you can,
> By all the means you can,
> In all the ways you can,
> In all the places you can,
> At all the times you can,

65

To all the people you can,
For as long as ever you can.[14]

4. The Spirit accompanies Jesus into the wilderness and Galilee (Luke 4:1–15)

a. The Holy Spirit filled Jesus (4:1)

Thus far, Luke has written about the role of the Spirit in affirming and authenticating Jesus, while preparing the readers to be aware that he is more special than anyone else who has benefited from the Spirit. Indeed, only the Messiah was envisaged as having such a privileged position and not even he was anticipated as enjoying such an integral relationship with the Spirit. That Jesus is described as being full of the Spirit indicates that success, even over the devil, is to be expected. Thus the early church writer Jerome, in his commentary on Isaiah 11:1, graphically writes, 'the whole fountain of the Holy Spirit descended and rested upon Jesus'.[15]

b. The Holy Spirit led Jesus (4:2)

That Jesus was led by the Spirit indicates his willing submission to God. More importantly, it signifies his status. It is because Jesus is the Messiah that the Spirit is leading him. The Spirit is not leading Jesus in order for him to function as Messiah but to indicate that he is Messiah. The Spirit does not accompany him because Jesus does not know the way but because he is the way. Luke provides this information not to demonstrate the association between leading and following, the superior guiding the inferior, but to illustrate to his readers that the destiny of the one is inextricably entwined with the destiny of the other. It is as if he is asking the question, 'What kind of person receives the attention of the Spirit in this way?'

Furthermore, the going of Jesus into the wilderness is to be understood as part of the divine agenda because of the presence of the Spirit. He goes with the Spirit; therefore, it must be appropriate. It was not a mistake on his part that resulted in his being tempted by the devil nor has he foolishly wandered into his territory.[16] This

[14] John Wesley's Rule, in G. Eayrs, A. Birrell (eds.) *Letters of John Wesley: A Selection of Important and New Letters with Introductions and Biographical Notes* (London: Hodder and Stoughton, 1915), p. 423.
[15] He is quoting from the fragmentary second century Gospel to the Hebrews.
[16] The wilderness was viewed by many Jews as the home of demons (Luke 11:24); similarly, water was viewed as being a fearful place for demons (Luke 8:33);

is God's plan, and the presence of the Spirit indicates to the readers that Jesus is walking in the centre of God's will. Ferguson writes, The Spirit 'serves as the heavenly cartographer and divine strategist who maps out the battle terrain and directs the Warrior-King to the strategic point of conflict'.[17]

This message is relevant for believers today also, for temptation is not always due to their placing themselves in danger of sin; it is not always their fault but often part of God's supervisory plan to strengthen them, albeit through adversity (1 Cor. 10:13). It is not that God tempts believers, or that he directs the devil so to do, or that he leads them into temptation, but that, when temptation occurs, it is accompanied by divine strength to overcome it (1 Cor. 10:13). Similarly, Jesus is partnered by the Spirit in the wilderness, and the Israelites are guided by God in the wilderness (Deut. 8:2). Elsewhere, Luke demonstrates the Spirit leading people (Luke 2:27; Acts 8:29, 39; 10:19–20). The message is clear – whenever and wherever the Spirit leads, it is always safe to follow. Not only does he know the way ahead but also he ensures that the destination will be beneficial.

Luke describes Jesus as being 'led by [*en*] the Spirit' (4:1) when Matthew (4:1) writes of his being 'led up by [*hypo*] the Spirit'. This is probably because Luke wishes to portray Jesus as constantly living in the sphere or presence of – or in association with – the Spirit, *en* often meaning 'in'. He is not superior or inferior to the Spirit; rather, they exist together in harmony and unanimity. Wherever Jesus goes, the Spirit goes as well. Even though, for Jesus, this involves a time of testing by the devil, it is comforting to the readers to realise that he is not alone. They can expect the same qualitative companionship of the Spirit in their personal tests to come. As with Jesus, who was led to the wilderness and not left there, so for them a similar prospect awaits. In the context of multiple spirits, the Spirit is to be recognised as an inestimable friend. As the Spirit is present at the start of the ministry of Jesus, so he also will be with believers as they commence their mission (Acts 1:8).

c. The Spirit ensures that the commissions he inspires will be completed

The association of the Spirit with John and Jesus in the fulfilment of their commissions indicates the same experience being anticipated

in *Test. Sol.* 5:11, the demon Asmodeus begs not to be sent into water. Thus, to enter the wilderness may have seemed presumptuous or foolish to the readers. The fact that Luke emphasizes the presence of the Spirit with Jesus militates against such an assumption.
[17] S. Ferguson, *The Holy Spirit* (IVP, 1996), p. 50.

by readers in their lives. The same Spirit is available and committed to enable them to complete everything God has prepared for them to do. Their responsibility is to ensure that they are appropriate vessels for the Spirit. The role of the Spirit in providing affirmation is borne out in the lives of others referred to in Acts (7:55; 9:17–18; 10:44–48). The Spirit has come to affirm believers when others are unwilling to do so, and to enable them to complete their Spirit-directed missions.

Similarly, although the devil clearly hopes to deflect Jesus from his mission, it is actually an opportunity for Jesus to defeat him at the beginning of his public mission. The devious plans of the devil are not only thwarted by the Spirit, in arranging this confrontation, but also are seen to be part of a higher agenda, determined by the Spirit. Although the devil may have anticipated surprising Jesus in the desert, it is the Spirit who has sprung the trap and the devil is the prey.

d. Jesus' power is identical to the Spirit's power (4:14)

When Luke records that Jesus returned in the power of the Spirit, he is referring to the fact that Jesus was functioning in the power of the Spirit. Nolland describes Jesus not as being 'ruled by the Spirit but operating in the sphere of the Spirit and with the power of the Spirit at his disposal'.[18] Luke does not reveal whether the power was manifested in healings, exorcisms or preaching. Although a reference to teaching is included in 4:15, followed by a description of his sermon in Nazareth, it is to be noted that the latter did not result in comprehensive conversions to Jesus; indeed, the desire of the crowd was to kill him. It is thus likely that Luke desires to establish the source of Jesus' power rather than its impact or administration. Jesus is functioning in nothing less than the power of the Spirit of God. The question to the reader relates to the kind of person who would be granted such a privilege in accessing the power of God.

The association of the Spirit with Jesus would have indicated to the readers that he did not function in human energy and authority alone, but also in the power and authority that was associated with the Spirit. The recognition that the Spirit partnered Jesus at the beginning of his mission would be a constant encouragement to the early believers as they began their missions without his bodily presence. The Spirit who walked with Jesus would be united with them in their quest to preach the same good news as that presented in Jesus' first recorded sermon in Nazareth. Although their

[18] Nolland, *Luke 1 – 9:20* (Word, 1989), p. 186.

commissions were different from his, the Spirit would partner them with the same quality of support as he gave to Jesus.

Luke describes Jesus returning to Galilee in the power of the Spirit, followed by his teaching in the synagogues. Elsewhere, Luke associates the Spirit with preaching (Acts 2:4, 14; 6:10; 8:29–30). It is thus no surprise that the following verses (Luke 4:16–30) record a sermon preached by Jesus in Nazareth. The significance of the reference to the Spirit is to demonstrate that Jesus is not functioning with a human agenda. Rather, he is commencing his public ministry in association with the Spirit. It is not that, before, he did not have the power of the Spirit and that now he does. Rather, Luke presents Jesus as operating in the context or sphere of the Spirit, with the power of the Spirit available to him to use at his prerogative. He completes his mission in companionship with the Spirit.

Luke 4:16–30; 12:8–12
6. The Holy Spirit commissions Jesus

1. Introduction

Although Luke's Gospel is addressed to Theophilus, it is not necessary to assume that he was the only person who was intended to read
it. Bock concludes, 'Any Gentile feeling out of place in an originally
Jewish movement could benefit from the reassurance Luke offered.'[1]
This statement helps to focus attention on the identity of the readers;
they are largely Gentiles who had traditionally been excluded from a
relationship with God; that was a privilege enjoyed mainly by Jews.
The question in the minds of many Gentiles therefore related to
whether that age-old fact was still true. Meanwhile, among the Jews,
there was a supposition that the Messiah may have had a bias towards
certain people. For many, there was an assumption (promulgated by
the religious Jewish leaders of the day) that women, the poor, the
sick and suffering (as well as Gentiles and Samaritans) had been
marginalised by God as well as by the rest of Jewish society; their
conditions were viewed by many as being indicative of God's hand
against them and of possible signs of sin on their part. There was
little expectation that Messiah would treat them any differently.

Life for the vast majority of people in the first century, especially
in Israel, was challenging at the best of times. Socially, they were
oppressed by richer people, they struggled with the burden of taxa-
tion (as much as forty percent of income), and were often hit hard by
famine, drought and disease. Life expectancy beyond forty years of age
was an uncommon feature. Their religious leaders were divided and
even antagonistic to one another. The generally wealthy Sadducees
wanted to maintain the status quo and offered little practical aid to the

[1] D. L. Bock, in *Luke 1:1 – 9:50,* vol. 1 (Baker, 1996), p. 15.

people, while the Pharisees and Scribes confused them with their innumerable and often complex interpretations of the biblical law, as evidenced in the extremely long Talmudic traditions (much longer than the OT itself). By way of example, the *Shabat*, which contains guidance concerning the observance of the Sabbath, is nearly one thousand pages long in its English translation. The notion of a God having time for ordinary Jewish people was a forlorn dream, especially when his apparent leaders sought to explain his will by often convoluted propositions. To many, it was assumed that God was more interested in legal minutiae than in simply loving ordinary people.

Turning to the political leaders brought them no respite since most were despotic, selfish, oppressive and dangerous. Herod the Great, who reigned at the birth of Jesus, was notoriously unstable and lived in fear of his life and throne. He terrorised Jerusalem, leaving it traumatised. To protect himself, he killed his grandfather-in-law, mother-in-law, nephew, two brothers-in-law, his wife Mariamne and three of his sons as well as countless others Jews, rich and poor, secular and religious. It was this man who arranged for the killing of the boys under two as recorded by Matthew (2:16). Apparently, this was so trifling a crime, in comparison with all his others, that it is not recorded in Jewish literature detailing his life. His son, Archelaus, was even worse and was deposed by the Romans who installed procurators, the best known being Pontius Pilate, whom the Jews hated because of his insensitivities to their customs.

Although many people today may be influenced by Christmas card scenes or sanitised films of the life of Jesus, life in the first century was often grim and scary. Perhaps worst of all was the fear of the future – it lacked hope. Over one hundred and fifty years earlier, they had enjoyed a brief time of independence but that was soon crushed by the might of Rome. Now, there was little to look forward to – except the dream that Messiah would come, perhaps in their lifetime, and rescue them. Yet, they had waited for so long and still he had not come. On top of this desperate dream was the lurking fear that they would be overlooked when he did arrive – after all, what did they have to offer him that could bring him pleasure? Would his first words welcome them or would they be pushed away by someone who had come for others and not for them?

Luke presents a gospel where such people are central and identified as being important.[2] God is viewed as touchable, the Spirit as on the side of the outcasts, and Jesus as touching the untouchable and

---

[2] Women (7:36–50; 8:1–3; 10:38–42; 13:10–17; 24:1–12; widows (2:36–37; 4:25–26; 7:12; 18:3; 20:47); the poor (1:46–55; 4:18; 6:20–23; 7:22; 10:21–22; 14:21–24; 16:19–31); children (8:42, 49–56; 9:37–42; 18:15–17); Samaritans and Gentiles

reinstating them into society as fully authenticated members. The message of salvation presented by Luke is inclusive of those who had assumed that they were excluded. Schnackenburg[3] describes Jesus as the one who 'liberates people from their ostracism'. The mission of Jesus is to provide wholeness in a comprehensive sense, and the Spirit is the one who signals that this message of hope to the helpless has received the approval of heaven.

The first occasion of Jesus' preaching was in the synagogue (4:15–16). This was the place where teaching normally occurred. The source of the sermons was the OT (in particular, the Torah and the Prophets), and they were delivered by religious leaders in the local community, although other men could also teach if permission was granted by the synagogue leader. Now, it was the turn of Jesus, and Luke introduces his readers to Jesus' first sermon. The astounding aspect of the message of Jesus is that it announces good news to the *poor*.

Furthermore, it is a message that receives a mandate from the Messiah who has been commissioned by the Spirit. Luke has presented Jesus thus far as having received the affirmation of John the Baptist (3:15–17), the Spirit, and the Father (3:22). However, not only is God on his side (2:40) but also his ancestry qualifies him for his role (3:23–38). Having bested the devil (4:1–13), he now speaks to the people (4:16–21). Given the fact that Luke informs his readers that the Spirit is partnering Jesus (4:14) and endorsing his words (4:18), one may be confident that his words are true. Those suffering can drink in the refreshing message of hope, from the one who has been endorsed by the Spirit himself.

The Spirit affirms the good news of Jesus as being a message of restoration and transformation for those who feel they have been hitherto excluded. Believers must not lose sight of the fact that the gospel is good news to all – and especially to those who have been hurt in the past, experience pain in the present, or fear the future. The Spirit who then supported a message of solace to those suffering still speaks the same supportive message today. The concept of suffering is redeemed by the Spirit as a valuable and integral element of the development of a believer. That the Spirit does not remove suffering may be significant in instructing believers to accommodate it into their lives with fortitude and joy, knowing that it was such for the prophets of the OT, for the spiritual champions of the NT (including Peter, Paul and Stephen), and for Jesus himself.

(3:4–6; 4:22–30; 7:1–10; 13:23–30; 14:16–24; 17:12–19; 20:15–16; 24:47); sinners (7:28–30; 15:1–32).

[3] R. Schnackenburg, *Jesus in the Gospels*, O. C. Dean (transl.), (Louisville: Westminster, 1995), p. 313.

2. The Spirit sets Jesus apart (Luke 4:18)

At the start of the sermon, Jesus quotes from Isaiah 61:1–2. Isaiah's message of hope is dedicated to those who have lost all as a result of exile but who are now promised political, physical, economic and religious restoration. An era is being promised that is beyond their wildest dreams (Isa. 61:3–11). Although their grief has plumbed the deepest depths, their exaltation and exultation are described in superlatives (Isa. 62:1–12).

The Spirit is the one who initiates this hymn of deliverance and endorses each verse. Before he articulates these prophetic promises, Isaiah identifies the fact that he has been anointed by the Spirit. The anointing by the Spirit was a common OT feature when people were set apart for the office of prophet (1 Kgs 19:16), priest (Exod. 28:41) or king (1 Sam. 10:1). It was God's way of marking an individual as the authoritative channel through whom he would minister. Thus, Isaiah demonstrates that his message of hope is related to his God-appointed prophetic status.

When Jesus states that he has fulfilled that ancient prophecy, the implication for his audience is clear. He is also claiming to be anointed by the same Spirit who anointed Isaiah. Although the Spirit had endorsed the prophecy centuries earlier, now the Spirit has validated the one who would fulfil it. The role of the Spirit is to affirm Jesus as a prophet before any prophetic ministry is described. Power, be it in miracles or proclamation, is not the only focus of this narrative in Luke; the identification and affirmation of Jesus as the bearer of this good news is also important. Jesus is presented as having a unique prophetic ministry, and the content of the prophecy is to be understood not only as a demonstration and proof of his person and his power, but also as a declaration of the acts of freedom that are integral to the salvation he has come to achieve. The acts affirm the message of which these acts are a part, while the Spirit affirms him, the messenger. The Spirit, who commissions him, validates him and his message. Therefore, people should listen to him and take heart that his message is trustworthy and true.

3. The Spirit offers hope to the hopeless (Luke 4:18)

Jesus' sermon fizzes with hope. It has the potential for electrifying the audience because it awakens dreams of long ago. Once, they knew they were God's people because the Spirit of God was with them, but he has been absent for many years. Now the words of the ancient prophecy are being spoken again and in fluent, confident and assertive tones. There may have been a nagging doubt, however, that this simply may be another forlorn dream; the presence of the Spirit should make all the difference. The question to be determined however is whether they will recognise the Spirit in the preacher; the tragedy is that most will not.

Jesus probably reads from Isaiah 58:6 and 61:1–2, though the message also reflects the prophecy of Isaiah 42:1–7, which articulates a message of hope for those who have none. Rather than view the contents of the message (Luke 4:18–19) as promising exclusively physical or spiritual restoration, it may be more accurate to identify it as being descriptive of the eschatological age anticipated by the Jews – an age when there would be a transformation of all aspects of life.[4] To a large degree, the individual restorative elements of such a promise were less important than the overall transformed life of which they were but representative aspects. The new era was to be a metamorphosis of life into a brand new and scarcely imaginable life to come. Such hopes filled the dreams of first century Jews.

Jesus, inspired by the Spirit, announces that such dreams were soon to be realised and the poor, the captives, the blind and the oppressed are identified as potential beneficiaries. Interestingly, Luke omits the reference to judgment and vengeance located in Isaiah 61:1. He has already referred to the concept of judgment (3:7–9, 17) and will do so again (9:51–56; 17:22–37; 21:5–36). However, for now, the message of the Spirit focuses on hope not heartache, joy not judgment, favour not fear, embrace not exclusion. This is a comprehensive package of good news with nothing negative to spoil its content.

The agenda set by the Spirit in the sermon is important for it reveals a ministry of freedom to the fearful. The message is to the poor, the spiritually captive and blind, resulting in their freedom from prisons of bondage and spiritual oppression. The Spirit supports a ministry to the outcast and the helpless. His is not a ministry to the mighty but to the marginalized; not to the rich minority in their palatial homes but to the poverty-stricken majority who have

---

[4] His offering sight is viewed by J. Nolland (in *Luke 1 – 9:20* [Word, 1989], p. 197) as having metaphorical and literal connotations; I. H. Marshall (in *The Gospel of Luke. A Commentary on the Greek Text* [Paternoster Press, 1978], p. 184) prefers a metaphorical interpretation only. Bock (in *Luke 1:1 – 9:50*, pp. 404–411) views it as descriptive of the eschatological age. M. Barker (in 'The Time is fulfilled: Jesus and Jubilee', *Scottish Journal of Theology*, 53.1 [2000], pp. 22–32) views the Jubilee (Isa. 58:6) as the ideal lens through which the ministry of Jesus is best understood. Thus, he concludes, Jesus spiritualized the Isaianic text, interpreting release from debt and slavery as forgiveness and release from the power of Satan.

little hope. The message inspired by the Spirit is good news for those who need it most.

One of the most important aspects of the Spirit as reflected in the OT is his companionship – in particular, in extreme situations. Thus, the psalmist (139:7) encourages himself by recognising that wherever he is and whatever the circumstances he may find himself in, the one constant is that the Spirit will be there too. Moreover, the presence of the Spirit is associated with the security that he brings to those for whom he cares (139:10). The Jews, however, had begun to doubt such ancient promises, let alone think about them (139:17–18); their assumption was that God had forgotten them. In response, the Spirit sought to whisper through Jesus that they had not been forgotten. The Spirit, who had endorsed the message of Isaiah that their physical exile was to end (Isa. 48:16), was also with Jesus when he announced that their spiritual exile was over. The reality however was that most would reject Jesus, the prophet of the Spirit, as their fathers had rejected other prophets commissioned by the Spirit centuries earlier (Zech. 7:12).

Tragically, the words of Jesus, inspired by the Spirit, resulted in the first signs of rejection by those he came to save. More painful was the fact that although the words appear to be accepted by the audience as potentially true, resulting in their amazement (4:22), the dream was shattered due to their assumption that such a person as Jesus could not possibly fulfil the prophecy. He was just one more ordinary Jew with aspirations that apparently mocked the sacred prophecy. The author hopes the readers will not make the same mistake, and will be able to trace the uniqueness of Jesus – as someone who is not merely the son of Joseph; on the basis of 1:35, Luke affirms that he has been birthed by the Spirit. Unfortunately, his own neighbours fail to see the shadow of the Spirit when they look at Jesus.

4. The Spirit and suffering (Luke 4:18)

The Spirit-worldview is different from that of many believers today, who assume a right to happiness and who expect God to infiltrate their lives with regular pleasant experiences. The notion that God could use suffering in their lives as an instructive and developmental aid is a shocking and even abhorrent notion to many. However, if it is not true, the experiences of the believers in Acts are cause for concern, for they do not fit the mould of the contemporary Christian worldview of many. What is of greater concern is that the experiences of the early believers appear to be intended to be

75

normative, and motivated according to the designs of the Spirit. Somewhere along the way, the role of the Spirit in association with suffering has got lost. Now, rather than suffering being viewed as a channel through which the Spirit chooses to empower believers effectively, it is seen by many as a channel through which the devil manifests himself, and which is, therefore, to be resisted at all costs.

This association of the Spirit with suffering is introduced in the OT. There, the Spirit empowered people to undertake extraordinary responsibilities that resulted in their being sustained in, or redeemed from, severely challenging circumstances (Judg. 6:34; 11:29). On other occasions, he is described as being present in times of suffering (Pss 51:11; 139:7), strengthening people on such occasions (Isa. 11:1–4), and offering hope after the suffering (Isa. 43:19; Ezek. 37:11–14). In particular, the Jews looked forward to the Messiah who was expected to be a Spirit-endowed person who would support those who were suffering (Isa. 42:1–5; 61:1–3).

This association of suffering with the Spirit is continued in Luke (1:15; 4:1–2, 15–19), the latter references being unique to Luke. In 1:15, an angel informs Zechariah that his son, John, will be filled with the Holy Spirit. However, his was to be a ministry that would result in misunderstanding (9:7–9), rejection (7:33) and uncertainty, as he himself wondered about Jesus and his own mission (7:18–20). His short mission would end in arrest (3:19–20) and execution (9:9) and he would die unaware of the success of the one he preceded. Although his role was uniquely important and affirmed as such by the Spirit (Luke 1:67–79), the course of his life was to be challenging as he experienced suffering on a number of different levels, specifically as a result of the mission that the Spirit had given to him. He achieved his objective in a context of authentic commitment to it, but this single-minded integrity was associated with adversity. The Spirit, who effectuated his triumph, drew him to his destiny through a sea of suffering.

In 4:15–19, the sermon preached by Jesus in Nazareth in the power of the Spirit at the commencement of his ministry further identifies 'the pattern of acceptance and rejection'.[5] One would assume that his message would have been well received by his audience. However, his hearers very quickly dismissed his words and demanded his death (4:29). The startling revelation, that he had come for the marginalised, appears to be the reason for his rejection by others who assumed that the Messiah would only come for them (4:23–28).

[5] M. W. Mittelstadt, *The Spirit and Suffering in Luke-Acts* (Sheffield Academic Press, 2004), p. 49.

Luke has crafted this narrative and its setting in his account carefully.[6] After the remarkable and self-affirming events at Jordan (3:21–22), Luke identifies the genealogical pedigree of Jesus (3:23–38), followed by his skirmish in the wilderness (4:1–13) that results in Jesus dismissing the devil and reminding him that he is no mere mortal to be tested; he is, after all, the Lord and his God (4:12). Thereafter, he enters his own home town with the Spirit and is initially welcomed by all (4:14–16). The long awaited mission is about to commence and, thus far, it appears that success and acclaim will be normative, all the more when heroes of the OT are associated with Jesus. He fulfils a prophecy from Isaiah, arguably the greatest OT prophet,[7] and Elijah and Elisha are paralleled with him (4:25–27), both of whom were highly honoured in Judaism.

As with John, however, his mission, so carefully delineated by Luke (4:18–19), does not meet with long-term affirmation. Although there is initial appreciation (4:22), it soon turns into vicious anger, outright rebuttal and physical expulsion from the synagogue and the city, culminating in an attempt to murder him (4:28–29). As Marshall indicates, 'the shadow of rejection hangs over the ministry of Jesus from the outset'.[8] It is possible that the question of the crowds, 'Is not this Joseph's son?' is the cause of genuine confusion, but backed by a readiness to accept the unthinkable, that a carpenter's son could be the Messiah. However, it is more likely that it is a question backed by malice, or at least one rooted in suspicion and a readiness to reject him as a mischievous upstart. The evidence that supports the latter conclusion is that they seek to kill him, even before the synagogue service has ended.[9]

5. Spirit-inspired messages are often associated with suffering (Luke 4:16–30)

Luke has recorded thus far the affirmation of Jesus by Gabriel (Luke 1:32), by Jesus himself (2:49), the Spirit (1:35), the Father (3:22) and even by the devil, who recognises his identity (4:9). Each of them affirms that Jesus is the Son of God, not of Joseph. Simeon, Anna, the angels and even the unborn baby John in Elizabeth's womb have all

---

[6] Bock, *Luke 1:1 – 9:50*, p. 399.

[7] See R. C. Tannehill, *The Narrative Unity of Luke-Acts: A Literary Interpretation.* Vol. 1 (Fortress Press, 1986), pp. 61–63.

[8] Marshall, *The Gospel of Luke*, p. 190.

[9] See also R. Brawley, *Luke-Acts and the Jews: Conflict, Apology and Conciliation* (Scholar's Press, 1987), pp. 20–21; Mittelstadt, *The Spirit and Suffering in Luke-Acts*, pp. 53–54.

testified to the status of Jesus, and Luke has also recorded that Jesus' ancestry goes back to Adam. The readers know who Jesus is and the implied question to them is, 'Why do the listeners in the synagogue misunderstand who his father is?' Misunderstanding on the part of those who listen to Jesus will be a constant companion to him in the months ahead (7:31–35) as it was for John the Baptist (7:33) and the prophets before him (4:24; 13:34; Acts 7:51–52; 28:25).

It is no surprise that the few who do understand his identity include demons (Luke 4:34, 41; 8:28), while those who are prepared to follow him include ordinary fishermen (5:11), tax collectors (5:27–28), a sinful woman (7:36–50) and those positively described by Jesus as 'babes' (10:21, RSV). Most of the people who knew him best, and the religiously inclined people who would have been expected to follow him as Messiah, have decided that he is an impostor. As Nolland concludes, 'the rejection in Nazareth is a "dress rehearsal" for the passion'.[10]

Although the rejection is cruel and painful, however, it is also startling, because Jesus has been anointed by the Spirit to preach good news. Now, both the bearer of that good news, and, by implication, the Spirit also, are rejected. It is not that the Spirit-agenda is flawed, but that suffering is an inevitable element of it, and the readers are not to miss this aspect of the agenda, especially where it relates to their journeys of faith. As with Jesus, walking with the Spirit often involves scenarios of suffering.

Despite the fact that both Jesus and John are participating in the greatest soteriological act to occur in this world, the achievement is associated with regular experiences of suffering, resulting in antagonism, persecution and execution. The Spirit institutes missions that result in challenging and even adverse trajectories.

There is a positive note, however, even in the midst of this pain. The suffering of the Spirit-envoys is controlled by the one who has sent them. The prison will not signal the end of the mission of John. He will reappear to witness to Jesus (Luke 7:22) and be witnessed to by Jesus (7:24–28). Also the attempted murder of Jesus will not succeed on this occasion. The Spirit has an agenda and Jesus will complete it despite the suffering along the way (13:32–33). The message to the reader is that the same Spirit who supervised the often-rejected Jesus will also supervise their lives, which are also destined to involve rejection (10:16).

In his second volume, Luke provides the story of Stephen, who functions as an example of a believer who was led by the Spirit (Acts 6:5, 10; 7:55). Although the Spirit is associated with his appointment,

---

[10] Nolland, *Luke 1 – 9:20*, p. 200.

his miracles and his sermon, it is the opposition and suffering of the Spirit-inspired Stephen that Luke concentrates on (Acts 6:9 – 7:60). What is more remarkable is that Luke presents Stephen in parallel to Jesus. Thus, as Jesus is led by the Spirit and dies a martyr's death, so also does Stephen. Stephen follows in the footsteps of the Spirit-inspired Jesus (cf. Luke 4:18, 28–29).[11] Each is led by the Spirit, is accused with the same charge concerning the temple (Luke 21:6; Acts 6:13–14), and dies a martyr's death.

The testimony of Stephen is both a warning and an encourage-ment. Stephen functions as an example of a believer who was led by the Spirit (Acts 6:5, 10; 7:55). Although there is a passing reference to the fact that he achieved signs and wonders (Acts 6:8), the imme-diate aftermath to the reference to Stephen's appointment, as one of the Seven, is that he experienced opposition followed by martyr-dom. The suffering was not illegitimate, nor symptomatic of weak-ness, nor indicating that the devil had won a battle. Rather, it more closely accentuated his being a follower of Jesus, and demonstrates the overarching sovereignty of God – in that it preludes the conver-sion of Saul who witnessed it (Acts 8:1) and the extended preaching of the gospel (Acts 8:4).

At the end of the sermon (Acts 7:55), Stephen is described as being 'full of the Holy Spirit' (cf. Acts 6:5), as a result of which he sees the Son of Man standing at the right hand of God,[12] as if to welcome him. His witness was empowered by the Spirit (Acts 6:10) but it resulted in his death at the hands of those to whom he witnessed. The same Spirit who enabled Stephen to see heaven, also enabled him to face death.[13] The message to the readers is clear. To be led by the Spirit assumes the possibility of suffering. Although the message of Acts is that the gospel triumphs, it is associated with the fact that it does so through suffering. More particularly, the Spirit who sets the agenda for the development of the church and assures that it will succeed, does so on a route often catalogued by opposition and suffering.

[11] S. Cunningham, *'Through Many Tribulations': The Theology of Persecution in Luke-Acts* (Sheffield Academic Press, 1997), pp. 206, 337–342; A. C Clark, *Parallel Lives* (Paternoster Press, 2001), pp. 177–183, 262–267; Tannehill, *The Narrative Unity of Luke-Acts,* vol. 1, p. 83; W. H. Shepherd, Jr, 'The Narrative Function of the Holy Spirit as a Character in Luke-Acts', *SBL Seminar Papers,* (1994), pp. 177–179.

[12] Whether this is to indicate a legal stance on behalf of Stephen by Jesus or to welcome him to heaven is uncertain. What is of fundamental importance to the readers (and Stephen) is that Jesus is also watching the Spirit-inspired Stephen; his suffering is not being missed by the Judge of the world, the one he is seeking to follow and emulate.

[13] C. K. Barrett, *The Acts of the Apostles,* vol. 1 (T. & T. Clark, 1994), p. 382.

Luke's catalogue of suffering for the protégés of the Spirit makes uncomfortable reading for some, especially if they harbour hopes that the Spirit's agenda for them will always revolve around pleasant experiences and result in pain-free lives. It is a painful lesson to learn that Spirit-anointed preaching does not always result in converts. Although Jesus had a unique vocation, there is little to indicate from the NT that his followers were expected to lead lives that are fundamentally different.[14] The Spirit does not inappropriately incorporate suffering as part of his agenda for those he guides but sometimes, through it, he enables the achievement of his goal. Luke records Jesus describing his life as 'my trials' (Luke 22:28), *peirasmos* (trial) being used in relationship to Jesus and his mission more by Luke than by Matthew, Mark and John put together.[15] Where Matthew and Mark merely echo Luke's recording of Jesus' request that his disciples pray that they should be protected from entering into trials, Luke repeats it (Luke 22:40, 46).

Suffering and opposition for Jesus are not accidents or malevolent intrusions caused by the devil. Rather, they are part of the Spirit's plan that will result in the mother of Jesus being emotionally pierced by a sword (Luke 2:35). Luke will have cause to refer to the pain caused by a sword later when he describes the death of Jesus' disciple, James (Acts 12:2). The identity of the pain anticipated for Mary is unclear. It is probable that the imagery of a sword piercing her inner being refers to the death or rejection of Jesus which she will feel like a sword through her own heart.[16] However one interprets the phrase, the fact remains that while there is much that would cause Mary to rejoice as a result of the inspired words from the Spirit, there is pain in the prophecy. Similarly, when Paul describes his life of suffering in 2 Corinthians 2:14–16 that was associated with his ministry, a ministry which resulted in people hearing the gospel, he concludes that the Spirit of God had been central to the enterprise (2 Cor. 3:3). Similarly, Luke associates suffering with being led by the Spirit (Acts 14:22). He identifies Paul's journey to Jerusalem to suffer as not only being prophesied by the Spirit (Acts 21:11) but also resulting from the leading of the Spirit (Acts 20:22).

Although Jesus was led by the Spirit to his victorious confrontation with Satan (Luke 4:1) and returned to preach successfully in the power of the Spirit (4:14), his sermon in Nazareth was not

---

[14] Acts 4:17–18; 5:17–18, 28, 40; 7:54 – 8:3; 14:1–5; 17:5–8.

[15] Luke 4:13; 8:13; 11:4 (Matt. 6:13); 22:28, 40, 46 (Matt. 26:41; Mark 14:38).

[16] Nolland, *Luke 1 – 9:20*, p. 122; Marshall, *The Gospel of Luke* , p. 123; see Bock, *Luke 1:1 – 9:50*, pp. 248–250, and R. E. Brown, *The Birth of the Messiah* (Doubleday, 1993), pp. 462–463 for a discussion of the options.

favourably received despite the presence of the Spirit on that occasion also. This was to be the first of many occasions when the leading of the Spirit resulted in pain not pleasure, a fierce rebuttal not a friendly reception, a murderous mob not a warm welcome. Similarly, the Spirit does not always lead believers on paths devoid of pain, but nor does he leave them to walk alone, for he is their constant presence.

In the lives of believers the Spirit is not only related to signs and wonders, but also to suffering and weakness. It is not the case that life lived in the shadow of the cross and life lived in the power of the Spirit are mutually exclusive. There is no contrast to be drawn between a theology of the cross and a theology of the Spirit. The former does not signify suffering and the latter glory. Both are complementary, involving suffering and glory; indeed, often glory is obtained through suffering. The Spirit, who is associated with many aspects of Christian spirituality, is also linked to the issue of suffering. He is the Spirit not only of power and triumph but also of power and triumph through suffering. The power anticipated in Acts 1:8 should be contextualized in the suffering associated with the witness to the gospel as reflected in the rest of Acts. Praying for more power needs to be recognized as simultaneously calling for more opportunities to exhibit it while embracing challenging situations.

On two later occasions, Luke records prophecies which result in warnings of challenging events to come. It is noteworthy that the Spirit inspires knowledge about these events though he does not remove them. By describing them, however, he prepares believers for what is to come. Through Agabus, the Spirit reveals that a great famine is to occur and he inspires the believers to care for one another (Acts 11:29–30). In Acts 21: 10–11, Agabus prophesies concerning Paul's fate in Jerusalem that will result in his being bound, arrested and placed in the hands of the Gentiles.[17] From 23:16 through to the end of the book, Paul's journey to Rome, largely in the hands of Gentiles, is detailed by Luke, the 'binding' being fulfilled in 21:33. As Tannehill notes, 'his arrest and trials are not an unexpected interruption of his plans but a part of what he must face to complete his ministry'.[18] Luke does not reveal why the Spirit reveals this information to Paul but the reader is under no illusion that Paul, in

[17] Although Agabus in Acts 21:11 states that Paul will be bound by the Jews, that is actually done by the Gentiles (22:30). It may be that the binding was also done by the Jews and that Luke has chosen not to record this. It is also possible that part of the prophecy was inaccurate – see also the apparent Spirit-inspired encouragement of some believers who advised Paul not to go to Jerusalem (21:4).

[18] Tannehill, *The Narrative Unity of Luke-Acts,* vol. 2, p. 266.

treading the path to Jerusalem as led by the Spirit (19:21; 20:22), is, as Stephen, following in the path of Jesus who also 'set his face to go to Jerusalem' (Luke 9:51, ESV).[19] His is a Spirit-charted journey that will involve suffering.[20]

An important element in the exploration of the Spirit in Luke-Acts is again to note the association of the commission of the Spirit with suffering. As Mittelstadt notes, 'Paul, in response to the multiple witness of the Spirit, willingly embraces imprisonment and its sufferings as a divine calling'.[21] Sufferings, whether for Paul or believers today are no surprise to the Spirit. It is not to be assumed that the suffering is to be understood as illegitimate or unexpected as far as the Spirit is concerned. He, who is in charge of all believers and their commissions, is also in charge of their destinies.

Elie Wiesel is an author whose writings have concentrated on the sufferings of the Jews caused by the Nazi regime in Europe in the 1940s. At the conclusion of a speech he gave on April 12, 1999 at the White House to the US Congress, he said, 'We walk towards the new millennium, carried by profound fear and extraordinary hope.' It is true that, sometimes, believers walk with the shadow of fear catching them up; however, the presence of the Spirit instils the light of hope that keeps those shadows at bay. Similarly, in 1899, Theodore Roosevelt said, 'Far better is it to dare mighty things, to win glorious triumphs, even though checkered by failure . . . than to rank with those poor spirits who neither enjoy much nor suffer much, because they live in a gray twilight that knows not victory nor defeat.'[22] The Spirit who guides us promises to walk with us on our journey and stay with us in times of achievement and times when we fail. His role as a guide is not always to lead us in green pastures, but also through the valley of the shadow of death. But even when the other end of the valley is a long way off, he promises still to be our partner on the way.

6. The Spirit provides support in times of confrontation (Luke 12:8–12)

In situations where they may have felt isolated, Luke informed his readers that the Spirit would be with them, inspiring them and empowering them (12:11–12). Their position of potential

---

[19] Tannehill, ibid, pp. 240, 259.
[20] J. Fitzmyer, *The Acts of the Apostles* (Doubleday, 1998), p. 677.
[21] Mittelstadt, *The Spirit and Suffering in Luke-Acts*, p. 124.
[22] H. Sidey, 'To Dare Mighty Things', *Time*, June 9, 1980.

helplessness in the face of opposition was to be re-categorised as one of supreme sufficiency because of the presence of the Spirit. Although their families may have betrayed them, the Spirit will buttress them. Although their neighbours may slander them, the Spirit will support them.

Luke records in chapter 12 a conversation between Jesus and his disciples, the core of which relates to opposition (12:1–3), fear (14–17), the potential for division (8–10, 49–53), the identification of one's eternal priorities (13–21, 54–56), anxiety (22–34) and preparation for his return (35–48). In these confusing times of instability and eventual crisis, the promise is given that the Spirit will provide inspiration. In particular, when it comes to knowing what to say when arrested for their message, Jesus guarantees that the Spirit will inspire them and empower their words.[23]

The Spirit does not remove the suffering but promises to be with believers in those times and to enable them to function appropriately as witnesses to the truth. The suffering, though malevolent, is not counter-productive, for the Spirit will ensure that the believers function successfully in it. Luke later identifies occasions when the Spirit does just that (Acts 7:54–56; 13:9–12). The first martyr, Stephen, who was led by the Spirit, is supported by him in the last moments on earth. The Spirit provides him with a vision which may be intended to reveal that Jesus is eager to be an advocate for Stephen, who has been judged by the Jews. Not only is Jesus identified as being aware of the crime committed against his servant, but he also joyfully receives him into his presence. Stephen's defence to the Jews may have failed but it was favourably received by Jesus. The Spirit enables Stephen to see the verdict of heaven before he receives the decree of the crowds.

Peter offers a similar promise to his readers – who are also being persecuted – by identifying the one who is with them as the 'Spirit of glory' (1 Pet. 4:14). The one who promises to elevate them into a new sphere of glory at the end of time is the one who promises to be with them when they are suffering. His presence is the reminder that another destiny awaits them, one that belongs to him and is therefore glorious. Because they belong to him, that will be their future vocation also.

Western believers have yet another reason to consider and learn from the experiences of those believers, mainly living in non-Western countries, who are experiencing phenomenal growth in the context of suffering. Their life trajectories are more in line with

[23] For a valuable enquiry into the use of *dei* ('it is necessary') in 12:12, see Mittelstadt, *The Spirit and Suffering in Luke-Acts*, p. 83.

those instituted by the Spirit for the believers in the early church. Last year, I listened to a pastor of a large church in Beijing tell me that suffering is not a major issue for most Chinese Christians. It's not that they don't suffer – they do. But it's not an issue that causes them to slow down in their walk with the Spirit or even think of going back. We in the West have prayed for them during their times of suffering and even asked the Lord to remove it. But they have done so less frequently. They accept suffering as normal to the life of the believer. The Chinese church has grown not despite the suffering, but because of it. Their heroes are those who are mainly now elderly Christians who were imprisoned for decades for their faith. Yet, they speak of those times as special times with Jesus. One who had been in solitary confinement for ten years described to me that those years were the most precious of his life. When suffering comes to us in our lives, even though it may be unnatural for us so to do, we need to consider the possibility of embracing it as the Spirit's way of refining us, teaching us and providing us with a platform on which to serve him.

John 3:1–10; 4:7–26; 7:37–39
7. The Holy Spirit and salvation

1. Introduction

Many believers fail to appreciate the significant role of the Spirit in salvation. Some have assumed his involvement in the lives of believers commences or, at least, significantly develops at a later stage in their Christian journeys after salvation. However, the message of Jesus, and that of the NT in general, is that the Spirit enables believers to be saved (John 16:8). As well as developing them later, he is centrally involved in the act of salvation itself (3:6). The Spirit is involved in the life of the believer from the start, not a second later (1 Pet. 1:2); indeed, it is he who convicts us of our sin in the first place. Although the Spirit actively sanctifies believers throughout their lives, it is important not to lose sight of the significance of the moment when this setting apart of believers first takes place at salvation. The Spirit is desirous of presenting believers cleansed and clean in the future, but he is also fundamentally involved in the initiation. The Spirit makes us clean and then continues to purify us thereafter. Therefore, it is important that we value his commitment to us, give him our thanks, worship him and remember that he who started the journey with us is committed to ensuring that we complete it.

John introduces his readers to a highly significant Jewish man named Nicodemus. In the following chapter, the readers are introduced to an insignificant Samaritan woman. It is difficult to imagine two more contrasting narratives. The first describes someone from the upper echelons of Jewish society who would have been respected and admired by many; the second relates to a woman, and a Samaritan at that, despised and rejected by the Jews as worth little more than the dirty dust on their sandals. He is a ruler of the Jews (3:1) whose name means 'victor over the people'. She, on the other hand, whose name is not even mentioned, is a water carrier (4:7).

He comes to Jesus in the cool of the evening (3:2), the appropriate time for appointments and discussions; she meets Jesus at midday (4:6) when the sun is at its hottest, the least suitable time for dialogue. Nicodemus had an excellent pedigree while she had a poor reputation.

Both are also introduced to the Spirit whose desire is to lead all to faith in Jesus, enabling them to enter the kingdom (or reign) of God and to worship as a result. Nicodemus relies on his natural birth, associated with water (3:5), a Jewish symbol of birth, to enter the kingdom of God while the woman relies on ordinary water to quench her thirst (4:9–11). Jesus offers to the former the Spirit as the one who facilitates an entrance into the kingdom of God (3:5–8). He offers living water to the latter, one drink of which will facilitate worship as inspired by the Spirit (4:24).

2. Nicodemus (John 3:1–2)

John reveals to the readers that Nicodemus is an important member of Jerusalem society. He was a Pharisee (3:1), a ruler of the Jews (3:1), a teacher of Israel (3:10), a member of the Sanhedrin (7:50), prepared to speak his mind (7:50) and courageous, in that later, he, with Joseph of Arimathea, anointed and buried the body of Jesus (19:39–42). He was also a wealthy man (19:39), given the amount of spices that he brought on that occasion. Because Jesus refers to him as 'the teacher in Israel' (3:10, original Greek), it is probable that he was a highly prestigious Rabbi.[1] Thus, the readers are introduced to Nicodemus who has come to talk to Jesus for he is intrigued by him. Jesus has some startling information to share with him that will destabilise him, but also has the potential of transforming him. That he collects the body of Jesus after his crucifixion indicates that such a transformation has taken place; a spiritual victory will occur in the life of the one called 'victor'.

Nicodemus acknowledges the divine message and source of Jesus (3:2), but Jesus provides him with the opportunity of recognising

---

[1] Although many have assumed that the reason for Nicodemus seeing Jesus at night was fear of being seen by others, this is unlikely. There is nothing in the narrative to indicate that Nicodemus was being cautious or concerned that his image would be harmed by seeing Jesus. Indeed, it appears that he may have been representing others in coming to Jesus (see his use of *we know*. . ., 3:2). It is likely that he sought a private appointment. The evening was the appropriate time for such a conversation, given that rabbis often undertook an occupation in the daylight hours; other than the Sabbath, teaching was often undertaken in the evenings when it was also cooler.

him as an even more significant person. He gives him the opportunity of recognising that he is not just someone sent from God, but God in the flesh, the Spirit being the one who can open his eyes to the truth. Jesus states that before people can enter or participate in the kingdom of God, they must undergo a process akin to birth (3:3).[2] Furthermore, Jesus suggests that being *born of water* is insufficient to facilitate entrance into the kingdom of God (3:5). The reference to water probably indicates natural birth.[3] This would have been significant for Nicodemus in that he would have assumed that being born as a Jew would have automatically qualified him for an inheritance in the kingdom of God (see 3:6).

a. Born of the Spirit (3:5)

Jesus then develops for Nicodemus a more complete presentation of the active nature of the Spirit in the process of facilitating entrance into the kingdom of God. Although Jesus does not elaborate on this, he does indicate that entrance into the kingdom of God involves a radical course of action that cannot be self-initiated; it needs the involvement of the Spirit. Indeed, the birth imagery implies passivity on the part of the one being born and thus entering the kingdom of God. The active agent is the Spirit. Thereafter, those to whom *the*

---

[2] There are two main possible meanings for the phrase *gennēthē anōthen*. Some prefer 'from above'; it is thus translated elsewhere in John and generally in the Synoptics and James. It is not the idea of repetition (*born again*) that is important to Jesus: rather it is a higher life that is to be imparted. Others however, have translated it as 'from the beginning'. Because Nicodemus' question (3:4) relates to a statement concerning a second birth, many suggest this is the most relevant interpretation. What is most important is that the change depicted is not only radical, but supernatural.

[3] Rabbinic sources show that terms like rain, dew and water are often used to describe male semen, thus indicating natural birth, an issue of significant importance to Nicodemus as the basis of his eligibility to be part of the Messianic kingdom. The phrase *born of water* may be connected with John's baptism (1:33) and could thus be understood literally as the cleansing needed prior to entrance into the kingdom. Nicodemus would thus be presented with the importance of accepting the validity of John's baptism of repentance for himself, a Jew. However, Jesus does not encourage him to repent of any sins, nor is sin the topic of conversation throughout the narrative. Although John records that the disciples – and Jesus (3:22, though see 4:2) – baptized many (4:1) in water and that John baptized many (3:23), water baptism is not a prominent feature of the Gospel; indeed, there is no reference even to the fact that Jesus was baptized. It is possible that *water* is referred to by Jesus in order to identify a purifying aspect of the Spirit. Water was associated with cleansing (Ezek. 36:25) and Jesus may be encouraging Nicodemus to recognize that despite being a member of God's people, he still needs to be cleansed, a process that may be achieved by the Spirit before entrance to the kingdom can be achieved.

Spirit gives birth bear the familial characteristics and nature of the Spirit (3:6). They become members not just of a new kingdom but of a new family. They are people of the Spirit, with all the privileges and responsibilities associated with that status. Most significantly, this means that insofar as they engage in a relationship with the Spirit, it is anticipated as involving an experiential dimension.

When one becomes a believer, one receives Christ and also the Spirit. Conversion is about a change in direction, a transformation, a judicial declaration including the forgiveness of sins. However, it is also about a commencement of a relationship with the Spirit. Justification is remarkable, as is forgiveness and adoption, but they all precede the never-ending opportunity to share in the life of God, as facilitated by the Spirit (2 Pet. 1:3–4). It is this social, experiential reality that is the goal of the believer. It is in this context that the love of God, as mediated by the Spirit, is experienced. In this dynamic matrix, we also give our lives and love to God.

Similarly, when Paul writes to the Galatians who are concerned that they may have made a mistake in following Jesus, he asks them about their experience of the Spirit (Gal. 3:2–5). They were afraid that their salvation was deficient and they felt a need to do something else to ensure that they were saved. To assure them, Paul simply reminds them of the presence of the Spirit in their lives. He is the evidence of their salvation, and he asks them when they received him. The answer is clear – when they became believers, they were joined by the Spirit. The moment they began to follow Jesus, the Spirit miraculously appeared next to them; there was no gap in time or space. He was there before they had chance to ask him to come, before they even knew of his existence; before they were ready for him, he was ready for them.

Furthermore, using the terminology of baptism, Paul identifies the Spirit as baptizing all believers into the one body (the church) and, then changing the metaphor, states that all were 'given the one Spirit to drink' (1 Cor. 12:13). The Spirit acts in two ways to make quite clear that believers are integrally bonded to him.[4] The terms 'baptized' and 'drink' are probably to indicate the experiential nature of this act. Rather than view the process of incorporation into the church as being merely based on an acknowledgement of certain theological facts, Paul anticipates that there will be a transforming dimension to this re-location, a dynamic feature worthy of such graphic verbs. Such a remarkable repositioning of one's life to

---

[4] Although some suggest that this occurs at water baptism or a subsequent experience of the Spirit, both are unlikely as the stress is on the entrance into the body of the church which occurs at salvation.

another plane of existence, from one family to another, assumes an accompanying experience. The latter may be expressed differently for each individual but it represents tangible evidence of change, a differential marker that Paul hopes for and expects when the Spirit enters the life of a believer.

In a similar fashion, he refers to the Spirit leaving his signature on the lives of believers (2 Cor. 3:3, 6). The Spirit has never intended being a silent partner in the life of the believer. It is not his plan to be the quiet visitor who creeps around our lives keeping out of our way, whose footprint is never seen, whose voice is never heard, whose presence does not disturb the air. His desire is to write himself into our experiences, leaving his fingerprint on all areas of our lives so that we know the practical effect of his influence. The supreme graffiti artist seeks to paint us with vivid colours and bold letters that reflect his presence.

b. The sovereignty of the Spirit (3:8)

After John records Jesus' words in 3:8, Nicodemus expresses astonishment. It is unlikely that he is confused by Jesus, even though Jesus uses words capable of two meanings.[5] After all, Nicodemus is a respected and learned Rabbi, well used to complex reasoning. Although the disciples may have failed to comprehend the intricacy and multifaceted nature of Jesus' words, it is likely that Nicodemus is an intellectual heavyweight. It is not the complexity of Jesus' argument that troubles him, but its content. He is perplexed not by the intelligence offered by Jesus, but by the implications of his insights. Jesus destabilizes him by calling into question the basis of his self-confidence and his perception of God's attitude to him – his birth as a Jew.

It is in this regard that Jesus cleverly compares the wind with the Spirit and, in doing so, two major points are made. As the wind does what it wants, so the Spirit is sovereign; more radically, as the wind may be experienced by all and anyone, so also the Spirit may be experienced by all, Jews and Gentiles. Jesus has come not just to give eternal life to the Jews but to the world (3:16). Similarly, the Spirit is the one who sovereignly imparts this divine life (6:63). Rather than assume that 'eternal life' (3:16) is solely a description of life that never ends, it is more appropriate to associate it with the eternal life of the Spirit. Such eternal life is characterised by the qualities associated with eternity and the Spirit of eternity himself.

---

[5] *Pneuma* can be translated 'wind' or 'spirit/Spirit'; *phōnē* can be translated 'sound' or 'voice'; *pneō* can be translated 'I breathe' or 'I move'.

3. The Samaritan woman (John 4:7–26)

Later, John introduces his readers to another who will benefit from the initiatory work of the Spirit. Unlike Nicodemus, she is not identified by name; she is simply a woman. The other details offered result in her being portrayed as someone who has been marred by life. She has little to offer the Messiah, who happens to pause for a drink of water from her well. Not only is she a woman but she is a Samaritan. As a woman, she is aware of her subordinate place in a male dominated society, of the limited opportunities she has to function in her religion and of her inadequacies and inferiority. As a Samaritan, she is excluded by the Jews as a member of a mongrel community, despised by them throughout a history of hatred and hurt. But there is worse to be revealed, for her life has been badly marred by broken marriages; she is socially and relationally disfigured, her life blighted with blemishes – a flawed and spoiled Samaritan woman. But John has one more item to divulge. She has a secret and Jesus knows what it is. There is little reason for her to feel proud about her situation and the shocking revelation to the readers is that despite knowing who she is, Jesus still talks to her. Jesus reveals that although she has had five husbands, her present partner is not her husband (4:16–18). In a Jewish context, she is not a likely candidate for a conversation with Messiah and at the bottom of the list of those who may be offered hope by him.

In contrast to Nicodemus who came to Jesus, however, this woman, who did not look for Jesus, is addressed by him and becomes the object of his interest. Indeed, if Jesus had not stopped at a well to rest and started a conversation with her, there is little to assume that she would have approached him. This is all the more likely given the antipathy of Jews to Samaritans and the fact that as a man, he would be assumed to be considerably more significant than she, a woman (4:9). Nicodemus came to Jesus, having witnessed his signs, but there is no suggestion that she knew anything about Jesus. However, she will be a sign to many others for she will point the way to Jesus (4:39–42). A racially unimportant and spiritually stained woman is prized by Jesus, who relates to others on the basis of what he can give to them not what they can give to him. She has little to offer but water, but Jesus has eternal water to dispense to her.

As a result of this meeting, she will be able to *worship in spirit and in truth* (4:24).[6] Worship is motivated and made possible

---

[6] Although *pneuma* could be translated 'spirit' or 'Spirit', the latter is the more appropriate translation in the context. When John records Jesus stating, *God is*

because of the presence of the Spirit. His presence in the life of the worshipper authenticates the worship offered. The geographical context of worship is less important than its content; the heart of the worshipper is more significant to God than external forms of worship. As God is identified with the Spirit, to truly worship God necessitates a context in which the Spirit is present. The Spirit is the one who facilitates worship by becoming intimately involved in and with believers.

The reference to truth relates to the role of the Spirit in facilitating worship that is authentic. Jesus is not suggesting that one should worship God in a correct formulaic way or with a particular liturgy or form of spirituality. He is saying more than that true worship is not based in error. In other words, he is not saying that there is a right way to worship God and a wrong way. It is more to do with identifying worship that is acceptable to God because of a relationship that has been established with him. The form of one's worship is much less important than the means whereby it is conducted and achieved. To worship God demands the help of someone identified with God, the Spirit. The Spirit enables believers to worship God in a way that is genuine, valid and authentic. After all, he is the Spirit of truth (John 14:17; 16:13). John thus confirms the Spirit as the one who authenticates worship. It is he who determines that worship can take place and who makes it possible. Worship takes place as a result of the Spirit, who initiates an open-door policy to God on behalf of the believer. As such, he presents believers as living temples in whom God chooses to dwell.

4. The Spirit of living water (John 7:37–39)

As in John 3:5, so also in 7:37–39, Jesus uses the metaphor of water in association with the Spirit in the context of salvation. It is no coincidence that these words of Jesus were uttered during the seven-day-long Feast of Tabernacles (7:2). It was popularly referred to as the Feast of Tents due to the fact that the participants camped in homemade shelters, erected on rooftops or in the fields (Lev. 23:34–36). It functioned as a thanksgiving for the harvests and an opportunity to remember how God had guided their forefathers during the forty years in the wilderness. Implicit was an anticipation of the arrival of the kingdom of God, when their 'exile' would

---

Spirit (4:24), he is not merely saying that God is non-material. Such a concept is obvious; rather, he is referring to the fact that God is associated with the Spirit. Similarly, to worship God demands the involvement of the Spirit.

finally be over and life-giving water would be available in abundance.[7] Little wonder that Josephus described it as the most popular festival held in the temple.[8]

It was at this feast that the ritual of drawing water took place on each of the seven days, reflecting the provision of water from the rock by God (Exod. 17:1–6). Water was drawn from the Pool of Siloam, and carried in a musical and formal procession through the streets of Jerusalem to the temple, where it was poured from a golden flagon on to the altar to cleanse it, prior to the offering of sacrifices. The procession was carefully timed so that it arrived at the temple just as the priests brought the first sacrifice to the altar during the singing of the *Hallel* (as recorded in Pss 113 – 118) by the temple choir. The memory of salvation in the past and salvation to come provided the ideal opportunity for Jesus to prophesy the fulfillment of this long-awaited hope. However, he stated that it would only be realized by those who believed in him. This was now no longer a prophecy only realizable by Jews – Jesus had radically altered the conditions whilst widening the constituency of those eligible to take advantage of this life-giving refreshment. Most importantly, the Spirit was to be the life-giving source for all people, regardless of their nationality or background.

The association of the Spirit with water is infrequently mentioned in the OT (Isa. 44:3; Ezek. 36:25–27)[9] though Jeremiah 17:13 identifies the Lord with 'the spring of living water'. However, the symbolism of the Spirit being poured out (Joel 2:28–29; Acts 2:17) may indicate a more common association between water and the Spirit than is explicit in the biblical text.[10] Central to the account, and to John 7:37–39, is the fact that the provision of the Spirit would not occur until after Jesus had been glorified. However, when the Spirit would be provided, it was stated that he would flow as living water 'from the heart'.[11] It is probable that the Spirit is anticipated as flowing from the heart of Jesus, to be received by believers (John

---

[7] Isa. 12:3, cf. Ezek. 47:1–12; Zech. 14:8 – both of the latter passages were read during the festival.

[8] Josephus, *Ant.* 8.100.

[9] It is interesting to note that some (later) Rabbis associated the practice with the pouring out of the Holy Spirit.

[10] See C. S. Keener *The Gospel of John*, vol. 1 (Hendrickson, 2003), p. 724 for further Jewish references and parallels.

[11] My translation. Note the original reading in John 7:38 is *koilia* (belly, cavity), a term sometimes used to represent the person concerned and even used synonymously with *kardia* (heart). G. R. Beasley-Murray, in *John* (Word, 1987), pp. 116–117, notes the possible allusions to the flowing of water from the side of Jesus at his death (John 19:34), the rock that provided water in the Wilderness (Exod. 17:1–6) and the river flowing from the temple (Ezek. 47:1–12).

7:38; 20:22).[12] Although the initial flow of the Spirit commences with Jesus, it is valid to deduce that, thereafter, believers are to take responsibility for the Spirit flowing through them to others within the Christian community and outside it (John 4:13–14). The issue to be determined is why Jesus chose water as a symbol of the Spirit. A number of suggestions may be offered other than the OT allusions between water and Spirit.

a. What is the significance of water?

Over seventy percent of the surface of the earth is covered by water. This was particularly appreciated by the public at large when pictures were beamed back from the Apollo space missions showing the vast areas of the oceans that covered the globe, resulting in it being named 'the blue planet'. However, much of it is undrinkable, resulting in the popular quotation from Samuel Taylor Coleridge's famous poem, 'The Rime of the Ancient Mariner' – 'water, water, every where,/Nor any drop to drink' – spoken by a sailor lost at sea. However, the inexhaustible and living water of the Spirit is freely available to all believers. It would be a tragedy if such a source of refreshing and refining was overlooked or ignored.

Some years ago, a ship sank off the coast of South America and the sailors transferred to a lifeboat where, for weeks, they languished on the ocean. Miraculously, they were eventually rescued. Their lips were parched and blistered and they were severely dehydrated, close to death. After a short time of recovery, they were asked why they had not drunk the water surrounding them. They responded with obvious incredulity as they had been floating in the Atlantic Ocean, the water of which is salty; to drink that would certainly have killed them. However, they did not realise that they had, in fact, been in the outwash of the Amazon River, which pumps fresh water two hundred miles into the ocean. Although they were surrounded by life-giving water, they had been oblivious to the fact and nearly died when all around them was all they needed to provide refreshment and to enable them to live. The invitation that Jesus offered in the first century is still available to us today. The Spirit is an endless resource of life-giving refreshment to us all and we should take advantage of him and enjoy all that he has for us.

[12] See Keener, who concludes that Jesus is the subject (*The Gospel of John*, vol. 1, pp. 728–729), and L. P. Jones, who believes that believers are the subject, in *The Symbol of Water in the Gospel of John* (Sheffield Academic Press, 1997), pp. 154–155; see also L. Morris, *The Gospel According to John* (Eerdmans, 1971), pp. 422–427, and D. A. Carson, *The Gospel According to John* (Eerdmans, 1991), pp. 323–325 for a full review of the options and support offered.

b. Water is indispensable to life

Water is crucial to the survival of the planet, not only for drinking but also to grow crops, feed animals and because it contains the fish that provide a major source of protein for most of the people in the world. When there is a dearth of water, diseases occur and death soon follows. In the first century, when drought was frequent and in the arid climate of Israel, where there were few rivers, a lack of water was devastating, because the vast majority of people lived in an agrarian society. With bread, it was viewed as one of the basic staples of life.[13]

In John 7:38, Jesus specifically describes the water he gives as *living*, symbolizing its freshness, constancy and flowing nature. This is to be contrasted with the sporadic rainfall that occurred from mid-October though mid-March in Israel. The quality of refreshing and life-giving water is regularly expressed in the Bible.[14] One of the clearest demonstrations of this feature is located in Exodus 17:1–6, where God provided water for the parched Israelites from a rock. Thus, water is an appropriate metaphor for the Spirit who 'gives life' (John 6:63) and rebirth (John 3:6).[15] Similarly, the Spirit is presented throughout the OT (Ezek. 37:14) and NT (2 Cor. 3:6, 16–18; Eph. 1:3–14) as offering a life-changing relationship with God in the context of also facilitating positive change and dynamism in the life of the believer. The 'flesh' is not capable of giving life (John 6:63); it is not possible to think oneself into the kingdom of God by way of reason or intellect or to enter on the basis of racial pedigree – it is a gift of the Spirit.

c. Water represents wisdom

Water was a common metaphor for wisdom in Jewish literature, especially as the wisdom that comes from God.[16] Similarly, the Torah and its teaching were described as water.[17] For water to be associated with the Spirit would have created in the minds of the hearers the notion of the Spirit of wisdom. It is he who now offers

[13] Gen. 2:10; Exod. 23:25; 34:28; Deut. 8:7–9; Amos 8:11.
[14] Pss 65:9–10; 104:13; 107:33, 35; Isa. 41:18; 43:20; Matt. 10:42; John 13:5.
[15] Although the RSV offers 'spirit' in 6:63, it more likely refers to the Spirit who gives life (so Keener, *The Gospel of John*, vol. 1, p. 694; A. J. Köstenberger, *John* [Baker, 2004], p. 219). It is difficult to imagine how a 'spirit' gives life and more sensible to understand Jesus' following words as referring to him speaking in association with the Spirit and life (6:63b).
[16] Sirach 15:3; 24:25; Exod. *Rab.* 31:3; Philo, *Somn.* 2.242–243; 1QS 10.12.
[17] C. S Keener, *The Spirit in the Gospels and Acts* (Hendrickson, 1997), p. 136.

himself as a personal guide and wise tutor to believers (John 14:16, 26; 15:26).

d. Water cleanses physically and symbolizes spiritual refining and renewal

Each of these concepts is common in the OT.[18] Ritual bathing was frequent in various Jewish contexts, especially in the Jerusalem temple and as demonstrated by the Qumran community on the northern shores of the Dead Sea, which had constructed an elaborate series of ritual baths for ceremonial purposes. The message of Jesus (and the rest of the NT) is that it is the Spirit who undertakes initially to set believers apart (John 3:5–6; 7:38; Rom. 8:14–17; Gal. 4:6) and then continually to refine them (John 14:26; Gal. 5:16, 25). Thus, in Titus 3:5, Paul identifies regeneration and renewal as works of the Spirit. The Spirit generates spiritual life. This does not refer to a rekindling or regeneration of life that was once present but had slipped away; this relates to a generation and creation of life. The Spirit initiates life where there was death, constructing potential out of nothing, a future out of a fatality. This is not simply a new start; this is the start of all that is new. All of this has been achieved as a result of God's generosity (3:16), the gift of eternal life from Jesus (3:6) and the Spirit (7:38).

d. Water is an eschatological symbol [19]

The concept of God sending streams and floods of water to a parched land was a frequent expression in Isaiah.[20] The symbolism of water was understood by John's readers as a life-giving source that was promised by God to transform the lives of the Israelites. It struck a chord in their hearts and hinted at that ancient hope that God's river of life would soon be flowing to them. Keener provides evidence which indicates that it is intrinsically likely that Zechariah 14 would have been one of the readings in the feast of Tabernacles.[21] The value of verses Zechariah 8–9 is that they describe the eschatological era to come, a period dominated by peace and the rule of God. They describe an occasion when a great river would be created, its source being in Jerusalem, which would then divide into two – one flowing

---

[18] Gen. 18:4; 24:32; Exod. 29:4; Lev. 15:13; Num. 8:7.

[19] The term 'eschatological' and its derivatives is used to refer to the end time when Jesus returns. The Jews understood that era as being defined when Messiah returns (as they still do).

[20] Isa. 21:14; 32:2; 33:16; 35:7.

[21] Keener, *The Spirit in the Gospels and Acts*, p. 158.

to the Mediterranean, the other to the Dead Sea. Abundant life-giving water would cover the land in the age of Messiah.[22] For Jesus also, the water identified with the Spirit in John 7 indicates spiritual renewal (Isa. 12:3), prophesied by the OT prophets, expected by the Jews[23] and now proffered by Jesus.

Interestingly, given the many references to water in John, it is no surprise that he is the only author who writes of the water that flows from the side of Jesus at his death (19:34). As the water leaves him, symbolic of the Spirit, the Messianic hope is fulfilled for the era to come, as symbolically, the Spirit is released to function in the lives of the followers of Jesus.

It is because of the characteristics associated with water in OT and Jewish history and life that Jesus associates it with the Spirit and with the sensational impact he is to have in the lives of believers. He is God's gift to people who are thirsty and he offers himself as an indispensable element in the delivery of spiritual life. As part of his involvement in the lives of believers, he shares his wisdom with them, cleansing, refining and preparing them for the future; indeed, his coming demonstrates that the eschatological age has already commenced.

---

[22] Ezek. 47:1–2 and Joel 3:18 also associate water with the Spirit and the new temple.
[23] See further Jones, *The Symbol of Water in the Gospel of John,* p. 156.

John 14:12–17; 15:26 – 16:7, 13–15
8. The Holy Spirit is the Paraclete

1. Introduction

John takes his readers on a roller coaster of emotional highs and lows that surely reflected something of the despair and elation, confusion and excitement, fear and euphoria of the disciples of Jesus, especially in his last few weeks on earth. Having healed a blind man (John 9:1–7), a miracle unknown in the OT or Jewish literature, Jesus is accused of being a sinner by the religious authorities (9:24). In contrast to a blind man, who 'sees' who Jesus is while still blind, the religious leaders, who can physically see, cannot (or choose not to) 'see' who he truly is. Having presented himself as the good shepherd (10:11), he is however accused by his potential flock of being demonized, mad and deserving of being stoned to death (10:20, 31). The sheep try to kill their shepherd. Having raised Lazarus from the dead (11:43–44), the religious leaders plot Jesus' death (11:53). Those who witness Jesus granting life seek to impose death. Having been welcomed by the crowds in Jerusalem (12:12), Jesus hides from them and leaves Jerusalem (12:36). Having apparently experienced triumph when entering Jerusalem (12:13), Jesus is troubled (12:27).

The reason for his pain is that the crowds have welcomed him as a miracle worker who raised Lazarus from the dead (John 12:18). Jesus realizes that they have accepted little more than that. To them he is merely a superstar, a wonder worker and potential king (12:39–40; Luke 19:37–38). Although Jesus states he is soon to be glorified (John 12:23), he associates that with service (12:26; 13:1–5, 12–20), his own death (12:23–25), crucifixion (12:32–33) and departure from this world (13:1), not with an earthly crown and palace. At this time, he is so troubled that he asks his Father to rescue him (12:27). And the crisis deepens. Although heaven affirms him (12:28), Judas betrays him (13:27); while God exalts Jesus (13:31), Satan enters

Judas (13:27). While Peter upbraids Jesus (13:7–8) and promises never to turn his back on him (13:37), he then denies him (13:38). It is at this point, after a catalogue of challenges and crises, that Jesus informs the disciples that he is to leave them and, not only that, but they cannot follow him (13:36). Instead of a physical partnership with Jesus, he warns that they will be expelled from synagogues and that people will think that killing them is the highest form of worship to God (16:1–2)

In this maelstrom of disturbing events, however, he tells them that he will return for them and, while absent from them, will prepare a place for them (John 14:2, 3). Even more significantly, he informs them that he will send someone to take his place, described as 'the Counsellor' (*paraklētos*, see also 14:26; 15:26; 16:7–11, 12–15) who will be their permanent companion and friend and the one who will empower them beyond their dreams. Although many believers think of the Spirit simply as a power or force that is often understood rather impersonally, the NT regularly describes him in personal terms. This is particularly the case in the Gospel of John.

The life-giving Spirit provides refreshing life, incisive guidance, personal cleansing and individual refining in this life as a foretaste of the life to come. The Spirit inspires hope in the hearts of believers in that he promises to be with them throughout their lives. This was graphically experienced by the disciples, who were afraid that in losing Jesus they were losing everything. In reality, fear was replaced by hope.

In his book *The Kite Runner*, Khaled Hosseini describes the fear felt by the main character whose father, Baba, died. He writes, 'I realised how much of who I was, what I was, had been defined by Baba and the marks he had left on people's lives. My whole life, I had been "Baba's son". Now he was gone. Baba couldn't show me the way anymore. I'd have to find it on my own. The thought terrified me.'[1]

The disciples also knew fear intensely as they considered a future without Jesus. After his resurrection, they waited for the promise of the Paraclete, who would take over where Jesus had left off and guide them into their futures. The same Paraclete has entered the lives of believers today; his touch is evident in their lives. He walks with them, leaving his footprints so they may follow him and walk in them. The promises concerning the Spirit to the disciples then are relevant to believers now: teaching (14:26), bearing witness to Jesus (15:26), leading into all truth (16:13), prophesying the future (16:13) and providing revelation (16:14).

---

[1] K. Hosseini, *The Kite Runner* (Bloomsbury, 2003), p. 152.

2. The Spirit empowers believers (John 14:12–14)

Jesus articulates the amazing truth that it will be to the advantage of the disciples for him to leave them, for then the Spirit will be sent in his place. Although Jesus had been of such great importance to them, he now says that someone is coming who can be of even greater benefit (16:7) to them and they 'will be active on the basis of his strength'.[2]

In 14:12–14, Jesus identifies one of the benefits of the arrival of the Spirit. Jesus promises that the works (*erga*) that he performed will be achieved to a greater degree by those who believe in him. Such works are best identified as miracles[3] and possibly also ethical acts.[4] It may be appropriate to recognize that anything that fulfils the will of God, as exemplified in the life of Jesus, may be identified thus. However, to suggest that believers will be able to achieve greater miraculous works than Jesus in terms of the dramatic impact caused is an unlikely interpretation of the text. Nor is Jesus promising that greater power will be available to believers than was available to himself. The significance of the promise is simply, though remarkably, that such authoritative power will be granted to believers who, corporately, will continue the ministry of Jesus throughout the world, not being restricted to one country or lifetime. This is because of the ongoing presence and empowering of the Spirit. In the absence of Jesus, it might be wondered how the development of the gospel would be sustained, let alone enlarged. Without the power base associated with the King of the kingdom, its growth would be in doubt. However, the Spirit grants power and authority to believers, the quality of which is identical to that owned by Jesus.

The reference to the Spirit (14:15–18) indicates that he is the

[2] R. Schnackenburg, *The Gospel According to St. John,* 3 vols (Burns and Oates, 1982), p. 127.

[3] Although some – B. Milne, *The Message of John* (IVP, 1993), p. 215; L. Morris, *The Gospel According to John* (Eerdmans, 1971), p. 646 – presume that 'works' could refer to the preaching of the gospel, this is not reflected in the text itself. Moreover, it may be argued that the plural 'works' would be an inappropriate way to express the preaching of the gospel. Significantly, the term is used elsewhere to relate to the miracles of Jesus, as identified in 14:10 (5:20, 36; 7:3; 9:3–4; 10:25, 32–33, 37–38). Furthermore, the use of the same term in 14:12, where Jesus first refers to the same works mentioned in v. 11 as being achieved by him and second refers to them as potential realities in the experience of the disciples, suggests a continuation of meaning (i.e. miracles). The following verses present a promise of Jesus in response to prayer, but the context is not of evangelism but the achievement of those same miraculous works.

[4] John 3:21 (7:7).

distinguishing feature in this promise. Even when Jesus has ascended, the purposes of God will still be made manifest through his follow-ers because they will be living in the age of the Spirit.[5] The ascension of Jesus did not signal the absence of divine presence. The emphasis in Jesus' promise is on the fact that fragile followers of Jesus will have the dynamic authority to emulate him. Indeed, because they are many, the potential of more examples of such authoritative manifestations of his power are to be expected. Thus, the greatness of the works is best understood in terms of the new context in which they are achieved. As the Spirit remained with Jesus (14:10), so also will the Spirit remain with believers.

Jesus makes a subtle but crucially important statement in that he affirms that the Spirit is currently *with* them but that soon, he will be *in* them (14:17). Jesus is not attempting to suggest that a closer proximity of the Spirit to believers will facilitate a greater release of his power in their lives. The Spirit has the capacity to exercise his power and authority whether he is a million miles or a whisper away. He does not function better or more easily by being closer to the area of need. The point that Jesus is illustrating is that the Spirit, until now, has never been described as being in anyone other than Jesus and John the Baptist (Luke 1:15). Not only will the Spirit be in the new Christian community but he will reside in each member of that community.

Jesus is expressing the fact that if they thought that the pres-ence of Jesus with them was remarkable, they should consider the consequences of the Spirit being in them. Similarly, the Spirit, who worked with Jesus and with the disciples before the ascension, is now described as working with the disciples but also in them. He is not a Spirit who simply anoints believers as the prophets anointed God's servants in the past; he operates from within. He is not just poured out upon believers, but he also fills them and, through them, blesses others. This is a new era that is being celebrated by this prep-osition *in*. Concentration should not be placed on the identification or even the achievement of such acts, but more on the fact that they are accomplished due to the power of the present Spirit.

Rather than try to compare and contrast the work of Jesus in the disciples and the work of the Spirit in believers, it is more appropri-ate to see the former as providing examples of how the latter may function. In a real sense, Jesus is no less present in the life of the believer than he was present with his disciples when he walked in Israel. In fact, because he and the Spirit are inseparable, he is as much

[5] cf. M. M. B. Turner, *The Holy Spirit and Spiritual Gifts Then and Now* (Paternoster Press, 1996), p. 338.

present in the believer's life as is the Spirit. It is not that Jesus is in heaven but the Spirit is on earth or that Jesus is our advocate there while the Spirit supports believers here. The Spirit is the presence of Jesus in our lives. The often quoted words that a believer is someone who has 'asked Jesus into his or her heart' is not as far from the truth as might be imagined. Although Jesus is not literally residing in one's heart, it may be concluded that he is closer to believers than that – that testimony is simply an illustration of something much more intimate. The Spirit is in us, around us, alongside us and ahead of us; working in us, for us and through us; on our side and against our enemies; with us and ensuring that we are with him.

3. The Paraclete

The Greek word used to refer to the Spirit by John is *paraklētos*, often translated as *Counsellor*. It is not used by any other NT author but was widely used before John.[6] Given that the word is capable of a number of translations, it may be more appropriate to use the transliteration of the Greek (*paraclete*) rather than offer a translation. Nevertheless, a number of translations could help define characteristics of the Spirit. Fundamentally, the metaphor is intended to leave the reader awestruck by the comprehensive nature of the conscientious compassion of the Spirit for believers.

a. The Spirit is 'alongside believers'

The term *paraklētos* is made up of two elements that may provide an insight into its meaning, referring to one who has been called (*kaleō*) alongside (*para*) another. Although the breakdown of a word and its etymology may not necessarily reveal its best translation in a given era or context, it can provide some insight to its meaning. The word *paraklētos* was used in various ways in the first century and these will be explored later. However, a fundamental role of the Spirit is to be 'alongside' believers, and he is thus best able to comprehensively support them. He is never so far from them that if they stumble, he will not be able to catch them. The term is not intended to define the exact location of the Spirit in relation to the believer. John is not attempting to determine the physical proximity of the Spirit to believers as being in spatial terms, but to identify that he is as close to them as possible. Indeed, in John 14:17, the Spirit is

---

[6] T. G. Brown, *Spirit in the Writings of John* (T. & T. Clark, 2003), pp. 170–180.

defined as being in the believer while Paul speaks about the believer being in the Spirit (Eph. 2:18). On other occasions, different metaphors will be used of the Spirit in relation to believers in an attempt to explore more fully the comprehensive care of the Spirit for those to whom he is committed. This term *paraclete* should therefore be understood as offering further reinforcement for this truth.

A number of commentators have suggested that John uses the term to identify the Spirit as fundamentally being a comforter or consoler of believers. However, the references in John do not easily reflect this.[7] Indeed, although the initial reference to the Spirit being sent may have been encouraging to the disciples who feared loneliness without Jesus, once the resurrection had occurred, there was no hint of their being despondent or in need of consolation. On the contrary, they were anticipating the promise of Jesus being fulfilled in Jerusalem and regularly visited the temple, praising God as they did (Luke 24:53). Thus, although the RSV translates *paraklētos* as 'comfort' (Acts 9:31), there is little to indicate on that occasion that the believers needed comforting by the Spirit. On the contrary, the believers were not discouraged or downhearted but encouraged because the church was being built up (Acts 9:31). One reason for the notion of the Spirit being a comforter may go back to the translation of the term by Wycliffe from the Latin *comfortare*, though even this actually means 'to be strengthened' rather than 'to be comforted'. It is more accurate to view the Spirit as mentoring, counselling, inspiring and encouraging believers, although this may undoubtedly, on occasions, include the act of providing comfort.

b. The Spirit is another Paraclete (John 14:16)

The value of a leader being replaced by another to ensure that the progress of the group continues is recognised in ancient and modern societies. It happened with Moses and Joshua (Deut. 34:9) and Elijah and Elisha (2 Kgs 2:9–10, 15), and it regularly occurs in modern leadership scenarios also, both secular and Christian. The way Jesus describes the Spirit as being *another Counsellor* (John 14:16) indicates that he is to function similarly to the way Jesus related to his disciples. As Jesus was sent by the Father (3:16), so was the Spirit (14:16); as Jesus was with the disciples, affirming and supporting them (3:22; 13:33), so will be the Spirit with believers (14:16–17); as Jesus taught and trained the disciples (14:26), so will the Spirit mentor believers (7:14–15; 8:20); as Jesus led his disciples into

---

[7] See further discussion by C. S. Keener, *The Gospel of John*, 2 vols (Hendrickson, 2003), vol. 2, p. 955.

truth (18:37), so will the Spirit guide believers into truth (16:13); as Jesus convicts the world (3:19–20), so will the Spirit (16:8); as Jesus walked with the disciples, so will the Spirit partner believers. The companionship of Jesus with the disciples will be no less immediate than the relationship of the Spirit with believers.

There are two terms that could have been used by John for *another* (*allos* and *heteros*). Although the distinction should not be over-pressed, the latter often refers to another of a different kind, the former identifies another of the same kind; it is *allos* that is used in John 14:16. The Spirit is not another, different kind of counsellor; rather, he is the same kind of Counsellor as was Jesus, exhibiting the same quality of care and wisdom. Jesus, who is described as a Paraclete in 1 John 2:1, is represented by John as supporting believers while in heaven to the same degree and with the same intimate commitment as does the Spirit on earth. Rather than think of them as two individuals working in two areas of the universe, it is more appropriate to understand the message that John seeks to present – believers are comprehensively cared for wherever they are, in heaven or on earth; believers are never alone, for the Paraclete is with them.

Furthermore, John is not simply suggesting that Jesus is now in heaven while the Spirit is on earth, a role-reversal on their part. Nor is he intending his readers to assume that he functions in heaven on behalf of believers (Heb. 7:26) while the Spirit functions on earth supporting them. It is not that the Spirit has taken over from Jesus because he has relinquished his intimate relational role with believers. Rather than assume discontinuity, it is more appropriate to acknowledge continuity of support for believers by both the Spirit and Jesus. Both are integrally linked with the support of and ministry to believers. Whereas Jesus (and the Spirit) offered this in Jesus' life on earth, now, because of his ascension, the Spirit (and Jesus) will continue it. To try and compartmentalise the work of Jesus and the Spirit is unwittingly to betray an arrogance that assumes that the inexplicable can be explained by human intellect. God is gracious and, through the NT writers, paints pictures to allow us to grasp truths that are actually beyond our understanding. He wants us to enjoy and experience them, and to be committed to them but not necessarily to comprehend them. Rather than seeking to understand and trying to systematise the concept of the divine shepherding of the church by Jesus, the Spirit and the Father, believers should first experience and be exhilarated by that truth. Then, and only then, should they engage in the exploration of the doctrine, acknowledging that although the mystery stretches their intellect too much, they should enjoy the journey of discovery and anticipate the possibility of being transformed as a result.

c. The Spirit is sent to believers (John 15:26; 16:7)

In John 14:16, Jesus is described as requesting the Father to give the Spirit to his followers. In 15:26, however, Jesus declares that he will send the Spirit from the Father while in 14:26, John declares that the Father will send the Spirit in the name of Jesus; 16:13 simply declares that the Spirit will come. One must guard against any suggestion of a divine hierarchy. The Spirit is described as God in 4:24 and there is no suggestion that he is viewed merely as an impersonal force or lesser member of the Godhead to be commanded to do whatever the Father or Jesus desire. The provision of the Spirit is not a unilateral act on the part of Jesus or the Father but part of the divine plan to take care of believers in the physical absence of Jesus.

That the Spirit is not able to come until Jesus goes (16:7) needs careful consideration. John is not indicating that Jesus and the Spirit cannot function concurrently. Nor is he simply (or even) suggesting that the Spirit takes over from Jesus, thus releasing Jesus to undertake another responsibility (as if he could not handle both). It is more likely that Jesus is indicating that the role of the Spirit will not be clearly manifested or appreciated by believers until Jesus ascends. Then, the Spirit will be more obviously demonstrated as continuing the work initiated by Jesus through the church. The worldwide ministry of the Spirit will be unmistakably evident. Despite the absence of Jesus, the church will still develop, but now by the Spirit functioning through believers.

d. The Spirit is an advocate for believers (John 16:8–11)

At times, John represents the role of the Spirit with the believer as that of a mediator, broker or advisor (16:8–11) and *parakletos* is able to bear this interpretation.[8] In secular Greek, the term is often used forensically, to refer to a lawyer who legally defends another or a friend who supports another in a legal context.[9] In Roman law, a person was generally accused by a private citizen rather than by a prosecutor chosen by the State, though advocates were provided to offer a defence, as well as witnesses for and against. However, as well as using witnesses to support and accuse the one on trial, Jewish law also generally adopted the practice of an advocate (to defend) and an accuser (to prosecute). The notion of someone functioning as an advocate, and chosen to do so by the legal authorities, was thus common in the ancient world.

The concept of advocacy was encouraging to believers then, as it

---

[8] Brown, *Spirit in the Writings of John*, pp. 180–234.
[9] See Keener (*The Gospel of John*, vol. 2, pp. 956–957) for a discussion of both uses of the term.

can be now. John has already revealed that they would be assaulted and even killed as a religious act (16:2), and Matthew and Luke describe believers being arrested and dragged before kings and governors, and flogged in synagogues, whilst being expected to speak on behalf of Jesus (Matt. 10:17–18; Luke 21:12). It is important to remember that synagogues did not function only as meeting places for teaching, preaching and worship but also as courts in which legal judgments were made. The removal of believers from the synagogues is probably related to a judicial action rather than their physical ejection. Clearly, there are times forecast when they will be liable to feel vulnerable, to be marginalised and to experience loneliness. In those times, both John and Matthew (Matt. 10:20) state that an advocate will stand by the side of believers; he is the Spirit.

At the same time, in the supernatural world, Satan (*satanas*, accuser) is described as functioning as an adversary of God's people (Job 1:6–12; Zech. 3:1–2; see also Rev. 12:10). The role of Satan is to accuse believers, pointing out their sins to God in the forlorn hope that he may eject them from his family. However, for every accusation, the Spirit provides a response to drown out the allegations of the enemy. He constantly stands between Satan and the believers; Satan may point his finger at them, criticise and censure them but he cannot condemn them, because the Spirit has the last word. Since he is God and therefore knows the mind of God, he knows that an eternal appeal on their behalf has already been accepted. Satan may have his day in court, but in truth, he is wasting his time. The advocate and judge have already decided the outcome in favour of the believer.

As individuals, believers are sometimes prone to convict themselves on the evidence of their actions, words and thoughts. They convince themselves that if they were to stand before God at that moment, they would be sentenced and punished. Believers, however, always stand before God and he is constantly aware of all that they do, say and think and is also cognizant of those shortcomings of which they are oblivious. Although they are deserving of divine condemnation, the Spirit acts as their advocate; he is on their side reminding the court of the sentence that was passed on Jesus who bore the costs and now sets them free.

Such a metaphor must not be articulated so as to suggest that if it was not for the Spirit, the believer would be judged by a holy God. Nor should one's position before the Father be assumed to be fragile and uncertain if it was not for the intervening presence of the Spirit. It is not that the Spirit is for us while the Father is ready to condemn us. In the OT, it was God who was the advocate on behalf of his people (Job 16:19–21; Jer. 51:10, 36; Lam. 3:58); in 1 John 2:1, it is Jesus. Father, Son and Spirit are all for us. Together, they function as the court in session. They are the advocate, judge and witnesses on our behalf. They shout down the opposing voices, eject the prosecution, silence the antagonists and throw out the case against us. This is not a sober time for them; it is not a solemn process that results in threats and accusations being rejected as a result of clever legal talk, astute argumentation or intelligent and incisive defensive manoeuvres. These are cases won with ease by the supreme intellect[10] but also the one who has initiated a complete salvation that no court or accuser can challenge, overturn or undermine.

It is also important to recognise that not only will the Spirit support believers but he is also prepared to condemn their critics, judge their judges and punish their prosecutors (John 16:8–11). Thus, as Jesus defended the blind man who was healed (9:35–41), the Spirit, who is his successor, will defend believers and be a witness against the world (15:25–27).

The Defenders is a name for a group of fictional, cartoon super-heroes, devised by Marvel Comics. They are presented normally as battling against mystic, supernatural challenges and always win, even when the odds are stacked against them. Although originating in 1971, their popularity remains. Indeed, there has been a resurgence of interest in such characters and their exploits have been transferred to the cinematic screen. It has fed an increasing desire to see superheroes with superpowers battling for the right against evil foes on behalf of innocent victims of evil.

We live in an age of turmoil and uncertainty, global terrorism and trauma, where news of atrocities is broadcast within seconds and beamed around the world. Life itself often appears increasingly insecure and frightening. Whether it be the first or the twenty-first century, people still need someone to believe in, someone who can guarantee their security. The Spirit offers himself as the constant one who provides all that we need to journey through life. The challenge that is presented and the invitation that is given is that we hold the hand that is offered to us and learn to listen to him as he guides us into the future and defends us in the present.

---

[10] Some scholars have traced a relationship between John's portrayal of the Spirit and the concept of wisdom in Jewish literature (see Keener, *The Gospel of John*, vol. 2, pp. 961–966). Similarly, the description of Jesus, in 1:1–18, is paralleled in Jewish Wisdom literature, including the notion of creation by the Logos/Wisdom (also Keener, *The Gospel of John*, vol. 1, pp. 367–387). However, it is difficult to be certain that John deliberately drew on Wisdom literature to describe the Spirit because the association between the Spirit and wisdom is limited in Jewish literature. However, for some readers, the suggestion that the Spirit functions similarly with God's wisdom in Jewish thinking would have been helpful to them in that it ties the Spirit closer to God, especially insofar as he reflects the perceptive quality and wise insight of God himself.

4. The Spirit guides believers into truth (John 16:13–15)

Although 'truth' refers to the intellectual knowledge of truths and moral guidance, the concept also refers to the fact that the Spirit will guide believers in seeking to live in a context of integrity and authenticity. Their lives are to be reliably supported and directed by the Spirit who is defined by covenant and faithfulness. The Spirit is not just determined to inform believers concerning that which they need to know for their benefit but also that which best defines the context in which God exists; theirs is a life that is encapsulated by the realities that characterise God, one of the fundamental ones being 'truth' or integrity, reliability and honour. Believers are safe in the knowledge that the one leading them embodies consistency and constancy, dependability and devotion to them, and fidelity and fondness for them. The Spirit is true as well as truth. He leads believers to know and express integrity but is also fundamentally and authentically genuine. As well as leading believers into truth (John 16:12), he is also the Spirit of truth (John 14:17).

There is no reason to believe that this promise is only relevant for the disciples of Jesus, especially since it is repeated in 1 John 2:20, 27. Thus, the Ethiopian official is enabled by the Spirit, through Philip, to understand the true import of Isaiah 53. Even though he was reading the sacred text, he did not understand it; he needed help and the Spirit provided it (Acts 8:31). Interestingly, the official uses the same verb to describe that he needs someone to 'guide' him (odēgeō) as Jesus does when describing the guidance offered by the Spirit (John 16:13). In Revelation 7:17, the word is also used of the Lamb who undertakes to guide believers. Now, the Spirit has taken it upon himself to be the personal tutor of all believers.

One of the roles of the Spirit is to underscore the person and clarify the message of Jesus to believers (John 16:14; Eph. 1:17; 3:5). The gospel which is ludicrous to Gentiles and scandalous to the Jews (1 Cor. 1:23) has little to commend it as a viable message of hope. However, the Spirit supernaturally asserts its authenticity (1 Cor. 2:10–14). Similarly, John 14:25–26 identifies the Spirit as the one who will teach the disciples everything and remind them of all that Jesus had taught them.

The Spirit also facilitates a comprehensive knowledge and appreciation of God (John 16:15; Eph. 1:17),[11] his power (Eph. 1:19) and his love (Eph. 3:16–19). Paul describes the Spirit enabling believers

---

[11] Much discussion has taken place as to whether *pneuma* here refers to the Spirit or the human spirit – some internal aspect of a person. The majority opinion of conservative scholarship is that it refers to the Spirit (A. T. Lincoln, *Ephesians*

to be able to accurately and experientially know certain aspects of truth concerning God, particularly relating to their salvation. A fundamental aspect of the Spirit is also to enable the believer to explore God; it is absorption with a discovery of God that gives the Christian life dynamism, and the Spirit is central in helping believers in the pursuit of that eternal quest. Coincidentally, the Spirit also enables believers to have a greater awareness of their hope and their place as his inheritance (Eph. 1:18). Their certain hope, which is supported by the Spirit, is that they will be God's inheritance. Such a destiny would be a forlorn dream if it were not for the Spirit, who forms reality out of doubt.

[Word, 1990], p. 57; G. D. Fee, *God's Empowering Presence* [Hendrickson, 1994], pp. 15–31).

John 16:1–11
9. The Holy Spirit convicts unbelievers

1. Introduction

Jesus speaks of the importance of love as a central theme for his followers (John 15:12–17), followed immediately by the fact that this concentration on love is often located in the context of hatred from those who oppose them (John 15:18–25). Jesus reminds his disciples that in this regard, they are following in his footsteps, for he also was hated and without a valid reason (John 15:25). But worse is to come. Jesus records (16:1–3) that this hatred will not only be intense but it will result in them being ostracised by their own people, refused permission to enter synagogues and even killed. Their killers will assume that their murderous deeds are equivalent to the highest acts of service to God, as did Saul (Acts 26:9–11). However, their deeds will not be overlooked by God for the Spirit, who sees everything, will respond accordingly (John 16:8–11). By the time John wrote his Gospel, towards the end of the first century, some Christians had succumbed to the virulent antagonism directed against them and ceased to follow Jesus.

2. The Spirit is on our side (John 16:7–8)

More significant for the readers, who are beginning to experience the malevolent opposition prophesied by Jesus, is John informing them that the Spirit is on their side. He will transform those who were once convinced that they were right to reject Jesus and the message offered by his followers. The Spirit, who is promised by Jesus as his replacement, will convince those who fought against the gospel that they were wrong to do so. Where believers have only human intellect, with all its shortcomings, to combat voices of derision, the Spirit has the wisdom of heaven available to him (John 14:26). Where Jesus' followers only have limited courage to speak confidently to those who dismiss them, the Spirit has divine authority available to him (John 15:26; 16:13). Whereas Christians have limited knowledge, the Spirit has the ability to always see the truth (John 16:13). While they may be unaware of the innermost feelings and thoughts of those who combat them, the Spirit has the capacity to make the self-secure tremble with conviction of sin (John 16:8).

The Spirit is committed to ensuring that the mission of Jesus will continue in his absence. As Jesus sought to bridge the gulf between sinful humanity and a righteous God, so also the Spirit functions as a mediator between the unbelieving world and its Creator. The Spirit powerfully convicts unbelievers who, without his intervention, would not be able to respond to Jesus, their sin acting as a deafening noise and an insurmountable barrier between them and the message of salvation.

3. The Spirit supports believers against the world (John 16:8, 11)

The term 'world' (*kosmos*) is used by John more than any other NT writer (105 times, mainly in his Gospel) and with a variety of meanings, including the created planet (John 1:10), humanity (John 8:12) and, most often, humanity in its opposition to Jesus (John 7:7; 15:18; 16:20). In 16:8, 11, he uses the term to describe those who have rejected Jesus. Despite their unbelief, Jesus reciprocates not by rejecting them but by dying for them (John 1:29; 3:16–17; 4:42). In 16:7–11, Jesus reveals that, when he leaves his followers, the Spirit will undertake the same function of helping people who reject the truth of the gospel to realise the remarkable fact that it is not only true, but that it is good news for them. In particular, the Spirit will convict and convince them of their sin and the fact that Jesus is their saviour.

Consider the consternation of the disciples leading up to these statements by Jesus. In the narrative provided by John, the disciples have experienced widely diverse emotions. In 9:1–35, John records that Jesus healed a blind man and identified himself as the light of the world. This was followed by an account of many believing in him (10:40–42) and the resurrection of Lazarus (11:1–44), leading to other Jews believing in him (11:45). However, the so-called triumphal entry into Jerusalem by Jesus (12:12–13) preceded the disturbing revelation that people are following Jesus simply because he was a miracle worker (12:17, 37). Instead of being sought for the light he can bring, people have clamoured to see miracles.

After this, Jesus is no longer presented by John as ministering or even functioning in public. Hiding himself from people prefaces the path to the cross (John 12:36). If Jesus was not always successful, what hope would his followers have without him? Although he speaks about homes in heaven (14:1–4), he indicates that they are to walk there on a path of suffering, experiencing the hatred (15:18) and persecution (15:20) of others, resulting in their excommunication from the synagogues (16:2) and their being murdered (16:2). The questions they must have faced relate to how to succeed in such circumstances without Jesus.

It is into this turmoil of emotions that Jesus injects a message of hope – the Spirit will be with them forever (John 14:16). He will enable them to fulfil their missions (14:12–15), teach them (14:26), remind them of Jesus (15:26) and enable them to emulate Jesus – in revealing the truth of the gospel and encouraging people, supernaturally, to place their faith in him. The miraculous attraction of Jesus resulted in people following him (John 1:26), including Peter and Andrew (1:40–42), Philip (1:43) and Nathanael (1:45–49). That ability to convince people of the validity of Jesus would now be made available to the disciples by the Spirit, in the absence of Jesus. The devastation they felt at the news that Jesus was leaving them and was to do so by dying was cushioned by the announcement that he was going to send to them someone as remarkable as himself. The Spirit would empower, authorise them and settle them in the knowledge that they were not going to be on their own in this alien world, for he would be their wise advocate, personal mentor and trustworthy guide.

The Spirit's work is for the benefit of an unbelieving world, that it would come to appreciate the wonder of Jesus, and the gulf between them and him caused by their sin (16:8–11). It is also for the benefit of the disciples, who are enabled to continue the work of Jesus. His ministry was effective because he was the Son of God. The question lurking in the minds of his disciples would be how they could carry on where he left off. How could they be certain that when they spoke, people would listen? Where they led, would anyone follow? John has the answer to these questions. The Spirit has come to earth to enable them and to go before them, working in the lives of those to whom they will speak, to ensure that the miraculous work of salvation will occur. He is to be their partner in mission, emulating Jesus and making it possible for them to be his effective followers. He is to be the best friend they will ever have, for his commitment to them will know no end.

The Spirit is partner to believers in their evangelistic mission by doing what they cannot do – enabling unbelievers to see their sin and their need of Jesus. Therefore, when sharing the gospel, it is important that we recognise that although our words and powers of persuasion may seem weak, our apologetic arguments insubstantial and our message powerless, the Spirit is already working in the lives of those to whom we speak. Although he will not force himself upon them, he has the capacity to convince them that Jesus is their only hope.

4. The Spirit of conviction (John 16:8)

One of the most difficult issues for many people to accept is that aspects of their lives may be morally wrong. This is compounded by the fact that the rules to determine correct behaviour are often disputed. God's standards for identifying acceptable behaviour are not a great cause of concern for unbelievers, nor do they feel any obligation to identify them, let alone keep them, and the perceptions of believers who espouse them are often rejected, ridiculed or ignored. Someone else is needed to help unbelievers gain a divine perspective on God's standards and the Spirit unilaterally steps in to the vacuum, providing them with the necessary conviction.

John 16:8 (*he will convince the world concerning sin and righteousness and judgement,* RSV) is capable of being understood in a number of ways, the word 'convince' (*elenchei*) being open to a range of meanings.[1] It could refer to the fact that the Spirit will convict unbelievers of their sin of unbelief (the most fundamental of all sins) or, more specifically, that because they choose not to believe, the Spirit will take responsibility for convicting them of their sin despite their rebuttal of such conviction. It is even possible that Jesus is suggesting that the Spirit will shame them into acknowledging their guilt or, less likely, convince the disciples of the guilt of the world. Basically, Jesus is indicating that the Spirit will reveal sin. As Bultmann states, 'He will uncover the world's guilt.'[2]

Allied to this is the probability that John is also referring to the commitment of the Spirit to identify the nature of sin, the divinely determined standard of righteousness and the fact of divine

[1] See D. A. Carson, *The Gospel According to John* (Eerdmans, 1991), pp. 534–539; T. G. Brown, *Spirit in the Writings of John* (T. & T. Clark, 2003), pp. 221–232.
[2] R. Bultmann, *The Gospel of John* (The Westminster Press, 1971), p. 561.

judgment.[3] The Spirit will help them deduce what they may not be able to do – identify that they have sinned and that such a condition is significantly harmful to their spiritual wellbeing. It is in the sense of 'exposure' or 'identification' that *elenchei* (convince) is used elsewhere in John (3:20; 8:46). It is not that the Spirit will persuade them of their sin so much as to wake them up to the fact that they have sinned. He will not argue with them about their sin but assert that they are sinners. His is a role of conviction of truth, not merely a gentle whisper that they amend their ways; it is a call to repentance, not a call for improvement.

The hoped-for consequence of such a revelation is that it will lead to repentance. However, there is no guarantee that this will occur. It did not always happen when Jesus revealed people's sin, and his followers should not expect any different. But what the Spirit does undertake to achieve is that unbelievers will have their eyes opened to the truth, whereupon they will have the opportunity to respond to the message of hope. The responsibility to enlighten them of their need and the salvation available through Jesus is undertaken by the Spirit. All he asks is that believers follow in his footsteps and demonstrate the truth of the gospel by their lives and words.

If people reject, ignore or are oblivious to Jesus, they will have lost the only true guide concerning the level of their spiritual worth (John 8:47; 10:4–5). He alone is the light of the world (9:5): if people turn away from him, they cannot benefit from his searchlight that focuses on their shortcomings and his grace; if their eyes are closed to the light he radiates, they fail to profit from such warmth and illumination. They are doomed to live in darkness, confusion, guilt and ignorance because the only authentic guide to behaviour and morality would have been discarded as irrelevant and meaningless.

In the light of Jesus being rebuffed, ignored or overlooked, it would be no surprise if he did not summarily punish the perpetrators. However, the Spirit takes up the challenge and continues the work of Jesus (John 15:22), highlighting personal sin, convicting people of their guilt, revealing their lack of righteousness and pronouncing judgment. The means of the conviction by the Spirit is not explained, though it could refer to being intellectually convinced or to other forms of encouragement to believe (via dreams or other events) that could lead unbelievers to accept the truth of Jesus.

The world that opposes believers has itself been put on trial by God and the judgment is certain. Although it tried Jesus and judged him as guilty, the Spirit has offered a retrial and concluded that

[3] G. R. Beasley-Murray, *John* (Word, 1987), p. 281.

the evidence is such that Jesus is innocent and the world is guilty. Believers need always to remember that those who may ignore or reject them have already been called to account for their actions by the Spirit; those who would put them on trial and excommunicate them have themselves been tried by the supreme Judge; those who persecute them have themselves been prosecuted by him. Their friend, the Spirit, demonstrates his absolute authority by his advocacy on their behalf.

5. The Spirit of righteousness (John 16:8, 10)

Polygraphs (lie-detectors) can now be purchased for the same cost as a meal in a restaurant. They work by measuring several physiological responses exhibited by people when they are asked a series of questions. Such responses relate to blood pressure, pulse, respiration and changes to one's skin. On the basis of these measurements, it is suggested that the trained reader can determine if set questions are answered truthfully or not. However, the reliability of the technology is uncertain. Although it is commonly assumed that polygraphs are generally accurate, there is little scientific evidence to support this assumption. Thus, although popular assessments have indicated 90-95% reliability, this cannot be established and some criminals have outwitted the polygraph, as established later on the basis of evidence gleaned from other sources. There is, however, one lie detector who is perfect in his ability to identify a lie, whether it be a sentence or a lifestyle. The Spirit convicts accurately, as no polygraph can. He is the perfect prosecution lawyer, who functions in the hope that salvation will be received by the sinner.

John records that the Spirit *will convict the world . . . in regard to . . . righteousness.* The term *righteousness* (a term only used by John in 16:8, 10) was well known to his readers. It is closely related to the concept of being right, authentic and virtuous. A righteous person, to a Jew, was someone who was worthy and maintained an honourable lifestyle, was committed to godly standards of behaviour and sought to function as an upstanding member of the constituency. In the OT and in Jewish society, righteous people were identified by their awe of God,[4] their piety and love for God[5] and their willingness to serve God and others.[6] Such people were described

[4] Exod. 18:21.
[5] Gen. 18:23, 26, 28; Deut. 4:8; Job 15:14; Ps. 37:16, 30–31; Prov. 15:28.
[6] Ps. 37:21; Mal. 3:18

as being trustworthy[7] and fruitful, living according to the Torah[8] and exhibiting behaviour that was both ethical and relational. Throughout the NT, the term is used as a contrast to disobedience, being descriptive of good behaviour.[9] This righteous lifestyle is integrally linked with an ongoing relationship with God and is used as a definition of character, lifestyle and attitude that is reflective of him.

The issue to be determined relates to who is being identified by the Spirit as being righteous in John 16:10. It is possible that it refers to the work of the Spirit in establishing the standards of right and wrong that enable people to know how to live and thus determine their personal righteousness. In this regard, the Spirit would assert that the level of righteousness of unbelievers was completely inadequate. The Spirit would thus be described as convicting unbelievers of their unrighteousness. At the same time, the Spirit acts as a defence lawyer for believers, affirming that they are righteous and right to follow Jesus. However different from those of others, their lifestyle, if adopted in obedience to Jesus, is correct. The Spirit acquits them, declaring them to be righteous.[10]

Given that Jesus relates this work of the Spirit to the fact that he will be leaving this world (John 16:7), however, it is more likely that John is describing the fact that in his absence, the Spirit intends to convince people that Jesus is righteous. Even though he is absent, and therefore cannot be scrutinised in order to establish this fact, the Spirit takes the initiative to enable people to accept that Jesus is the epitome of righteousness. Even though he died as a criminal, the Spirit acquits him as sinless; as Godet writes, although 'Good Friday attributed sin to Jesus . . . Pentecost reversed the sentence'.[11] Although he was born in obscurity and was surrounded by ordinary sinful humanity, the Spirit vindicated him by reminding people that

[7] Philo, an important Jewish historian and philosopher living around the time of Jesus, uses the term to mean 'accurate' (*De Op. Mun.* 1; *Quo. Det. Pot. Ins. Sol.* 121) and 'deserved, just' (*Leg. All.* 1.87; 2.18; 3.30, 191; *De Pos. Cai.* 32, 88). Thus, Noah was proved to be righteous by his actions (*Quo. Det. Pot. Ins. Sol.* 123, 170; *De Mig. Abr.* 125), and Abraham by his trust in God (*Quis Rer. Div. Her.* 94). Josephus, another Jewish historian living in the first century, generally uses the term to describe that which is just, honest or correct (*Wars* 1.13, 230, 544; 2.135, 139, 145; *Ant.* 1.72, 158, 199; 2.151, 172).

[8] *1 Macc.* 2:50; Philo, *Ps. Sol.* 3:7; *Leg. All.* 3.77, 79; *Quo. Det. Pot. Ins. Sol.* 123, 170; Philo, *Gen.* 1:10, 76; 2:48; *Ex.* 1:21: 2:27; b. *San.* 110b; Mid. *Ruth* 1.

[9] Matt. 5:45; Mark 2:17; Luke 1:17; Acts 24:15; Rom. 3:10; 1 Pet. 3:12, 18; 1 John 3:7; Rev. 22:11.

[10] Keener, *The Gospel of John*, 2 vols (Hendrickson, 2003), vol. 1, p. 1034.

[11] F. Godet, *Commentary on the Gospel of John Vol. 3* (T. & T. Clark, 1877), p. 176.

THE MESSAGE OF THE HOLY SPIRIT

he exhibited a lifestyle that was dominated by perfection. Every action, word and thought was presented flawlessly. The Spirit is dedicated to enlightening those who cannot see, startling them with the unique righteousness of Jesus.

Given the uncertainty that surrounds the translation of this verse,[12] it is possible that the Spirit is engaged in each activity – demonstrating that the righteousness of unbelievers is not good enough, while that of believers is appropriate, and proving that the righteous life of Jesus was divinely authentic.

6. The Spirit of judgment (John 16:11)

The Spirit is not only involved in exposing the sin of unbelievers but also in denouncing the ruler of the world, the devil. The role of the Spirit is not to fight the devil and overcome him by a superior force of power so much as to judge him. His is a moral authority over the devil, a judicial condemnation, a presenting of a legal case that results in the devil being found guilty. Of course, the Spirit has considerably more power and authority than the devil, but the message presented by Jesus is that the devil is being authoritatively condemned because he has broken the rules. This is not a battle of two equals where the devil wins some skirmishes but loses the war. This is a forecast of the demise of the devil, who has foolishly chosen to ignore the will of God.

Ruler of the world he may be, but he is way down the list of superior forces and the supreme Ruler has called him to account. He is now simply living on borrowed time, awaiting his judicial review, which will result in divine justice being established and his demise being enacted. His failure is assured, for God's judgment has been declared. The one who judged Jesus, even though Jesus was superior to him, who condemned him unfairly (John 12:44), even though he was innocent, is himself under sentence of eternal death for his crimes against humanity and God. Not only does 'the prince of this world' have no authority over Jesus in his presence (14:30), but also the Spirit ensures that he has no authority when Jesus is absent (16:11). Any diabolic judgment against Jesus or his followers has no validity, for the evidence presented is not only unimpressive and meagre but also groundless and unjustified. The devilish judge who precociously and illegitimately accuses believers is himself judged by the Spirit who has the court of heaven on his side.

[12] Brown, *Spirit in the Writings of John*, pp. 229–230.

7. The Spirit of grace

The ministry of the Spirit, as recorded by John in these verses, although serious and sobering, is, in fact, a gracious act on his part. If he did not guide unbelievers to recognise their guilt and the judgment awaiting them, they would march unwittingly to desolation of an eternal nature. It is also a sign of his grace on behalf of believers, in that he chooses to help them undertake their mission of leading people to Jesus. A major problem for believers is that those to whom they speak are spiritually deaf and blind; thus, they cannot easily respond to the message concerning Jesus, for they are unable to see or hear him. John (1:5, 9) states that although the light shines, many people are not able to respond to it (1:10–11). Even where people are provided with opportunities to see the supremacy of Jesus, they remain blind (John 8:12–58; 9:1–39) and worse, are oblivious to their blindness (8:59; 9:40–41). Even when they try to see the truth, they cannot do it on their own.

They need the help of the Spirit, as did Nicodemus (John 3:1–8). The Spirit operates in a forensic way, judicially convicting unbelievers of their sin and guilt, and declaring judgment on them as a prosecuting counsel. The Spirit helps them identify their need of a saviour because of their sins and their precarious spiritual position. He clearly presents Jesus as their route to righteousness and the devil as the root of their problem. The tragedy occurs when they reject that help, remain blind but, nevertheless, assert that they can see.

Part Three
The Holy Spirit in the book of Acts

Acts 1:8; 4:1–31; 6:8 – 7:60; 13:4–12
10. The Holy Spirit and evangelism

1. Introduction

A fundamental significance of these verses is that they confirm that
the promises offered by Jesus – concerning the role of the Spirit in
inspiring believers to speak in challenging circumstances – were
authentic (Luke 12:12; 21:15). This is particularly important because
of the socio-religious climate of the day. This was an era of change
and insecurity and a time when believers felt increasingly vulnerable. They were experiencing situations that they had not anticipated,
and destabilizing emotions, such as fear, confusion and uncertainty,
were increasingly present in their lives. Compounding this was
the fact that Jesus had still not returned. Their worry related to
whether anyone was able to help them in his absence. Luke provides
evidence that the Spirit is able to offer them valuable support, by
writing about it in his narrative of events. The earliest Christians had
specific need for the support of the Spirit in their evangelism.[1] The
problems they experienced often related to their marginalization by
the State (Acts 21:33; 24:27), Graeco-Roman religions (19:23–29)
and philosophies (17:17–33), as well as Jewish abuse (2:13), rejection
(13:8, 45; 14:2) and persecution,[2] socio-economic problems (11:28)
and demonic oppression (16:18).

---

[1] Acts 8:14–15; 10:9 – 11:18 (esp. 10:15, 22, 28–29, 34–35, 45; 11:1–3, 17–18).
[2] Acts 4:3; 5:17–18, 40; 6:11–13; 7:54–60; 8:2–3; 9:23–24, 29; 11:19; 12:1–3;
13:50; 14:4–5, 19; 16:19–25; 17:6–7; 18:5–6, 12–13, 17; 20:3; 21:27–36; 22:22–23;
23:2, 12–15; cf. S. Cunningham, *'Through Many Tribulations': The Theology
of Persecution in Luke-Acts* (Sheffield Academic Press, 1997), pp. 337–342; E.
Bammel, 'Jewish Activity Against Christians in Palestine According to Acts'
in R. Bauckham, (ed.), *The Book of Acts in its First Century Setting. Volume 4.
Palestinian Setting* (Paternoster Press, 1995), pp. 357–364; also B. Rapske, *The*

2. The Spirit inspires confident witness to Jesus (Acts 1:8)

Menzies identifies the power derived from the Spirit in Luke-Acts as related to prophetic witness and proclamation rather than to miracles.[3] This emphasis on inspired and empowered speech is manifested in the lives of the disciples (Luke 24:44–49; Acts 1:8), Philip (Acts 8:4–12, 26–40) and Paul (Acts 20:22–28). Thus, while Paul concentrates on the role of the Spirit being the source of the life of the kingdom of God – while also noting his empowering of believers (Rom. 15:19; 1 Cor. 12:4–31; 14:1–33) – Luke offers the perspective that the Spirit enables believers to proclaim the kingdom of God forcefully and effectively.

Commencing with the promise relating to the Spirit in Acts 1:8, which indicates that the Spirit is to be imparted to the believers, Luke explicitly relates how this was fulfilled in the lives of Peter, Stephen, Barnabas and Saul, while also recording fulfillments in the lives of countless other believers. The identity of this empowering force is clarified in relation to evangelism that is characterized by boldness (4:13, 31) and wisdom (6:10). Though their message does not always result in acceptance, it is nevertheless accompanied by joy being experienced by the evangelists (13:52). The contents of the message and its presentation are described as being a cause of wonder (4:13; 13:12), unstoppable (6:10), associated with supernatural phenomena (6:15; 7:55–56; 13:9–11) and anticipated as having no national boundaries. Such momentous advance and authority is due to the dynamic presence of the Spirit in the lives of the believers. Indeed, such is the added benefit of the power of the Spirit that Jesus requires his followers to wait in Jerusalem for the Spirit. Only when he comes will the evangelistic mission begin in earnest, with the Spirit directing its agenda and empowering their witness.

Although Acts 1:8 provides a remarkable promise for the potential of the gospel being presented to the world, its original hearers may have viewed such a prospect with rather less enthusiasm than modern believers. The city of *Jerusalem* and the region of *Judea* were inhabited by Jews who had not proved themselves to be ready listeners to Jesus. Furthermore, the people of *Samaria* were their

---

Book of Acts in its First Century Setting. Volume 3. Paul in Roman Custody (Paternoster Press, 1994), pp. 115–435.

[3] R. P. Menzies *The Development of Early Christian Pneumatology* (Sheffield Academic Press, 1991), pp. 161–77, 258–62; F. L. Arrington, *The Acts of the Apostles* (Hendrickson, 1984), pp. xxxvii–xl; R. Stronstad, *The Charismatic Theology of St. Luke* (Hendrickson, 1984), pp. 13, 52, 55, 72, 80; J. B. Shelton, *Mighty in Word and Deed. The Role of the Holy Spirit in Luke-Acts* (Hendrickson, 1991), pp. 125–27.

enemies[4] and *the ends of the earth* was to be identified with areas that signalled the unknown – each brought challenges to would-be witnesses of Jesus. This was a challenging vocation and one that needed the inspiration and empowering of the Spirit to enable it to be undertaken at all, let alone to be done successfully. The provision of the Spirit is therefore to be contextualized in the challenging nature of the commission.

To witness to one's faith in Jesus in the first century world was to put oneself in the position of facing ridicule, opposition and even death. The ability to engage in evangelism therefore was not for the fainthearted. The promise of the Spirit was not that the situation in which one witnessed would be easy but that the resources with which one would be able to do so would be enhanced. Thus, the believer is exhorted, through the examples of others in the church, to believe the promises concerning the supportive role of the Spirit in evangelism and to engage in it. Success was not always guaranteed but the resourceful Spirit was.

The first evangelistic sermon that results in the joy of three thousand becoming believers (2:41) was in response to mocking of the opposition (2:13), while the last recorded sermon to unbelieving Jews (28:17–28) was as a result of Paul being arrested and sent to Rome. Nevertheless, as demonstrated by the final word of Acts, 'unhindered' (RSV, *akōlytōs*), Paul achieved his objective, opposed but unrestricted. Even though the backdrop of the mission related to his being arrested, enduring a storm and a shipwreck, and experiencing the danger of being executed and a snake bite, the Spirit ensured that the destiny he had determined for his envoy would be achieved.[5] The promise of Acts 1:8 which indicates that believers will witness on behalf of Jesus in Jerusalem and then throughout Judea, Samaria and to the ends of the earth, including Rome,[6] is fulfilled by the end of Luke's narrative. The prophecy of Isaiah 49:6, quoted in Acts 13:47, is also fulfilled as a result of the Spirit's involvement in believers.

The Spirit sent Paul and Barnabas (13:2, 4), some of the most highly qualified people in the church, to be engaged in mission. It is a salutary reminder that to do the work of an evangelist or a

[4] H-J. Klauck, in *Magic and Paganism in Early Christianity* (T & T Clark, (2000), p. 14. writes, 'Samaria was a transition zone, geographically and religiously speaking, from Judaism to paganism.'

[5] See further D. Marguerat, 'The Enigma of the Silent Closing of Acts,' in D. P. Moessner, (ed.), *Jesus and the Heritage of Israel* (Trinity Press, 1999), pp. 284–304.

[6] J. A. Fitzmyer, *The Acts of the Apostles* (New York, 1997), pp. 206–207; for a wider discussion, see D. L. Bock, *Acts* (Baker, 2007), 64–67.

missionary is an exceedingly high calling. Although all commissions of the Spirit are intrinsically equal, there has been a tendency in recent years to see less emphasis on evangelism, especially in the West, and a greater emphasis on other ministries. The danger of evangelism being viewed as less important than it was in the early church is one of which believers need to be aware. All who are involved in sharing the gospel should receive the fullest support from the church. The Spirit has set his seal on this task and the church must see it as its responsibility to commission such people wholeheartedly and prayerfully (13:3).

The church can learn from other organisations that exist to save and to serve those in dire need. The US Department of Homeland Security has a number of agencies that function to protect the lives of others. One of them is the US Coast Guard service. In a section headed *Commitment to Mission*, the following is included, 'Our mission puts us in harm's way . . . We conduct ALL missions professionally and enthusiastically. We think ahead, plan, and prepare for each mission. We do not take shortcuts. Everyone contributes to mission success. We set the standard that others follow . . . Our Challenges are great, but we are greater.' That should be a target and aspiration of equal relevance to believers today in their evangelistic mission.

3. The Spirit empowers believers to present the gospel to everyone (Acts 1:8)

The believers are commissioned to go to Samaria and beyond (as well as to Jerusalem and Judea). The good news of Jesus is now to be shared with all. The mandate of the Spirit is to move outside national boundaries and enter into areas that were previously prohibited. The early believers may have been intrigued to hear that the Gospel was to be presented to people who were not Jewish. Many would have assumed that the good news offered by Jesus was only to be made available to Jews. In his commission to his disciples, Jesus had specifically stated that they were to go to 'the house of Israel' and to 'enter no town of the Samaritans' (Matt. 10:5–6, ESV). Later, Matthew (15:24) records Jesus announcing that his mission was 'only to the lost sheep of Israel'.

The significance of this is that there was little expectation by Jews or Gentiles that the Messiah would say or do anything positive to Gentiles. However, the Spirit declares a different agenda to common perceptions and identifies the Gentiles as potential recipients of the grace of God. In particular, Matthew records that the Messiah will proclaim justice on behalf of the Gentiles (Matt. 12:18), though the actual expectation of most Jews was that Messiah would pronounce judgment on the Gentiles, resulting in their destruction. Such a remarkable message of hope to those who have none is supported by the fact that it follows the reference to Jesus being filled with the Spirit. It is not that the Spirit gave Jesus the idea to include the Gentiles or that the Spirit changed his mind to include Gentiles, instead of only Jews. The point of the proclamation is to identify that the inclusion of the Gentiles is authentic for it has the highest support – the Spirit himself.

The heart of the Spirit has not changed now from that prophecy fulfilled by Jesus then. He is still desirous of all coming to faith. Thus, he empowers believers to witness from Jerusalem to Rome, to include Jews, Samaritans and Gentiles, royalty and rulers, politicians and persecutors. Luke identifies the Spirit as inspiring Philip to speak to the Ethiopian official about Jesus (Acts 8:29) and Peter to speak to the Gentile centurion (10:19). The Spirit motivates the mission that soon became dedicated to the Gentiles (13:2, 46–48; see also 16:6–7), and the decision of the Jerusalem council to welcome Gentiles into the family of God (15:28).

Thereafter, the Spirit announces his desire to accept non-Jews into the church by filling them on notable, public occasions (Acts 8:14–17). The Jewish believers who witnessed Gentiles receiving the Spirit after Peter had preached to them (Acts 10:44–45) were 'astonished', while the Gentiles 'were glad' (13:48). The OT indicated that the Spirit was to be given in the *eschaton* ('last days') but, significantly for God's covenant people (Isa. 11:1–9; 32:15–20; Joel 3:1–5), to enable them to be a light for the nations (Isa. 2:1–4; 42:1–9; 49:1–6). There was no expectation that the Spirit would be given to unbelieving members of God's people or Gentiles. However, the Spirit welcomes all into the family of God and does it in the public gaze of many observers. He delights in the fact that many should witness his expansive plan of salvation.

4. The Spirit provides power to witness in the context of suffering (Acts 4:1–3)

The earliest chapters of Acts contain a great deal of information that illustrates the rapid progress of the gospel, though the first recorded healing results in suffering that is increasingly associated with the missions of envoys of the Spirit (Acts 4:3). The response to the questions of the crowd that follows the healing of the paralysed man includes a reference to the suffering of Jesus (3:18) and the rejected prophets of God (3:22–23). This is followed quickly by the arrest and imprisonment of the apostles (4:3) and a strident set of questions by the Jewish leaders, concluding with threats against the believers by the religious leaders (4:21, 29). The Spirit who empowered them (Acts 1:8; 5:32) did so because of these and other challenges to come, as prophesied by the Spirit in the OT (4:25).

Luke records that Peter defends himself before a seriously important selection of dignitaries, including rulers, elders, scribes (probably referring to the Sanhedrin) and, more elevated than anyone else, Annas, the High Priest, with Caiaphas, and John and Alexander, members of his family (Acts 4:5–8).[7] In the presence of such high-powered authority, even a confident person would be intimidated. However, the initial sentence of Peter indicates that far from being cowed or frightened, he is secure and speaks authoritatively. Less than two months previously, the same leaders clamoured for the crucifixion of Jesus and the death of his disciples. Then, Peter denied he knew Jesus and fled. Now, he identifies that Jesus is alive, resurrected by God (4:10) and the cause of the miracle of the recent healing (4:10). Not only that, but he blames them for the death of Jesus (4:11) and concludes by telling them that salvation is only available through Jesus (4:12). Such astounding courage is either foolhardy or founded on an indisputable fact – someone else is on his side, the Spirit (4:8).

Jesus promised his followers that the Spirit would provide courageous witness when it was most needed, particularly when confronted by opponents of the gospel. Matthew refers to the 'Spirit of your Father' (Matt. 10:20), while Mark and Luke refer to the 'Holy Spirit' (Mark 13:11; Luke 12:12). Luke states that the Spirit will teach believers what to say while Matthew and Mark refer to the fact that the Spirit will speak through them, their words being his. However slightly different the references to the Spirit and the promises may be in the Gospels, the message is clear – when believers speak, they will do so in the presence of and with the active help of the Spirit. The promise to inspire those he commissions is now fulfilled in the experience of Peter and the early believers (Acts 4:8), and even affirmed by their opponents, who recognise their boldness and eloquence, despite their being uneducated and ordinary men (4:13). Similarly, the confidence of the believers in the efficacy of their preaching is due to the Spirit on whom they rely (4:31).

---

[7] Although Annas was High Priest earlier, from AD 6-15, he fundamentally controlled the High Priesthood through five sons, two sons-in-law (including Caiaphas [18–36]) and one grandson whom he arranged to be appointed to the role of High Priest. It is also possible that because Annas had been removed from the post by the Roman procurator, some Jews may have still viewed him as the legitimate holder of the office.

Because of him, the level of suffering will neither obstruct their ongoing witness, nor necessarily be removed by the Spirit.

Some believers are attracted to the notion of functioning in the power of the Spirit but are less keen on fulfilling the commission for which the power is granted. For the early believers, they were commissioned to witness on behalf of Jesus and preach about the kingdom of God. If they undertook those commissions, then they were granted power by the Spirit. The power was not theirs to own, to keep for when needed or to use for selfish ends. The power would be manifested when the agenda of the Spirit was being fulfilled. It takes a promptness to witness to result in the power to witness. Similarly, it was only when the people spoke the word of God that they experienced boldness (4:31). Furthermore, the commissions were to be undertaken in challenging circumstances. Indeed, that is why the power was particularly valuable. If there is an absence of a readiness to suffer, however, there is little reason to expect the sustenance of the Spirit.

5. The Spirit's support in preaching does not always result in salvation (Acts 6:8 – 7:60)

This divine aid does not always result in positive responses by those who hear the gospel. Luke provides information to this effect in Acts 6:11–14 and 7:54–60, which are located at the beginning and end of Stephen's speech before his religious accusers. The Spirit filled him and provided wisdom, as a result of which he spoke perceptively and incisively (6:10). Those opposing him could not refute his declaration; he was too clever for them. Some people are naturally experts at winning arguments, convincing their audience of the wisdom of their perspectives. It may be due to their intellectual prowess, persuasive speech or the credibility of their case. But Stephen was up against the Jewish intellectuals of the city, with academic credentials and the ability to rationally, logically and accurately prove their point. However, on this occasion, they met their match for Stephen has a significant advantage, the Spirit of wisdom feeding him information, stimulating his intellect and demolishing the validity of their responses.

Although the Spirit empowered his speech, however, it resulted in his martyrdom not mass conversions, though one man present, Paul, may have later remembered what he had heard. Moreover, in his defence, Stephen refers to his hearers as those who *always resist the Holy Spirit* (Acts 7:51). Luke thus addresses the issue of suffering experienced not just by those who are commissioned

127

and empowered by the Spirit but also by the Spirit himself, who is 'resisted' by people. Not every witness inspired by the Spirit resulted in a positive response. However, even when the apostles were persecuted and driven from Antioch (13:50), the believers 'were filled with joy and with the Holy Spirit'. The Spirit who commissioned them (13:2, 4) was with them through their suffering and filled them with delight (13:52).

6. The Spirit provides timely words (Acts 13:4–12)

In response to the Spirit (13:4), Paul preached in Cyprus, where he was confronted by Elymas,[8] a Jewish magician who pretended to be a prophet (13:6) and who sought to distract Sergius Paulus, the proconsul, from discussing the gospel with Paul (13:8). The Spirit, who sent Paul, now instructs him to sternly accuse Elymas of being a fraud, devilish, unrighteous and antagonistic to God (13:9–11). These are forceful accusations, insulting and defamatory but true. Paul's authority and accuracy have their source in the Spirit. The evidence of this is that he prophesies that he will become blind and it happens, resulting in the proconsul coming to faith in Jesus (13:12). Of interest is the statement that Paul 'looked intently at' Elymas (13:9, ESV), prior to saying anything to him.

The word used (*atenizō*) is often used by Luke, including in Acts 3:4, where prior to Peter asking the lame man to look at him, 'directed his gaze at him' (ESV). It is not clear from Luke, but it is possible that in the process of looking, the Spirit revealed to Paul and Peter what they were to say and do. It was important that they took time to be silent, to pause and then to follow the divine instructions facilitated by the Spirit. For Peter, the Spirit provides guidance to pronounce healing that was supported by a prior revelation of the Spirit and not based on mere hope or presumption.

7. The Spirit expects obedient witnesses

When in Acts the Spirit directs people to speak, there is no hesitation on their part even when the message they are to impart is confusing to them. Thus, the instruction that Philip is to speak to the Ethiopian official results in his running to obey (Acts 8:29–30).

---

[8] Luke refers to him as Bar-Jesus (13:6) which means 'son of Joshua' and Elymas (13:8). It is possible that Elymas is a Semitic word that may be interpreted 'magician'.

When the Spirit instructs Peter, a Jew, to speak to a Gentile centurion, an unlawful act according to Jewish laws (Acts 10:28),[9] he goes (10:29), even though it involves a journey of over thirty miles. Despite the message going against his traditional beliefs concerning segregation, he obeys the Spirit even though it involves him proclaiming a new revelation of inclusion (11:12). On arriving and meeting Cornelius, he takes little time to state his conviction that 'God does not show favouritism' (10:34) and consequently speaks to him about Jesus.

Similarly, when the Spirit guides Saul and Barnabas to undertake a mission, not only are they willing to leave the thriving church in Antioch immediately but the other leaders in the church there are prepared to support them in this venture. This is demonstrated by their laying hands on them and praying for them, prior to sending them to follow the guidance of the Spirit, 'acting as believer-priests on behalf of God'[10] (Acts 13:1–3).

8. The Spirit inspires signs and wonders as part of the evangelism undertaken by the believers

The presence of the Spirit in evangelism is not only identified in verbal preaching and teaching about Jesus. It is also manifested in Spirit-initiated signs and wonders. The association of miracles with evangelism was common in the ministry of the early church, as reflected in the book of Acts. Such manifestations of the Spirit were often valuable when accompanying and complementing the preaching of the gospel, for they enabled believers to powerfully engage in the task of presenting the supremacy of Christ and of authenticating the gospel, especially in the context of other power-based religions.

In Peter's sermon to Cornelius and his family, he associates the Spirit with power and relates it to the healing ministry of Jesus (Acts 10:38). The same Spirit is active in the lives of the believers as they preach the good news of Jesus. As a result, they witness remarkable supernatural acts of healing which draw people to hear their message of hope. Although salvation does not always occur (14:8–19), such supra-normal acts dumbfound opponents (4:13–14) and attract many to become willing listeners to the apostles (3:11–26; 8:4–8; 28:7–10). Many of these come to faith after witnessing the miracles (4:21–22; 9:32–42; 13:4–12).

Luke traces a theme of supernatural activity resulting not only in

[9] M. 'Ohol. 18:7; Jub. 22:16.
[10] Bock, Acts, p. 440.

people coming to faith in Jesus but also in many physical healings being experienced. Paul provides a theological framework for these manifestations and for the expectation that they may occur again. The Spirit is identified as the one who facilitates such supernatural activity through believers (1 Cor. 12:7–11, 28). When people are confronted with the gospel, there is often a significant transformation in their lives. It may be exhibited in a conviction of a need of God, sorrow for one's sin or a desire for God's forgiveness; it may result in a willingness to sacrifice and turn from a particular lifestyle in order to become a Christian; it may involve a willingness to surrender one's own ambitions in order to follow Jesus; it may be accompanied by a supernatural resolution of a physical or emotional issue. Indeed, A. H. Anderson, speaking of evangelism in the Majority World, describes healing and exorcism as 'probably the most important part of evangelism' and 'church recruitment',[11] resulting in significant numbers of people coming to faith as they witness the reality of God in their midst. Similarly, L. G. McClung describes signs and wonders as an 'evangelistic door-opener',[12] especially where medical aid is limited. E. Y. Lartey also identifies this, particularly in the African context where healing and the imposition of sicknesses and curses have also been present in much tribal religion,[13] while P. Y. Cho identifies it as a major reason for church growth in Korean Pentecostalism.[14]

[11] A. H. Anderson, 'Global Pentecostalism in the New Millennium', in A. H. Anderson, W. J. Hollenweger (eds.), *Pentecostals after a Century* (Sheffield Academic Press, 1999), pp. 216 (209–223).

[12] L. G. McClung, 'Spontaneous Strategy of the Spirit. Pentecostal Missionary Practices', in L. G. McClung (ed.), *Azusa Street and Beyond: Pentecostal Missions and Church Growth in the Twentieth Century* (Bridge, 1986), pp. 74 (71–81).

[13] , E. Y. Lartey 'Healing: Tradition and Pentecostalism in Africa', *International Review of Mission* (1986), pp. 75, 47–50.

[14] P. (D.) Y. Cho, 'The Secret Behind the World's Biggest Church', in L. G. McClung, Jr., (ed.), *Azusa Street and Beyond* (Bridge, 1986), pp. 99–101 (99–104).

Acts 2:1–12
11. The Holy Spirit at Pentecost

1. Introduction

These verses describe the coming of the Spirit to the believers on the day of Pentecost. While Luke's first volume begins with the birth of Jesus, his second commences with the birth of the church. It was a particularly auspicious occasion. Although the Spirit functioned in the lives of some people in the OT era (Ps. 51:11) and lived with believers before Pentecost (John 14:16–17), he did not initiate the church until the day of Pentecost. Furthermore, the ministry of the Spirit on behalf of and through believers is much more comprehensive after Pentecost than before. Given the uniqueness of this occasion, Luke chooses to emphasise certain important issues whilst ignoring less central aspects. It is important to recognise the significant aspects of this momentous event and retain them as being of vital importance for his readers and his overall message.

Thus, Luke does not identify the location of the meeting place, nor the number or identity of all the believers (though he records that 120 were at a previous meeting [1:15]), nor does he describe what they were doing. There is no indication that they were praying for the Spirit to come (or even praying – though the reference to corporate prayer on a previous occasion [1:14] has encouraged some to assume they were also praying now), engaging in any spiritual activity or expecting anything supernatural to occur. There is no suggestion that the followers of Jesus were hiding in the upper room when the Spirit came.[1] On the contrary, Luke records that after the

---

[1] Many believers assume that the followers of Jesus were frightened prior to the day of Pentecost, hiding from those who were planning to arrest them and do to them that which they did to Jesus. However, they have mixed up the events prior to the day of Pentecost with the emotional turmoil and sense of stomach-churning

ascension, the disciples 'returned to Jerusalem with great joy. And they stayed continually at the temple, praising God' (Luke 24:52–53).[2] They were not sorrowful but straining to start their missions; not looking to the past but to the future; their hearts were not empty but expectant for what was to come; their hopes were not dashed, but they were determined to obey their risen, ascended Saviour. He had told them to stay in Jerusalem and wait for an enduement of power (Luke 24:49), so wait they would.

A fundamental purpose of the book of Acts was to signal that the eschatological aspirations of the Jews were now realised; the Spirit (and the kingdom of God) had come. The Spirit who was anticipated in the future (Joel 2:28) is now present, the evidence being the experience of his presence in the lives of believers. Once, the Spirit had been rarely experienced; now he has franchised all believers to manifest him in their lives personally and for the benefit of others. Little wonder that the Spirit's coming was so exciting to the early believers, whose lives took on a dynamic character that was often accompanied by miraculous phenomena.

2. The Spirit is in charge of his own agenda (Acts 2:1)

The statement, *When the day of Pentecost had come* (2:1, RSV), is not simply intended to specify the identity of the day, thus locating it in early June. The significance of the word used for *had come* in Greek (*symploroō*) is that it relates to the idea of fulfilment. Luke is indicating to the readers that the Spirit came when the time had been fulfilled, at the right moment, at the specified time. The believers had not prayed the Spirit down. He had come at the predetermined moment, in order to fulfil a divine plan. He had identified this date in his divine diary and was keeping his self-imposed appointment.

The readers lived in an era that assumed that deities determined one's destiny. For the Jews, this was supported by the history of Israel as recorded in the OT. God had shown himself to be the one who had led them from Egypt to Canaan. Thereafter, as a result of the leadership of godly prophets and kings, he had guided them. The Gentiles also believed in the central motif of providence, as a result

---

panic and depression experienced by the disciples prior to the resurrection of Jesus. In the latter, the followers of Jesus were frightened, but this was not the case after his resurrection.

[2] Similarly, F. F. Bruce, in *The Book of Acts* (Eerdmans, 1975), pp. 55–56, explores the possibility that the room, in which they were residing, may well have been in the temple precincts, an understandable location for the three thousand people who later accepted the message of Peter (Acts 2:41).

of which the gods fulfilled their purposes with regard to people. There was thus a common belief that, to a very large degree, the future was out of one's personal control; it could not in a meaningful way be fulfilled unless a divinity had set the agenda.

Luke introduces his audience to the one who has set the agenda for the church. Indeed, this is a central theme of the book of Acts in which he will use eleven different Greek words that indicate the idea of fulfilment (1:16; 2:23; 4:28; 5:38–39; 13:29, 33; 21:14). It is this that ensures the value of the book as an evangelistic tool to people who believe in a pre-determined destiny set by a supernatural force. Thus, Luke agrees with Jews and Gentiles who thought of history as unfolding according to a divine plan. However, he identifies the planner and facilitator of the agenda as being the Spirit. It is he who determines the schedule of events.

As the events on the day of Pentecost were extraordinary, even disturbing, it is possible today that the Spirit may upset our plans or cause us to reassess our ways. It may prove to be a destabilising moment when he visits us afresh. However, not only is he uniquely creative but he is also trustworthy. His controlling influence in our lives is not one that will lead us to despair or fear; rather, his relationship with us is, in essence, based in love (2 Tim. 1:7). He works with and through us; he does not force or hurt us.

3. The Spirit introduces a new initiative (Acts 2:1)

The fact that the Spirit chose to come on the day of Pentecost is, of course, highly significant. Fundamentally, the feast of Pentecost, or Weeks (Exod. 23:16; 34:22) was associated with the end of the barley harvest, occurring fifty days after the feast of Unleavened Bread that incorporated the day of Passover. It was a time of celebration and thanksgiving for God's provision.[3] Luke does not clarify why this particular feast was to be the chosen time at which the church was established, though the symbolism would have been clearer to Jewish readers. That the Passover was the context of the death of Jesus is surely no coincidence. The feast at which the Passover lamb is sacrificed was the time when Jesus, the Lamb of God, was also sacrificed. The feast of Pentecost also included a day when sacrifices were offered to God as thanksgiving for a successful harvest (Exod. 23:16; Lev. 23:15–21). It was a time of in-gathering of all varieties of crops, a time for bringing together all that God had created.

---

[3] It was also known as the day of firstfruits (Num. 28:26), a motif used in connection with the Spirit by Paul (Rom. 8:23).

133

Similarly, on the day of Pentecost, the Spirit assembled all believers for the first time, identifying them, with all their differences, as members of God's special creation and absorbing them into his family.

The feast of Pentecost was also later viewed as an occasion when the people celebrated the giving of the law to Moses, though evidence is lacking to certainly relate this to the first century era. However, the feast provided the opportunity to re-commit oneself to keeping the law. It may be appropriate to recognise in this event therefore that a new lawgiver, the Spirit, was being presented to God's family – not a written code but a personal guide who would not live in the pages of a book but be written in the hearts of believers (2 Cor. 3:3–6).[4] Similarly, the feast of Pentecost celebrated the establishment of the Mosaic, Noahic and Abrahamic covenants by God with the Israelites (*Jubilees* 1:1–2; 6:19). Now, however, a new covenant was being ratified, having been established by Jesus and affirmed by the Spirit. A new age was being introduced in which a new people (the church) and a new patron (the Spirit) were being announced to the world. A new wind was blowing, a new fire had been started and the Spirit was central to both.

The Spirit is fundamentally creative, facilitating opportunities for initiative and development. Because he is imaginative, it is incumbent on believers to ensure that they follow him as he leads them. Since he is resourceful, it is to be remembered that any task he entrusts can be achieved, for he only commissions those to whom he also commits himself. He is capable of guaranteeing that objectives he sets can be achieved. He is, after all, the Spirit of power and authority (Acts 1:8).

4. The Spirit is given to all believers (Acts 2:4)

Acts 2:1–13 describes the events that occurred on the day of Pentecost in fulfilment of John 7:37–39, in which Jesus prophesied that the Spirit would come after Jesus had been glorified (see also Acts 1:6). Even more importantly, this was to fulfil the ancient prophecy recorded in Joel 2:28–32. Luke himself makes the association between that promise and the events of Pentecost (Acts 2:17–21). Prior to Pentecost, the disciples had received the Spirit, to a degree (John 20:22), possibly to empower them (John 20:23) in

---

[4] It may be of interest to note that while 3,000 Israelites died in judgment after the giving of the law (Exod. 32:25–28), 3,000 became believers after Peter's sermon that followed the giving of the Spirit (Acts 2:41).

the period between Jesus' death and the arrival of his replacement, the Spirit.[5] However, on the day of Pentecost, the disciples were to experience a completely different dimension of the involvement of the Spirit in their lives, superior to anything they had experienced before.

Luke commences his second volume by reminding the readers of the promise of Jesus (Luke 24:49) prior to his ascension that he would baptize all believers with the Holy Spirit (Acts 1:4–5). It is important to recognize the descriptions offered by Luke in this respect (Acts 2:1–4). Not only were *all* the people together, but the Spirit filled *all* the house, filling *all* of them, *each* of them hearing the deafening sound of a gale-force wind, experiencing tongues of fire on their heads and speaking in tongues. Following this, in Peter's sermon, he offers the same promise (2:39), identifying the bestowal of the Spirit as a gift to all who will repent of their sins and receive the forgiveness of Jesus (2:38). He later affirms the reality of this event in a statement to the Jewish religious hierarchy (5:32). In his letter, John, who was there on the day of Pentecost, offers the same promise to his readers. They also have been given the Spirit who abides in them (1 John 3:24; 4:13).

Various terms are used for this initiatory expression of the Spirit: being clothed with power (Luke 24:49); baptized with the Holy Spirit (Luke 3:16; Acts 1:5); filled with the Holy Spirit (Acts 2:4); receiving the Spirit (Acts 2:38; 10:47); and the pouring out of the Spirit (Acts 2:17; 10:45). Although this is so, the same event is being referred to, namely the presence of the Spirit in the life of believers as affirmation that they have been forgiven and are now living as obedient disciples of Jesus.[6] As far as the above references from Acts are concerned, they confirm that the recipients of the Spirit were authentic believers.

It was inevitable that the Spirit would come into the lives of those who had previously been followers of Jesus at a later point than he did with regard to new converts because, as Jesus had said (John 7:39), the Spirit would not come until he had been glorified (Luke

[5] Some believe that this reference relates a prophecy by Jesus that would be fulfilled on the day of Pentecost. That Jesus breathed on the disciples and said 'receive the Holy Spirit' is then to be understood as a symbolic act that would be realized later on the day of Pentecost. Alternatively, others believe that two distinctive endowments of the Spirit are recorded, the one here at the resurrection of Jesus, the other on the day of Pentecost.

[6] Luke is not suggesting in Acts 5:32 that the Spirit is given as a reward for one's obedience, but that such readiness to obey is indicative of his presence (cf. 5:29). Paul will later develop this by teaching that not only does the Spirit affirm the fact of salvation to believers but he also supervises their spiritual development.

24:49; John 14:16, 17). Now, that promise was being fulfilled for the disciples on Pentecost,.

What is of significance is that there is no immediate association of the giving of the Spirit with any function on the part of the believer. He is not described as being given in order to enable the believers to fulfil a commission or undertake a responsibility. In these verses, the presence of the Spirit is identified as being the evidence of a transformation having already taken place. Fundamentally, the Spirit is a gift from God to the believer.[7] He comes primarily to authenticate their relationship with Jesus. Although he will later empower them and thus enable them to fulfil their God-given commissions (Acts 1:8), initially his involvement in the life of believers is to fill them with himself. He wants to do them good before he facilitates their being able to do good to others. He blesses them with his presence before they bless God with their praise (Acts 2:11). He wants them to be the recipients of the ancient promise before he empowers them to share that promise with others.

In the OT, the Spirit partnered people when they had a commission from God that had to be completed, often prophecy, and when that had been achieved, the Spirit left them (Num. 11:25–26). In a similar way, the Spirit inspired the OT prophets for specific issues, remaining with them temporarily until the commission had been effected. Now the Spirit had come to stay, not for a short time but permanently.[8]

This provides a timeless message to the readers who lived in times of extreme insecurity in a localised and global sense. In particular, believers had in recent years begun to experience emotions that they had not expected when they chose to follow Jesus. The political and religious authorities had begun to pressurize them and persecute them for their faith and this caused fear, uncertainty and confusion for many. Many had begun to count the cost of their new-found faith and had decided that the price was too high; others had wavered in their commitment because they wondered if they had made a mistake when they left their previous religion, which was often less isolating; still others wondered where God was in the midst of their trials. Their lives appeared to be out of control and their destinies seemed to be increasingly determined by the dictates of others. This was an era of change and insecurity.

---

[7] See also Luke 11:13; John 7:39; 14:16–17; Acts 2:33, 38; 5:32; Gal. 3:13–14; 1 Thess. 4:8.

[8] The Spirit is described as being 'upon' Simeon (*ep' auton*, Luke 2:25), suggestive of the fact that the Spirit was not permanently indwelling him. Similarly, the Spirit filled Elizabeth and Zechariah, enabling them to prophesy (Luke 1:41–42, 67), though there is no indication that this filling was constant.

It was a time when believers felt vulnerable because of the rule of their leaders that had consequences for the well-being of ordinary people.

Luke has an important message to present. For believers, increasingly excluded by society, the presence and support of the Spirit from the moment they became Christians was a welcome encouragement and one that resulted in an anticipation of provision for their futures. Thus, it is no coincidence that fire and wind accompany his coming. Both represented the presence of God in the OT (Exod. 3:2; 2 Sam. 22:11), as well as his capacity to infuse new life (Ezek. 37:9–14), to protect (Exod. 13:21; 14:21), to provide for (Num. 11:31) and to cleanse (Isa. 6:6–7). These divine characteristics are not to be overlooked in assessing the significance of the presence of the fire and wind in association with the Spirit in Acts 2:2–3.

5. The Spirit fills believers (Acts 2:4)

The description of the believers being *filled* with the Spirit is a favourite for Luke. It is used as a synonym for the terms 'receive' (Acts 2:38) or 'baptize' (Luke 3:16) in association with the Spirit. There is no suggestion in Luke that having once filled believers, the Spirit may not fill them again. In fact, having been filled with the Spirit on the day of Pentecost, Peter, John and others are specifically recorded as being filled again (4:31). The term *filled* is useful in that it helps to describe some aspects of the impartation of the Spirit to the believer in that it is comprehensive. Similarly, in 2:33, the Spirit is described as being poured out, the implications of lavish overflowing being clear. There is no suggestion that the person who is filled with the Spirit needs replenishing due to the Spirit leaking out; nor should the term be taken to imply that the Spirit is best understood as a fluid.

The words used by Luke are for the purposes of creating pictures that are descriptive of the involvement of the Spirit in the lives of believers. As such, they are best understood metaphorically. Central truths that relate to each of them include the fact that the Spirit's involvement in the lives of believers is comprehensive, experiential, personal and expected to make an impact on them and those around them. The Spirit is not a doctrine to be affirmed or to be debated so much as a person to be enjoyed and experienced. He is not a powerful force so much as a personal friend, not simply a reservoir of energy but an energetic advocate ministering to us, for us and through us.

6. The Spirit communicates through believers (Acts 2:4–11)

The evidence of the Spirit having come to believers on the day of Pentecost was that they spoke in other tongues (2:4). That others understood what they said indicates that, on this occasion, they spoke in known languages (*xenolalia*) (2:7). Some have suggested that in Acts 2:6, the speaking in tongues was accompanied by a miracle of hearing on the part of the observers, resulting in their being able to understand the content of the tongues, though this is not clear from the text. Other than Acts 2:6, the NT indicates that an earthly language is not being assumed by the writers when they refer to tongues (1 Cor. 14:2, 6, 13, 19). In Acts 2:11, the translation of the tongues is described as relating to the mighty works of God. The Spirit thus manifested his presence in the lives of believers by verbal communication.

It is possible that this supernatural ability to speak in unknown tongues is the reason for the mocking reaction of some of the bystanders. However, it is more likely that, in a cosmopolitan city where many languages would have been spoken, the ridicule relates to the content of their speech. There seems to be little reason for people to mock their ability to speak other languages.[9] What is more likely is that they did so because the believers were excitedly expressing all the great things that God had done. Other than the hysterical, ecstatic worship of some pagan cults, most Jewish worship of this time was solemnly liturgical. For the believers to be rejoicing in God would have been unusual and was thus categorised dismissively. Furthermore, most Jews would have found it incongruous that ordinary Galileans should be praising God since there was no widespread concept of the dynamic presence of God with them in their own lives. Indeed, most had assumed that he had forgotten them.

It is to be noted however, that in contrast to the mockers, many were amazed (Acts 2:12) and, after Peter's sermon, three thousand came to faith (2:41). Most significantly, Peter identifies the speaking in tongues as a fulfilment of Joel 2:28–32, which refers to people prophesying on behalf of God. Peter viewed the content of the tongues, as understood by the hearers, as being prophetic. Ordinary believers were privileged to speak on behalf of God. In the OT, few people were anointed by God to be prophets and even fewer to function as a prophetess. But now, all believers are called to this

---

[9] It seems that there was some animosity between the cosmopolitan Jews who lived in Jerusalem and the conservative country-folk from Galilee. Not only was there a distinction in the dialect (Matt. 26:73) but more general differences led to a certain patronising attitude to the latter by the former.

sacred duty – to speak the message entrusted to them by God. On this occasion, it was tongues (also Acts 19:6); elsewhere, it will be through preaching (Acts 4:8, 25, 31), revelation (Acts 5:3–9; 13:9), wisdom (Acts 6:10; 15:28), visions (Acts 7:55–56), supernatural direction (Acts 8:29; 13:2) and prophecy (Acts 11:28; 19:6; 21:11).

Luke does not explore the reason why the Spirit chooses that his arrival should be accompanied by tongues. However, since (prophetic) speech was the most common occurrence when the Spirit was manifested in the lives of people in the OT, its presence here is understandable. It is not described by Luke as proof for the presence of the Spirit in the life of a believer. Rather, it functions as the outpouring of the activity of the Spirit through a person in mission activity to unbelievers, cutting across barriers of language. The emphasis on mission will be a major aspect of the work of the Spirit in the church in the chapters to come. Here, Luke demonstrates that inspired speech is the first act of the Spirit. That the believers are seen to be speaking foreign languages miraculously indicates the priority of the Spirit and his pro-activity in ensuring that cross-language evangelism takes place.

The Spirit inspires and enables believers to speak on his behalf in a variety of ways. This may involve all forms of communication available to us, be it spoken or written. The Spirit desires to speak more often than we might expect. What may be even more startling is that he wishes to speak through *us*. Our role is to listen for him and then to communicate his message, be it in a church or the office, the home or the school, amongst Christians or not, in a declaratory mode or as a whisper, to a group or an individual. His desire is to reveal Jesus and our privilege is to be part of the process.

7. The Spirit establishes a new community (Acts 2:38–39)

The coming of the Spirit on the day of Pentecost provided the basis for a racially undivided community, demonstrated by the expansion of the Christian community to include Samaritans and even Gentiles. Those outside were now included. Indeed, Peter includes such a hope in his sermon (Acts 2:39). Ramachandra, referring to Acts 10:9–23, concludes that the day of Pentecost resulted in 'the stupendous sight, unimaginable in their contemporary world, of a Jewish peasant and a Roman centurion living together under one roof'.[10] The Spirit affirmed those whom others were wishing to exclude.

[10] V. Ramachandra, *The Recovery of Mission. Beyond the Pluralist Paradigm* (Eerdmans, 1996), p. 269.

In the OT, only certain people (mainly Israelite men) benefited from these experiences with the Spirit. After the day of Pentecost, increasingly, the Spirit would be filling the lives of men and women, irrespective of culture or nationality; Luke traces the history of this progression in Acts. Little in their scriptures would have indicated to Jews that the Spirit would be given to anybody other than themselves (Isa. 11:1–3; 32:15; Ezek. 36:24–28; 37:14; Joel 2:28–29). At best, other nations would be drawn to Israel, who would then reflect God to them (Isa. 60:3–14).

The implication that Gentiles would be able to experience the same quality of relationship with God as did his people is rarely articulated in the OT. Zechariah (14:16–17) prophesies that the nations are to worship God, but it will be as a result of divine compulsion, failure to do so resulting in severe punishment. But the Spirit demonstrates that God desires direct and intimate relationship with all people and not just Jews. Thus, it is no surprise that although the initial fillings by the Spirit are of Jews, both Samaritans and Gentiles will also be recipients. Although such a momentous occasion is initially presented with reference to Jews in Acts 2:1–4, the outworking of such a revelation will include opportunities for others to similarly receive the Spirit.

Thus, Jewish believers are presented with the reality that Samaritans are also accepted by the Spirit (Acts 8:14–19), as are Gentiles (Acts 10:44–47; 11:15) and even killers of Christians (Acts 9:17). Given the ancient rivalries and hatred between Jews, Samaritans and Gentiles, it took a sensational act of the Spirit, witnessed and affirmed by Jewish leaders of the church, to ensure that age-old, divisive resentments were divinely removed from the minds of all concerned. The Spirit dictated the new rules of his community and ensured that all believers knew them. This fundamental work of the Spirit to create a diverse but united community (1 Cor. 3:16) needs greater emphasis among believers, who, unfortunately, are increasingly divided. Unity is not a negotiable element on the agenda of the Spirit, nor should it be valued as a doctrine devoid of reality by believers today.

The phenomenon of tongues is valuable as a sign that the tongues speaker is now part of a charismatic community and therefore is expected to function in charismatic ministry. In particular, whenever speaking in tongues was experienced, in its historical setting in Acts, it removed barriers of class and race, affirmed non-Jews as valid members of the new Christian community and allowed for the integration of all into the newly constituted community of God (Acts 10:46; 11:15). In this regard, it may be viewed as a reversal of Babel. There, language became the reason for the disintegration of the society, whereas now, in the initiation of the church, a reconstitution of history by the Spirit has occurred. Macchia identifies it as the 'first ecumenical language of the church',[11] demonstrating the unity available to believers because of their common experience in Christ, as facilitated by the Spirit. It indicates the centrally important issue to Jesus (John 13:34–35; 17:21–23) and the Spirit (Eph. 4:2-3) – the unity of the church. The Spirit's gift of tongues is thus a means of reminding individuals of their equal status within the church, breaking through all racial and economic divisions. As a sign, it also highlights the fact that the Spirit functions through weakness, that all believers can benefit from his resources and that his gifts do not result from human endeavour or natural talent.

The Spirit is interested in inclusion, providing an opportunity for unique cooperation and harmony. Thus, he initiates a community that includes women, men and children, young and old, multi-racial, culturally varied and nationally diverse. The church, as initiated by the Spirit, is a medley of people who are privileged to stand with each other, to relate to each other, to minister together on behalf of the Spirit and thus to reflect God and his purposes.

[11] F. D. Macchia, 'Babel and the Tongues of Pentecost: Reversal or Fulfilment? – A Theological Perspective', in M. J. Cartledge, (ed.), *Speaking in Tongues: Multi-Disciplinary Perspectives* (Paternoster Press, 2006), pp. 47 (34–51).

Acts 5:3–9; 8:29–40; 10:19–23; 11:12–15; 13:2–4; 16:6–10
12. The Holy Spirit guides believers

1. Introduction

When my daughter, Anna-Marie, was very young, I was driving to the airport with her to pick up my wife. 'Why doesn't God speak to me?' she said. I knew what she meant. As Christians, we talk about God speaking to us but we have very limited notions as to how he does. Perhaps he will speak through a sermon, prophecy or personal Bible reading. Few of us expect an audible voice or an angelic visitation. But the fact is, he's everywhere and I'm learning the importance of identifying when he does speak so that I can respond to him, whatever he says, however he says it. Paul anticipates the same when he writes to the church in the bustling metropolis of Rome and reminds the believers that God whispers his presence throughout his creation (Rom. 1:20).

The notion of God guiding people in their lives was an aspiration of the Israelites. Although they had the law, many of them desired a personal tuition and leading that resulted from the Spirit of God intimately coaching them and helping them plan their future and live righteously (Ps. 143:10). The realisation of such a hope was partially experienced by the Israelites in their travel from Egypt to the Promised Land (Isa. 63:14). The anticipation was that it would happen again to a greater degree.

In the years before the time of Jesus, there grew a belief, particularly among Jewish rabbis, that God still spoke from time to time.[1] This conviction largely developed in the absence of prophecy, since God had not spoken through an authentic prophet for four hundred years. It was borne out of desperation to hear from God

---

[1] M. *b. Sot.* 33a.

again. The voice of God, or more accurately, 'the daughter voice of God' (*bath-qol*)[2] was described as the 'echo of God's voice'. In the absence of prophetic revelation, the desire to hear from God increased and Jewish Christians would have been familiar with such a hope – to hear from God. Now, the dream was a reality for believers because of the Spirit. They had waited centuries for it to happen and when the Spirit came on the day of Pentecost, the prayer was answered – the Spirit had come to guide them personally, passionately and perfectly.

2. The Spirit offers personal guidance (Acts 5:3-9)

The book of Acts provides a number of examples of the Spirit guiding believers. Peter is advised by the Spirit when Ananias and Sapphira lie to him about the amount of money they gave to the apostles (Acts 5:3, 9). Although the message to the church in Jerusalem and the readers of Acts is that the Spirit is omniscient, the parallel lesson is that believers are accountable to him. He is, after all, *the Holy Spirit* (5:3) and *the Spirit of the Lord* (5:9). Philip was guided by the Spirit to speak to an Ethiopian official (8:29) and Peter was advised by the Spirit to go to a Gentile centurion, Cornelius (10:19; 11:12). Nothing in their earlier lives would have indicated that it would have been appropriate for them as Jews to dialogue with Gentiles, let alone offer them the possibility of salvation and baptism. They needed supernatural confirmation that such an action was appropriate and the Spirit provided it.

On occasions, the information revealed by the Spirit may be completely new, because of a situation that has arisen that demands an innovative strategy to address it. Guidance may not always be available from the Bible, but the ever-present Spirit is a valuable instructor in such circumstances. Thus, none other than the Spirit provides the sensational revelation that the church is to be multi-racial (Eph. 3:5–7). That plan which had not been disclosed previously, and was thus a 'mystery' until the Spirit revealed it, provided an opportunity for a fulfilment of Jesus' promise that the Spirit would lead believers into truth. This was more than the Spirit reminding the believers of what they already knew; on this occasion, the Spirit clarified truth that had been suppressed by years of assumption that God's heart was only for the people of Israel. Similarly, the Spirit commissions Saul and Barnabas (Acts 13:2, 4) to undertake a mission that resulted in them preaching to Jews initially

---

[2] Josephus. *Ant.* 13:10.3.

(13:4–43) but then to Gentiles (13:46 – 14:28; esp. 13:46–47). Again, an exceedingly unusual mission, that was to include preaching the gospel to Gentiles, was supported by a supernatural impulse of the Spirit. This was later confirmed by the Spirit at the Jerusalem conference that met to discuss the mission to Gentiles (15:28). Thus, he who operates with better than a photographic memory and can remind us of what we once knew also, on occasion, offers new revelations that will help in our spiritual development.

When Paul was in danger of not going in the right direction, the Spirit interrupted his plans and guided him to go to Macedonia (Acts 16:6–10) and later to Jerusalem (20:22–23). Although readers may be desirous of knowing how the Spirit guided Paul, that is clearly of limited importance to Luke, who is more interested in enforcing the point that the Spirit was in charge of the direction of his mission.[3] Indeed, it may have been unhelpful if Luke had identified the Spirit's method of guiding the apostles. The Spirit is more creative in directing his delegates than even the examples offered by Luke. Some principles may be gleaned from the account. The apostles did not sit around waiting for direction; they used their initiative, relying on the Spirit to divert their plans when appropriate. Secondly, they were prepared to acknowledge his involvement in their journeys, attributing the changes of direction to him. For them, there was no accident or coincidence when it came to the guidance of the Spirit; he was in charge of the map. Finally, they obeyed the promptings of the Spirit.

On occasions, Paul identifies information he shares as being inspired by the Spirit even though it is not reflected in the Scriptures. Thus, when he gives advice to widows, he states, 'I think that I . . . have the Spirit of God' (1 Cor. 7:40).[4] However, it is not clear as to whether the advice is given because the Spirit has specifically guided him or whether he gives it as one who acknowledges his relationship with the Spirit. If it is the former, he is referring to occasions when he has no Scripture to refer to as the basis for giving advice, and thus

[3] It is possible that prophecies provided the necessary guidance, or that external circumstances, which made travel impossible, were interpreted as indicating the hand of the Spirit.

[4] G. D. Fee, in *God's Empowering Presence* (Hendrickson, 1994), p. 140, suggests that Paul is viewing the Spirit as 'not the guarantor of Paul's words, but of Paul's life, which makes these words more than simply one man's personal opinion'. Thus, he believes that Paul is not claiming the Spirit to be the source of a revelation but that the Spirit is the ultimate ground for ethical decisions. Although the latter perspective is true, the fact that Paul indicates his belief that he has 'the Spirit of God', on this occasion, suggests that he believes that in the absence of Scriptural revelation, that which he advises has the support of the Spirit. Thus, he identifies the witness of the Spirit in the decision-making process.

relies on the Spirit to guide him (when he has a Scriptural basis, or refers specifically to a revelation given by Jesus, he identifies it [1 Cor. 7:10; 9:14; 11:23; 14:37; 1 Tim. 5:18]). If the latter, he is referring to occasions when he gives advice but he does so as one who has sought to listen to the Spirit in the past, though he recognises that it is not guaranteed to be authentic or infallible.

Paul's words in 1 Corinthians 7:25 are also capable of being interpreted in either way. As an apostle, it would be assumed that he intends his advice to be viewed as trustworthy and therefore to be accepted. However, elsewhere, he does concede that others should be free to test messages that purport to come from the Spirit (1 Cor. 14:29). On balance, because of the reliance on the Spirit that he is seeking to stress, and given his apostolic authority, probably he is here expecting his readers to accept his views as those that have been transmitted to him by the Spirit; any examination of them should lead the believer to affirm them as being authentic. In this regard, Godet's suggestion that Paul is simply offering advice that can be accepted or rejected by the readers 'as purely optional' is unlikely.[5]

3. The Spirit guides believers in diverse ways (Acts 16:6-10)

It may be no coincidence that Luke uses two different descriptions to depict separate occasions when the Spirit guided Paul and his colleagues, with reference to his eventual preaching in Macedonia (Acts 16:6–7); thus, they were *forbidden by the Holy Spirit* (16:6, ESV) and later *the Spirit of Jesus would not allow them* (16:7). It is possible that the way the guidance was presented was different on each occasion, warranting the change in vocabulary.[6] The Spirit is cognizant of the fact that believers exist in different life settings that demand a personal agenda on his part to ensure that they receive all they need to cope in their particular situation. The Spirit is creative and caring enough to treat believers as individuals, offering guidance in ways that are appropriate to their temperaments and life situations.

Paul also notes that the Spirit seeks to guide believers with regard to their lifestyles (Col. 1:9–10). The Spirit not only identifies God's ways but enables believers to walk in them (Eph. 3:20; Col. 1:11). This follows the OT precedent where Joshua was enabled by the Spirit to operate with such a quality of wisdom that the people obeyed him (Deut. 34:9). The Spirit also offers guidance with regard

---

[5] F. L. Godet, *Commentary on First Corinthians*. First published 1889 (T.&T. Clark); reprinted by Kregel, 1997, pp. 396–397.
[6] So F. F. Bruce, *The Book of Acts* (Eerdmans, 1975), p. 327.

to practical aspects of life. Thus, those who made the garments for Aaron were described as being aided by 'a spirit [or Spirit] of skill' (Exod. 28:3, ESV; *pneuma sophias*, LXX) while Bezalel was enabled by 'the Spirit of God . . . to make artistic designs for work in gold, silver and bronze . . .' (Exod. 31:3–4).

As I write, I have just returned from a prayer meeting that is held at our college on Tuesdays at midday, in the middle of the lecture programme. In it, we welcomed our final year students back to college from month-long placements that they had undertaken. They had traveled both far and near and been involved in churches, para-church organizations and other settings that had enabled them to prepare for their futures, to put into practice some of the lessons learned at college, and to discover new ways of benefitting from the guidance of the Spirit. Three of them offered a brief account of their time on mission. Each of them acknowledged being stretched, but also spoke of the resources of the Spirit that they relied on, some of which were revelations to them, and all of which reminded them of the personal care of the Spirit who is dedicated to them. They had discovered that the Spirit had exercised a divine creativity and led them as individuals in paths suited to them.

The Spirit may choose to speak through the language of the Bible (Col. 3:16), but he may as easily speak in other ways including prophecy, circumstances, sermons, conversations, inner compulsions, visions, dreams and even, though rarely, an audible voice (John 15:7–12; Acts 15:27). The guidelines in the Bible are recognized as being valuable but so also are other occasions when the dynamic and transforming Spirit may speak to believers. Sometimes, the Spirit provides guidance through circumstances (Acts 16:10) while, on other occasions, he uses people to offer direction (Acts 13:2–3). That is not to suggest that the Spirit is superior to the Word or the Word to the Spirit. The Spirit and the Word function together, on occasion the former through the latter but also sometimes spontaneously and without specific reference to the written Word. Pinnock writes, 'There are many notes on the Spirit's keyboard which we often neglect to sound,' resulting in our not taking the opportunity to hear him more often.[7]

A sense of balance and sensitivity is needed, however; the Bible without the Spirit can result in barren exegesis, but to emphasize a quest for the Spirit without the balance of the Word can degenerate into effervescent emptiness. Where the Spirit speaks outside the written Word, caveats must be instituted carefully in order to check

---

[7] C. H. Pinnock, *Flame of Love. A Theology of the Holy Spirit* (InterVarsity Press, 1996), p. 121.

for errors in the listening process. The Spirit will never contradict the Word and extra-biblical revelation must be assessed in the context of the Christian community, which has itself been developed by the Spirit and the Word (1 Cor. 12:3; 14:29; 1 John 4:1–3). The Spirit and the Word functioning in the Christian community is the ideal framework to counteract imbalance and to recognize the intrinsic value of any revelation.[8] An example of the Spirit-community model in identifying the will of God is reflected in Acts 15:22, 28, where the role of the Jerusalem community is prominent in arriving at the conclusion to welcome Gentiles into the church. Where there was uncertainty and limited scriptural guidance, the believers looked to the Spirit to facilitate the correct conclusion.

4. Believers should listen for and to the Spirit (Acts 8:29–40; 13:2–4)

The Bible is an influential guide (Ps. 119:9–11) but believers are also to be led by the Spirit (Rom. 8:4; 1 Cor. 2:13) as he speaks on other occasions. It is not that the Bible and the Spirit are separate and contrasting sources of influence, guidance and wisdom. The Spirit who inspired Scripture also facilitates preaching and teaching which is dependent on it. However, he also predates it and has the capacity and desire to influence the lives and spirituality of believers dynamically and energetically in ways that include the Bible, but may also be additional to it. Although the Bible is a fundamentally important source of guidance, it does not exist to provide answers to every question that may be posed. It was originally written for readers who existed in ancient cultures and eras that are inevitably different for those living in later generations. Therefore, to view it as the neat basis for all decision-making for all times, even with reference to the life and practices of believers, is not always appropriate. Principles may be gleaned and applied, but care in providing contextually-appropriate guidance is always necessary.

The recurring theme in the seven messages to the churches in Revelation is, 'hear what the Spirit says' (2:7, 11, 17, 29; 3:6, 13, 22). Sometimes, he provided particular guidance to local churches that

[8] In the evangelical world, the Spirit largely has been viewed in the Bible as manifested in terms of affirming propositional truths and in the establishment of church offices. Protestants have tended to assume the Bible as the basis for the ministry of the Spirit, while Catholics have preferred the magisterium. However, while accepting that the Spirit fundamentally speaks through the Bible, he is also able to speak through the prophetic voice; the challenge for believers is to identify when the latter is authentic.

147

differed from messages offered to others. However, the expected consequence of hearing the Spirit was an obedient response. The Spirit offered encouragement and exhortation, support and censure, promises and prohibitions, pledging himself to them but expecting them to prioritize his words in their lives. The Spirit who is rarely silent, and who chooses to speak to believers, anticipates that they will be listening for him and responding accordingly. He may not reveal all that one would like to know, but he will provide all that one needs.

When exploring the fact that the Spirit guides believers, care must be maintained in order to guard against following an impulse that may not be from the Spirit. Furthermore, it is dangerous if it is assumed that one should not engage in normal activities of life without a preceding word of the Spirit. The Spirit is not to be identified with a controlling force who does not allow any independent activity on the part of believers. There have been too many documented accounts of believers who have failed to engage in perfectly legitimate activities because they have not 'heard' from the Spirit. At the same time, some believers have been encouraged to enter into relationships or undertake responsibilities because they have felt 'constrained' by an impression that they have assumed to indicate the guidance of the Spirit. The Spirit rarely forces believers to engage in activities; rather, he graciously encourages us to be involved in pursuits that, though challenging, will be supported by his enabling power and grace.

Listening for and to the Spirit is an issue of significant importance for Christian leaders. It is incumbent upon them to be messengers of the Spirit, thus necessitating a prior dependency on and disclosure by the Spirit. As importantly, it is their privilege and responsibility to help others in the process of hearing the Spirit so that they can actively walk with him. Walking with the Spirit is not assumed by Paul to be a partnership in which the Spirit speaks only when asked to, nor does he anticipate that the Spirit will only speak when absolutely necessary, or infrequently. The relationship expected by Paul between the believer and the Spirit is one in which the former takes the responsibility of listening to the latter, as a blind person may listen to the guidance of one who can see the way ahead. This delicate process of dialogue is one that needs careful consideration and sensitive teaching to ensure that it is put into practice.

5. Hearing the Spirit accurately is of crucial importance (Acts 11:12-15)

He speaks and so must be listened to. This demands the development of a personal relationship with him, learning to recognize his voice and to respond to his guidance.[9] This is a high calling. Eternal life may be a free gift of God (Rom. 6:23) but it is a life that demands being led by the Spirit of eternal life. Paul is not replacing a harsh law and replacing it with a soft, easy, indulgent set of rules. The expectations of the Spirit are those that belong to eternity and excellence; nothing less than his standards will do. It is a much more rigorous lifestyle to which believers have been called, that needs the enabling power of the Spirit to adopt it. It is the Spirit who is the believer's guide and it is he who must be obeyed.

[9] John 14:16–17, 26; 15:26; 16:7; Acts 1:2, 16; 4:25; 8:29; 10:19; 11:12; 13:4; 15:28; 20:22–23; 28:25; Rom. 8:14–27; Gal. 5:17–18; Eph. 1:16–17; 3:4–5.

Part Four
The Holy Spirit in the Epistles

Romans 8:1–13, 14–23, 26–27
13. The Holy Spirit opposes the flesh and affirms believers

Having spent time exploring the guilt of humanity (Rom. 1:18–32) and the justice of God (2:1–11), Paul introduces a discussion on the place of the law in determining one's spiritual status with God (2:12 – 3:20) before presenting the importance of faith in achieving righteousness (3:21–25), which is the basis of one being justified (5:1–21). Thereafter, he exhorts his readers to recognise that being justified anticipates an ethical life-change, with consequent responsibilities on their part to ensure that it occurs (6:1–23). It is at this point that he identifies the role of the Spirit in guiding believers in their new lives. Instead of the law which was the guide for God's people, Christians are offered the Spirit, who is a personal, immediate, dynamic and perfect guide.

1. The Spirit opposes the flesh and expects believers to do the same (Rom. 8:1–13)

a. Introduction

In these verses, Paul explores probably the most fundamental issue relating to people then and now, including believers. It is a perennial problem of life for everyone, and it relates to moral and ethical aspects of life. It relates to how one can know what is the proper action to take, the correct decision to make, the right word to say, the appropriate thought to think – and then to determine how one can do what is the best. In short, this defines the battle between good and evil, a conflict that was present in the Garden of Eden and which continues to create havoc in the lives of individuals and communities. Paul has a simple but profound proposal to offer his readers in these verses, that will

153

enable them to determine these issues. First, he introduces them to two antagonists, the flesh (*sarx*) and the Spirit (*pneuma*). Then, he identifies believers as being on the side of the Spirit (who will be their guide in the decision-making process and who will enable them to achieve their aspirations). Finally, he exhorts them to walk closely with the Spirit and declare war against the flesh, whereby their potential dilemma will have the opportunity of being resolved satisfactorily.

b. Believers are free (Rom. 8:1–2)

Paul starts the section (8:1) by noting the foundational status of believers. They are no longer under condemnation; they are free (8:2). Believers are no longer bound to the mangy dog of sin that rubs against them and sullies their lives, nor are they to be viewed as trying but failing in a constant, nervous fight that leaves them battered and bruised. Paul presents a much more victorious scenario, in which the Spirit enables them 'to revolt against the usurper sin with a real measure of effectiveness'.[1]

He has already identified them as being justified (Rom. 3:21–24). Now, he explores a new element in their standing before God. It includes the fact that they are freed from the guilt and consequent condemnation of sin. But also, they are delivered from the power of that sin over them. Thus, his use of the word *Therefore* (8:1) relates to his argument in 6:1 – 7:25. Because they have been justified, there is no fear of them being guilty because of deeds done in the past. Because of their relationship with God, nothing and no-one can hold them accountable; sin is no longer their landlord and any outstanding debts have been paid by their new owner. Here, however, he is interested in exploring their lives *after* justification. Who will care for them in the future, enabling them to fight temptation and overcome sin? Who will stop the flesh convincing them they cannot overcome it? Who will develop within them the confidence to believe that they can win the battle over sin? Who can lead them to victory but also enable them to fight and defeat the fleshly foe? It is no wonder that the answer to all these questions – the Spirit – is mentioned fifteen times, in most verses from 8:1–16.

c. The Spirit and the law (Rom. 8:1–4)

Not only are believers not to follow the dictates of the flesh, but also they are to remember that the law is no longer to be their guide, for

---

[1] C. E. B. Cranfield, *The Epistle to the Romans Vol. 1* (T. & T. Clark, 1975), p. 378.

the Spirit is their superior mentor. When he speaks of the law, Paul often, as in Romans 7:4–16, refers to the OT law, in particular, the Torah. This was prescribed by God for his covenant people, to set the standard for lifestyle, failure to keep it being covered by the sacrificial system. Ongoing sacrifices for the covering of sins are now no longer necessary, since the sacrificial death of Jesus has atoned for the sins of the world. In Romans 2:29, Paul acknowledges that the law confirms the racial identity of the Jew, particularly demonstrated by a physical surgical operation (circumcision). However, since the death of Jesus, the Spirit marks the spiritual identity of the members of a renewed Israel, as prophesied (Jer. 31:3–34; Ezek. 11:19; 36:26–27; 37:1–14), confirmed by spiritual internal surgery, not external circumcision (Rom. 1:21; 2:15; 5:5; 6:17). Thus, Paul describes believers as having been discharged (released) from the law, having died to it (7:4),[2] resulting in the possibility of a new, fulfilling life in the Spirit (7:6).

Paul is not stating that the law was valueless; indeed, he describes it as holy (Rom. 7:12), spiritual (7:14) and good (7:13, 16), identifying important purposes of the law. It pointed out sin and identified the standards expected by God (7:5, 7, 13); it also established that he is holy and just. However, it has limitations and thus Paul refers to it as weak (8:3). It acted as a very good standard for the behaviour of the Israelites, consistently pointing out their failings and identifying punishments. However, it could not provide power to facilitate improvement. Thus, because of the weakness of the people to keep it, the law locked them in a circle that led to condemnation.

Furthermore, although the law offered valuable guidance to the covenant community of God in the past, now since Jesus has died, a better guide is available – the Spirit, who indwells every believer. Paul taught that the law had now been superseded as the ethical guide of the believer (Rom. 10:4; Gal. 3:2–5, 19–29; 4:4–7; 5:1, 5). As well as drawing attention to the new guide, Paul draws a contrast between the old law, as defined by words and letters (and therefore, to a degree, external, impersonal and lifeless), and the new life of the Spirit (characterized by internal, personal and vital components).

God gave the law to the Israelites as an act of grace, not judgment. It declared that they were sinners, unable to achieve God's

---

[2] Paul builds on the analogy of the significance of the death of one partner in a marriage to the marriage relationship. He argues that, because of a believer's union with Christ, it is as if he or she died when Christ died. As a result, a change has occurred in the relationship with the previous partner, the law. Now, believers are free to engage in a new relationship with Jesus, who replaces the law. As the law was an integral element of the old covenant, now the Spirit is the integral replacement in the new covenant. Believers no longer need the law; they have the Spirit.

standards on their own. However, one of the main purposes of the law was not merely to encourage them to achieve acceptance by good deeds, but to help them realize that God desired relationship with them. That relationship was based on his grace towards them, not on their efforts towards him.

For Paul, the Spirit provides the most sensational insights and privileges for the believer. He is a better resource than the law for a number of reasons. The Spirit offers specific guidance, being able to advise the believer in multiple situations, his advice sometimes being more precise and explicit. He is a superior guide since he is God and not merely a code book of conduct. As contrasted with a book of regulations, he is associated fundamentally with relationship, not rules. The Spirit brings a person into relationship with God whereas the law can only provide the standard expected by God and warn of the consequences of disobedience. The Spirit acts as a personal guide and influence whereas the law is impersonal. The Spirit points out sin but also provides strength to overcome it, and power to obey his promptings, whereas the law only highlights sin and condemns the sinner (Rom. 7:7–11; Gal. 3:10). The advice of the Spirit is contemporary, relates to issues relevant to the lifestyle and context of believers, is available without having to consult a handbook of laws, is not confined to issues relevant to ancient ceremonial or religious topics, and provides an internal and loving influence. Finally, the Spirit acts as an ever-present guide while the law, inasmuch as it is a collection of books, is less immediate. The Spirit is less an empowering force or power and more an enabling friend and mentor.

Paul specifically states that it is because of the Spirit that 'the just requirement of the law might be fulfilled in us' (Rom. 8:4, ESV). It is not that the Spirit is given to enable the believer to keep the law. Rather, he is stating that those requirements laid down by the law have now been fulfilled in the believer because of what Jesus has already achieved on our behalf, the benefits of which have been transmitted to us by the Spirit. They have been fulfilled in the sense that believers base their relationship with God on faith that Jesus has done everything that is needed. The Spirit's presence in their lives is the confirmation that their God-given faith has been accepted as that which was needed to commence a relationship with God. The Spirit whispers the words of assurance that friendship with God has been established. There is nothing more to be done. The cross has now taken centre-stage, the Spirit introduces the believer as a child of God, while the law bows out, having done all it could.

The purpose of the law (to encourage relationship with God by faith, in the context of an understanding of his holiness) has now been achieved. The law demanded holiness; the Spirit now makes believers holy by applying to them the gift of salvation as achieved by Jesus on the cross. Those who walk with the Spirit (that is, believers) have passed God's standard, not on their own merits but on the basis of faith. They have passed the exam without even having to sit it. If they had, they would have failed it anyway, but God passed them at the cost of the sacrifice of his Son, who passed it for them.

The purpose of the law was to identify sin and its consequences, and to point to Christ. It has achieved what it was designed to do. It can now leave the rest of the believer's journey to the Spirit who has been given through faith (Gal. 3:14). Christ, who has redeemed us from the burden of the law (Gal. 3:13), is now our custodian, not the law (Gal. 3:24–25). Now as heirs of God (Gal. 4:1–7), it is the privilege of believers to be mentored personally, not by an external law code, however good, but by the Spirit of God himself. It is no wonder that Paul regularly uses the concept of freedom to define the new life of the believer (Rom. 7:3; 8:2; Gal. 4:30–31; 5:1, 13). Of course, this does not refer to a freedom to sin. On the contrary, this new relationship, in which the Spirit takes it upon himself to be the coach for every believer, has serious consequences. This new freedom is for the purposes of attaining righteousness (Rom. 6:20); believers are freed from slavery to sin in order to be bound to God's standards and will. Therefore, in the battle against the flesh, believers are to take advantage of their new, influential and empowering resource and mentor – the Spirit, who has replaced the law and its limited ability to facilitate change in the lives of those who sought to keep it.

d. Flesh and Spirit (Rom. 8:5–8)

In Romans, Paul uses the Greek term *sarx* (translated variously as 'flesh', 'sinful nature' or 'human nature') on a number of occasions but in different ways, the difference in use being particularly notable in chapter 8. Sometimes, it refers to the characteristic of being human (Rom. 1:3; 4:1; 8:3; 9:5, 8), and human effort (Gal. 3:3). However, on other occasions, it is clear that he is using *flesh*, not to refer to the physical body and mortality, but to describe something much more malevolent and malignant that militates against God in a way that makes it indivisible from sin; indeed, the term 'sin' is often synonymous with 'the flesh' (8:4–9, 12–13; 13:14). In this respect, to live a life dominated by sin is equivalent to living a life controlled by the flesh. It is as if flesh and sin gang up on the believer and make it difficult to live as a follower of Jesus – so difficult that one wonders how it can be achieved. It is in this context that the Spirit, who was mentioned just four times in chapters 1–7 (only eight times

157

in chapters in 9–16), is now presented pervasively throughout this section (twenty-one times in 8:1–27)[3] as the one who provides the force that not only rescues believers but enables them to take territory previously held by the flesh and sin in their lives.

In Romans 8:5–13, Paul contrasts the Spirit with the flesh, identifying the incompatibility of the two and the tension that causes. A life influenced by the Spirit is focused on those aspects of life that are important to the Spirit, while it also has a different destiny to a life focused on a sinful agenda (8:6). Paul identifies his readers as people of the Spirit and not of the flesh (8:9). As such, a lifestyle characterized by the word 'flesh' is inappropriate for them for it describes a way of life that is not influenced by the Spirit. Such a life may be grossly immoral or mildly displeasing but the depth of decadence is not the issue; it is a life that is devoid of the Spirit and thus cannot please God (8:8), however moral the person concerned may be. Indeed, whether they realize it or not, such people are in a state of enmity with God (8:7), for their lives are devoid of the presence, influence and power of the Spirit.

e. Believers are in the Spirit (Rom. 8:9)

The complete re-location of believers is clearly expressed in Romans 8:9, where Paul describes them as being in the Spirit while also referring to the fact that *the Spirit of God lives in* them. These apparently contradictory phrases are to be appreciated for what they are – descriptions that emphasize the integrated involvement of the Spirit with the believer (1 Cor. 6:17). The intimate association of the Spirit with the believer is heightened in that the Spirit is described as being *of God* (this, in 8:9, is the first occasion in Romans where Paul refers thus to the Spirit). It is none other than God who resides within the believer. Not only that but he *lives in* them (8:9), indicating a tangible experience of God, not merely an intellectual acknowledgement of divine truths. Intimacy of relationship, not merely a rational response, is the ideal expected by Paul when he refers to the Spirit dwelling in the believer. The sense of privilege but also of challenge for believers is remarkable.

Paul, however, has more to say about the privileged position of believers. He emphasizes their spiritual elevation by stating that, as well as the Spirit, Christ also is in them, by the presence of the Spirit who is described as *the Spirit of Christ* (Rom. 8:9). The value

---

[3] Cranfield (*Romans Vol. 1*, p. 371) identifies these references to the Spirit in chapter 8 as being, 'much more often than in any other single chapter in the whole NT'.

of this for the readers was that it helped them appreciate the character and personality of the Spirit. To describe him as being *of Christ* reminded them of Jesus, his actions, deeds and words; his care, compassion and love; his power, authority and presence. Clearly, the Spirit is expected by Paul to function in the lives of believers as did Jesus with the disciples. Indeed, the Spirit is equivalent to the presence of Christ in the life of the believer.

Now, Paul moves to the climactic consequence of his train of thought. Their new life has commenced; now, he talks about the end of their lives. In Romans 8:10, he notes that although their physical bodies are to die[4] as a result of sin, the Spirit[5] of life has been given to them as a result of righteousness (obtained on their behalf by Jesus and granted to them at salvation). Paul encourages them by stating that their final resurrection is guaranteed since the same Spirit who raised Jesus from the dead, guarantees to raise them from the dead (8:11). Paul affirms that the Spirit confirms their eternal status rather than simply enlivens them throughout their lives on this earth. He is not here encouraging them to take advantage of the power of the Spirit to improve their lifestyles; he will come to this in verse 12. Here, he is caught up with the glory of the position of the believer. The Spirit comes into the lives of believers at salvation and does not leave them; then, at death, the Spirit transforms them as he transformed Jesus.

This comprehensive salvation results in their being placed in a capsule of care that will ensure that they are ushered into the presence of God with the same quality of love as experienced by Jesus. Paul is not interested in exploring how this happened with reference to Jesus; simply to note that it did and that the same miracle of grace awaits the believer.[6] Given this certainty and the lavish provision of

---

[4] Some suggest that this death is that which occurs at salvation when believers 'die' to sin, meaning that they are no longer dominated by sin or subject to the reign of sin since they are now members of a new reign, or kingdom. However, it functions as a clearer contrast if it refers to physical death.

[5] The term 'spirits' in 8:10 (RSV) is actually in the singular form 'spirit' (*pneuma*) in the Greek and this changes the meaning considerably. Since words in Greek do not take a capital letter unless they begin a paragraph or are proper names, it is not certain whether Paul is referring to the Spirit (ESV, KJV) or the life force (spirit) of a person (NIV, NASB). However, elsewhere in 8:1–11, the same word (*pneuma*) is translated 'Spirit'. Therefore, it is more likely that the same translation ought to be offered here. In particular, the same Greek phrase is translated 'Spirit of life' in 8:2.

[6] J. D. G. Dunn, in *Romans 1–8* (Word, 1988), p. 445, writes, 'The believer escapes neither this body of death nor the death of this body, but God's acceptance, life and power are not subject to sin or death, and when sin plays death as its last card God's Spirit will trump it.'

the Spirit (8:12–13), Paul reminds the readers that the presence and commitment of the Spirit demands righteous lifestyles.

f. Believers, all of whom live in the Spirit, are expected to be different (Rom. 8:9–11)

These glorious facts concerning the lavish commitment of the Spirit to believers are not intended to result in the readers congratulating themselves on their relationship with God, nor are they merely to encourage them. They are to act as motivations for action, providing incentives and inspiration to be more Spirit-controlled and less flesh-friendly. Similarly, if the word *ei* (if) is translated as 'since', in 8:9–11, the positive nature of Paul's perspective of the believer is considerably heightened.[7] The Greek word *ei* is capable of being translated 'if' or 'since' and it is often the context that determines the most appropriate meaning. In these verses, given Paul's desire to encourage the believers to recognize their relationship with the Spirit and thus to benefit from it in their fight against the flesh, it is more likely that 'since' is the correct translation; it provides an explicit assurance to the modern reader, rather than uncertainty. He is not sowing doubt into their minds as to whether the Spirit is in them. Rather, on the basis of the presence of the Spirit, he establishes their identity and security as children of God. The Spirit is their identifying mark that they are children of God. Therefore, as a result of the Spirit's certain relationship with them, they are not only against the flesh by default, but also they are not tied to it anymore, and furthermore, they have the authority and power of the Spirit to overcome it.

It takes effort for believers to achieve what the Spirit desires. Holiness is not natural nor does it automatically occur the longer one remains a Christian. It takes determination and an intentional strategy to gain victory over evil and to reflect integrity and goodness. An old Cherokee Indian once told his grandson about a battle that goes on inside everybody, a battle between two wolves, one of which is evil, the other being good. The grandson listened and was then quiet, finally asking his grandfather, 'Which wolf wins?' His grandfather responded, 'The one you spend time with and look

---

[7] So Dunn, *Romans 1–8*, p. 443; see Cranfield, *Romans Vol. 1*, p. 388; C. K. Barrett, *The Epistle to the Romans* (A. and C. Black, 1973) p. 158, offers 'as is indeed the case'; Rom. 8:9, RSV – 'But you are not in the flesh, you are in the Spirit, [*since* (not merely "if")] the Spirit of God really dwells in you'; 8:10, RSV – 'But [*since* (not merely "if")] Christ is in you . . .'; 8:11, RSV – '[*Since* (not merely "if")] the Spirit . . . who raised Jesus . . . dwells in you . . . he . . . will give life to your mortal bodies.' These are positive not negative or doubtful assertions.

after.' The challenge for believers is whether we choose to spend time with those things that harm us and hurt the Spirit or with the one who wishes only to do us good.

When Jawaharlal Nehru made a speech to mark the end of the long struggle for Indian independence from Great Britain on August 14 1947, he stated the following: 'The achievement we celebrate today is but a step, an opening of opportunity, to the greater triumphs and achievements that await us. Are we brave enough and wise enough to grasp this opportunity and accept the challenge of the future? Freedom and power bring responsibility.' Similarly, the freedom and power initiated by the Spirit are great privileges that carry with them the possibility of targeting the future creatively and strategically, intentionally determining to build on the potential that they offer for the benefit of all and to the glory of God. He went on to say, 'As long as there are tears and suffering, our work will not be over.' The Spirit of compassion walks with all believers in order that they may see through his eyes and react as he would react at the world in which they live. The work is ongoing and sometimes a struggle; it is certainly a challenge, a mixture of trials and triumphs, but we walk with the Spirit.

g. Believers who are alive in the Spirit are expected to put the flesh to death (Rom. 8:12–13)

The flesh from which believers have been set free has the nasty habit of resurrecting itself. Believers have the authority to remind it and themselves that it has no right to be alive; rather, they are encouraged to reckon it as dead (Rom. 6:11) and if it refuses to listen, it must be forcibly laid to rest again and again and again. Throughout the process, the Spirit promises to provide the courage, confidence and inner strength to succeed in this activity (8:13). At the same time, the Spirit reminds believers that however loudly the flesh claims to be their lord and master, and to be in control of their lives, it is trespassing on ground claimed by God and inhabited by the Spirit.

The Spirit of life has energy and vitality to vanquish all that is associated with death (Rom. 8:2). He has enabled believers to be what the law could not achieve – that is, justified (8:4). He enables believers to do what they could not achieve – that is, be sanctified (*put to death the misdeeds of the body*, 8:13). The resources for victory are immediately available for believers because the Spirit is instantly and directly present. Sin and flesh have been condemned by God (8:3). This conjoined parasite that takes advantage of human weakness to succumb to temptation and brings pain to people is doomed; it exists in a vicious circle of vice and victimization, but it is destined to be damned. Believers are provided with the opportunity of participating in its demise by putting it to death with the power of the Spirit, prior to its final destruction by God. Although this is a battle, it must never be forgotten that the enemy has actually been defeated. The victory is to be daily established, claimed and proclaimed as much as it is to be achieved. As Lloyd-Jones concludes, 'The church is not primarily a hospital, it is a barracks . . . Realize what God has done to you, realize what you are . . . and march with your heads erect as those who were once "in the flesh".'[8]

Paul is not calling for believers to surrender to the Spirit so that he can mortify the flesh on their behalf. He is calling for a robust stand against sin, in partnership with the Spirit. This is a joint declaration of war on the flesh by the Spirit and the believer (Phil. 2:12–13; Col. 3:5–9). The term Paul uses for *put to death* (*thanatoute*) is placed in the present tense in Greek; he thus anticipates an ongoing action of putting the flesh to death continuously rather than a once-only, quick, decisive act. From Romans 12:1 onwards, Paul identifies how one may put into operation his commission to them, as a result of which they will be fulfilling the Spirit's sanctifying agenda for them, doing 'what is good and acceptable and perfect' (12:2, ESV). Paul identifies such a lifestyle not only as a sacrificial enterprise on the part of the believer, but also one that may be identified best as a 'spiritual act of worship' (12:1).

Elsewhere, he speaks of the implications of not heeding to the practical guidance offered by the Spirit with regard to sanctification (1 Thess. 4:8). There, in the previous seven verses, Paul explores the importance of sexual chastity in the believer's life. The one who has been given to them is privy to all that happens in a believer's life. To conduct oneself immorally despite the presence of the Spirit is to disregard him; it is to act as if he is not there, to continue to sin without a care that he is conscious of what is happening.

2. The Holy Spirit affirms believers as God's children (Rom. 8:14–23)

a. Introduction

Paul has been declaring the difference the Spirit makes in the life of believers (8:1–13). He has contrasted life influenced by the Spirit and an existence which is dominated by selfishness (which he calls

---

[8] D. M. Lloyd-Jones, *Romans: The Sons of God* (Banner of Truth, 1974), p. 131.

'the flesh'); the former pleases God (8:8) while the latter does not (8:7). While the former results in believers benefiting from the life-giving Spirit (8:10–11), the latter results in people existing in hostility to God. It is a stark contrast.

Now, he begins to unfold a new truth that will prelude the climax of 8:31–39, in which his presentation concerning the privileged position of believers culminates with the affirmation that the superlative love of God for them ensures a quality of security that is unparalleled. He has already established that believers are justified and reconciled (5:1–21), released from the law (7:1–25) and its condemnation (8:1), and enabled to keep God's law by the Spirit (8:2–13). Now, Paul declares the role of the Spirit – to establish the believer as a child of God. The Spirit places believers within the very focus of God and grants them the privilege of experiencing God's love intimately, enthusiastically and eternally.

Paul verifies these concepts by using the act of adoption to demonstrate that even though not naturally children of God, he unilaterally chooses that they be so, adopting them into his family. Believers have been enabled to experience being God's children, as did the Israelites in the past, but also in the present to a much higher degree. Now, the Spirit involves himself in the process, resulting in an adoptive bond that is more akin to the relationship enjoyed by the Father and his son, Jesus. Now, they are identified as being fellow heirs with Jesus and are encouraged to speak of his Father in the way he did when on earth.

Adoption, as a legal act, was not practiced by the Jews, and thus Paul is probably reflecting Roman adoption when he refers to it in this passage. He clearly chose this image because it indicated a number of important features present in the relationship of God with believers, not the least being that it parallels the OT picture of God adopting the nation of Israel. Adoption resulted in an ending of the previous relationship to one's natural parents, including the cancellation of any debts. The new father would provide the adopted child with the family name and the promise of being entitled to an inheritance, certified at adoption. Thereafter, adopted children enjoyed an equal relationship with their adoptive father as natural born children, becoming heirs, given new names and thereafter legally protected in their new relationships.

b. The Spirit leads believers (Rom. 8:14)

Paul states that those who are influenced and guided by the Spirit have demonstrated that they are privileged to be identified as the children of God (Rom. 8:14). He is not suggesting that being guided

163

by the Spirit is due to an increased level of spirituality on their part but simply indicating that those who are the children of God will be led by the Spirit of God; that is the Spirit's decision and their delight. He is not affirming their righteousness, as the basis on which they may be presumed to deserve such personal guidance, but highlighting God's righteousness, as a result of which he chooses to graciously guide (Ps. 23:3); it is not because of our goodness that he leads us but because of his. Having chosen us, the Spirit undertakes now to guide us.

The idea of the Spirit leading believers would have been significantly encouraging to Paul's readers, many of whom previously would have experienced only coercion by malevolent forces, human or spiritual. For the Spirit of God to take the responsibility for leading them would have been a singularly welcome fact. Perhaps, some would have doubted Paul in making such a claim that God would lead them. The common presumption was that deities only guided a few, exceptional individuals, who deserved such personal attention and care. That the Spirit should lift a finger to touch their lives or point out the way ahead, tap them on their shoulder or take their hand and lead them gently in his way, whisper directions or guard them from the precipice, was a dream come true. Perhaps because of natural doubts that such concepts may have indicated presumption on their part, Paul does not reduce his enthusiasm in declaring the truth: children of God are led by the Spirit. Since they are the former, they should not be surprised at the latter, even though it is inexplicable and extraordinary that the Spirit willingly should choose so to do, and in such a warm, intimate and individual way.

c. The Spirit provides release from the past and hope for the future (Rom 8:15)

Consequently, Paul encourages his readers not to live as if they were slaves but to enjoy the confidence associated with being children of the Father. Furthermore, he reminds them that the one who arranges this transfer of ownership is not a spirit of bondage or fear but of adoption (8:15). A minority of slaves held authoritative positions in Roman society, though most did not, many being mercilessly treated. The fundamental factor for all slaves was that they were not free, however, nor was there anything other than a slim chance that they ever would be free. They were chained to their destinies, having no control over their futures; theirs was a life of bondage and fear.

Paul uses this concept of *bondage* (8:21) as a definition of this present age (8:19–25) in contrast with the eternal life to come; although believers live in the present age, they belong to the future. This world is not their home; they are free to look to the future and let it determine and resolve the present. The Spirit is the one who beckons the believer into the future and to experience it in the present – not to fear it but to be free to enjoy it as an ecstatic experience prepared for them by God. Paul declares that the Spirit will not lead them into fear but into freedom: not freedom from responsibility as children of God, but freedom to be children of God; not freedom to sin, but freedom to be able to do all that one was unable to do before the Spirit's empowering.

The promise that the Spirit will not lead believers into fear (8:15) is valuable to Jewish readers because fear of displeasing God by breaking his law was a major issue in their relationship with God (Heb. 10:26, 27, 30, 31). At the same time, non-Jewish readers believed in gods who often reacted to their actions disproportionately and arbitrarily. However, love, not fear, characterizes the relationship of the Spirit with believers.

d. The Spirit affirms our adoption by God (Rom. 8:15)

The term translated *sonship* (or 'adoption') (Rom. 8:15) is used five times in the NT[9] and never in the OT,[10] though it is one of the oldest expressions of social harmony and love dating back to the Babylonian and Egyptian empires. For Jewish readers, the reference to the concept of children of God would have struck a familiar chord. They were aware that the term was used of the relationship of the Israelites with reference to their being the sons of God (Isa. 10:22, 23[11]) and to the inheritance of God.[12] Non-Jewish readers had little, if any, belief in a deity that was prepared to be intimately involved with them as Yahweh was to the Israelites; their gods were generally apathetic toward their existence, much less prepared to acknowledge that they were significant enough to relate to.

Paul develops a concept which is startling in its simplicity and, at the same time, staggering in its reality. The Spirit in believers is God's guarantee that he owns them as his children. Before believers have the opportunity to improve themselves, God adopts them, then binds himself to that adoptional process and commits his Spirit

---

[9] Rom. 8:15, 23; 9:4; Gal 4:5; Eph 1:5.

[10] Although the term is not used, the practice is referred to (Moses, Exod. 2:5–10; Esther, Esth. 2:7).

[11] Quoted by Paul in Rom. 9:27.

[12] Deut. 32:9; 1 Kgs 8:51; Ps. 33:12; Isa. 63:17; Jer. 10:16; Mic. 7:18.

to live in them. The Spirit who was given to us when we became Christians is the eternal evidence that our adoption is certain. He is a watertight guarantee that our adoption is certain, immediate and eternal (Eph. 1:13-14). The Spirit of adoption not only releases the resources of God for the one adopted but is also a reminder that the divine declaration of adoption cannot itself be reversed.

This astounding assertion that God has adopted believers to be his children is verified by the Spirit and confirmed by his presence in their lives, Paul defining him as none other than the Spirit of adoption (Rom. 8:15). Jesus provided the possibility of adoption when he died on the cross, while the Spirit activates it experientially. The Spirit – who dwells in believers and owns them (8:9) – asserts, at the same time, that they have been adopted into the family of God. Because he is in their presence, they are in the presence of God.

One of the most remarkable aspects of adoption is that it results in God placing himself in the vulnerable position of being hurt and even rejected by his adopted children. Fatherhood brings pleasure but also potential pain. The pleasure of seeing the first steps of a baby is to be contrasted with the pain of parents who see their child taking the first steps towards rebellion. The pleasure of children sharing smiles with their parents is also sometimes followed by the slamming of a door, the determined refusal, or the angry expletive. Parents allow themselves to be vulnerable because they love their children more than their children know. God does the same, only to a greater degree. He, who knows exquisite happiness and joy as God, willingly adds potential pain to his perfect existence by providing believers with the privilege of being adopted. It is a remarkable fact that not only does God grant this, but he also gives his Spirit as the timeless affirmer of it. Too often, doubt and sin cause believers to question the validity, security or inviolability of their adoption. It is thus an incredibly powerful verification by the Spirit, who provides the quality of confidence that enables believers to name God as their Father.

e. The Spirit encourages believers to cry 'Abba, Father' (Rom. 8:15)

The word cry (krazein) is a particularly powerful term that is rarely used by Paul. Other than this verse and Romans 9:27, where he quotes Isaiah 10:22–23, the only occasion is in Galatians 4:6 (ESV) – 'God has sent the Spirit of his Son into our hearts,[13] crying, "Abba!

---

[13] The reference to the Spirit coming 'into our hearts' is a fulfilment of the prophecy in Ezekiel 11:19, in which the prophet looks forward to a time in the future when God promises to 'put a new spirit' in his people. To the person of

Father!"' The fact that the term is thus used on two occasions to articulate the same truth concerning adoption, and rarely elsewhere, demonstrates the emotional and supportive intensity of the affirmation that God is truly the Father of the one articulating the term. Indeed, the statement in Galatians 4:6 strengthens the concept further by identifying the Spirit as being 'the Spirit of his Son'. The description 'Spirit of his Son' is only used here in Pauline literature. It seems that Paul, in linking the Spirit with the Son, is wanting to emphasize the fact that the Spirit in believers is none other than the same Spirit of the Son of God who loved them and secured sonship for them; theirs is a shared sonship with Jesus. There is no need to attempt to work this out intellectually or to try to determine the separate identities of the Spirit and the Son. Paul is not anticipating a theological enquiry as to how much overlap there is between the Spirit and the Son. Instead, he is anticipating an experiential response triggered by the intellectual and emotional perception that the sonship enjoyed by Jesus with the Father is now a reality for the believer also.

It is uncertain whether the 'cry' to which Paul refers is uttered by the believer or, less likely, the Spirit through the believer, Fee concluding, 'we speak as the Spirit inspires'.[14] Perhaps it is better not to attempt to separate the concepts. Paul is probably intending that readers recognize the integral involvement of the Spirit in the initiating and affirming of the adoptive relationship between the believer and God. The Spirit is to be recognized as inspiring believers to acknowledge that to refer to God as their father is a valid, not a presumptuous act. It indicates an ongoing certainty that although believers may be disowned by many, they are owned by the Father.

To use the term *abba*, employed by Jesus in his relationship with his Father, demands a great deal of confidence on the part of the believer. This assurance is made possible by the Spirit exerting a direct influence on the mind and the emotions.[15] Thus, the translation offered that the Spirit 'bears witness with our spirit' (Rom. 8:16, ESV) is appropriate, for it notes the recognition felt by the believer that a transformation has occurred. The Spirit acts as a reliable friend who affirms that such an experience is valid, certain and authentic and not presumptuous, self-manufactured or artificial.

---

the first century, the heart indicated the seat of the emotions and the centre of one's moral, spiritual and intellectual life; it represents the central core of one's life.

[14] G. D. Fee, *God's Empowering Presence* (Hendrickson, 1994), p. 567.

[15] Similarly, in Rom. 9:1, Paul refers to the Spirit as assuring him that his description concerning the quality of their salvation in the previous verses is true.

Indeed, without that supernatural affirmation, to claim to be a child of God would be inappropriate and precocious.

For the Jew, faithfulness to God's laws was a reason one might define oneself as a child of God. The law was given as a gift of God to people he had already chosen (Deut. 7:6–8); keeping it demonstrated the actuality of that relationship, and was central to it (Deut. 7:11). For believers, in the absence of such an association with the law, a claim to being children of God is nevertheless valid, because the Spirit affirms such a status. It is he who declares that it has been initiated at salvation, as a free act of grace by God, and the believer can own it as a reality. The present tense used by Paul to describe the witness of the Spirit indicates that this is a continuous and constant affirmation. If anyone doubts such a declaration, they are encouraged to recognize that it is none other than the Spirit himself who makes it.

f. The Spirit enables believers to own God as Father (Rom. 8:15–16)

Adoption becomes the basis for knowing God (Gal. 4:8–9). It results in the one adopted being able to call God, '*Abba*, Father' (Rom. 8:15).[16] The word *abba* means 'father' and was used by Jewish children (young and old) of their fathers. Indeed, its popular use meant that for many Jews, it was an inappropriate term to use of God, dangerously close to being precocious or even irreverent. Jesus used this term, however, to address his Father, and invited the disciples to use the same term in the Lord's Prayer. It is in this respect that adoption may be appreciated as even more remarkable than forgiveness. To be acquitted of a crime would be a notable act, more so to be forgiven by the victims. However, to be taken into the family of those people as their adopted child, and accepted as an equal member with all their other children, would be a much more remarkable act of grace. Believers have not been marched into a monastery or forced into a fraternity, but welcomed into a family by way of adoption. They have not been conscripted, enslaved or employed, but adopted. The Spirit is the first friendly face to affirm that we have been received by our Father; thereafter, he walks with us to be with him, where we will be friends re-united with each other forever.

The concept of a father is capable of accommodating a number

---

[16] The Aramaic (*abba*) is translated by the Greek (*patēr*); both mean 'father'; also Mark 14:36; Gal. 4:6. Dunn (*Romans 1–8*, p. 453) suggests that it reflects 'a cry in which the pray-er delights to be able to address God in the same terms but in different words'.

of important features including love and care, security and safety, resulting in responses of fondness and respect, love and obedience. In them all, there is an offer of welcome that draws from us a question, 'Can it be true? Really? Is it safe to put my trust in the belief that I am a child of God; yes, even me?' The Spirit speaks in soft tones that it is true, always and forever.

Reference to the cry of the believer – *Father* (Rom. 8:15) – may be a silent or spoken acknowledgement by believers of our relationship with God. It may be articulated in times when fear grips our minds and clouds our sight – or when contentment fills our lives like a warm shaft of sunlight, and we acknowledge our happiness by thanking our Father for being our source of joy. Whatever the occasion, the Spirit continuously affirms to believers that the Father has willingly welcomed them into his family.

g. *The Spirit brokers an inheritance for believers (Rom. 8:17)*

Believers are to receive an inheritance that belongs to them as God's children. Thus, again, the word *ei* (if) (v. 17) may more helpfully be translated 'since' or 'because' ('since children, then heirs, heirs of God'). Believers are also described as being *co-heirs with Christ* (see also Eph. 3:6; Heb. 11:9; 1 Pet. 3:7). The description focuses the mind of the reader on the concept that believers have been exalted to the position of being able to benefit from the same resources of God as did Jesus. The identity of the inheritance is not explored by Paul; it is sufficient to know that it is synonymous with that enjoyed by Jesus.

Although this is to be realized fully in the next life, the guarantee is certain because of the quality and presence of the guarantor, the Spirit. Although some believers may not have been able to be freed from slavery, their destiny was affirmed by Paul as being one of freedom, initiated and guaranteed by the Spirit. They were encouraged to live with their minds not focused on the present (difficulties), but gazing into the future with the recognition that their destinies are eternal ones. The Spirit resides within them to affirm them as people whose destinies lie beyond this life on earth.

Paul asserts that an important aspect of being an adopted child of God is a willingness to suffer (Rom. 8:17). Indeed, the association between suffering and sonship was familiar in OT thought (Prov. 3:12). Paul is not declaring that believers must suffer in order to receive their adoption, but he is acknowledging that suffering may accompany it. However, it will not invalidate their adoption, nor should it be viewed as inappropriate for children of God to suffer.

169

On the contrary, their elder brother Jesus suffered and they are simply following in his footsteps. Suffering does not invalidate their right to be called children of God, such a position being determined by God, and assured by the Spirit, to be enjoyed eternally. His promise to them is that this suffering is to be considered in the light of the fact that, as the children of God, they will be glorified with him hereafter;[17] indeed, it is the prelude to that glory.

It is important that suffering, therefore, in whatever form, should not be automatically dismissed as an inappropriate aspect of a Christian life. Paul redeemed the concept of suffering as a platform on which one is able to reflect and to trust God for the benefit of those watching, be they other believers, an enquiring or hostile world, angelic beings or malevolent spiritual forces.

h. The Spirit is the 'firstfruits' for believers (Rom. 8:23)

Paul now moves closer to his conclusion (Rom. 8:31–39), when he will provide indisputable evidence that believers are safe in the family of God, because they have been welcomed by a God who has freely chosen them. Not only that, but he embraces them in supreme love that not only encapsulates them in an envelope of protection, but excludes anything that would seek to destabilize them. The one who seals that envelope is the Spirit who is described as their *firstfruits* (8:23). This term was regularly used in a sacrificial sense relating to the first of the flock, or the first of the fruits of the harvest that were given to God.[18] Here, Paul uses the term to describe a down payment of an inheritance to come. The feast of Pentecost celebrated the first fruits of the harvest (Exod. 23:16; 34:22; Deut. 16:9–12); the Spirit of Pentecost is himself the firstfruits to be celebrated as God's gift to the church.

As a metaphor, the phrase 'first fruits' needs to be interpreted carefully. It is not intended to indicate that someone better than the Spirit will be granted to the believer later, or that the believer only receives part of the Spirit at salvation. The intention of Paul is to enlighten the readers as to the significance of their salvation and, in particular, to establish that it is not restricted to life before death. On the contrary, death is the gateway into life as it was ever intended to be, the metaphor of the harvest indicating the motif of resurrection. Although redemption for the believers is yet to be

---

[17] Rom. 2:7, 10; 5:2; 8:21; 9:23; 1 Cor. 2:7; 15:43; 2 Cor. 3:18; 4:17; Phil. 3:21; Col. 1:27; 3:4; 1 Thess. 2:12; 2 Thess. 2:14; 2 Tim. 2:10.
[18] Exod. 23:19; Lev. 2:12; Num. 18:12, 30; Deut. 26:2; 2 Chron. 31:5; Neh. 10:37; Mal. 3:8.

fully manifested in the next life, the guarantee of that occurrence is the presence of the Spirit in the present; that the first fruits are being gathered in indicates that the full and final harvest is soon to come. Creation and believers are looking forward to being released from the bondage imposed by sin (Rom. 8:18–22), longing to be able to enjoy the full benefits of their salvation. Paul is grateful for the fact that as an insight and guarantee of that final salvation, the Spirit has been given to each believer. He provides a glimpse into the life to be experienced in its fullness, when our adoption is to be finally manifested. He is a flavour, a whisper, a breath of the future in the present.

My two most common prayers are 'I'm sorry' and 'thank you'. However, although I am increasingly aware of the privileges available to me as a child of God, I am also learning that the Spirit is encouraging me to avail myself of his resources to a greater degree than I have accessed them in the past. Because I am so grateful for all that I have received, I am sometimes reticent to take advantage of all that the Spirit makes available to me. I remember hearing someone relate a startling occasion when he awoke from sleep with the memory of a vivid dream. He had dreamt that he had been in heaven and was being shown around by an angel. He was taken to a room that was filled to overflowing with presents. On closer examination, he noticed that they were all addressed to him. On asking the angel for an explanation, he was told that they were gifts that were available for him if only he asked for them. It was only a dream but it resonates with the words of James (4:2), 'You do not have, because you do not ask . . .' As God's children, affirmed by the Spirit, we have been given keys to unlock treasures intended for us. To ignore them is not only foolish but borders on ingratitude. The sign of truly appreciating our adoption is when we rest completely on our Father and listen to the Spirit, who bids us to stay, enjoying all that is there for us as God's children.

Believers have become used to the concept of 'now and not yet' to describe the fact that, although they have received a great deal, as a result of their salvation there is more to come. Similarly, while some of the benefits of their relationship with God have become a reality, there are aspects that are yet to be fulfilled. However, although this is undoubtedly true, such a concept can be dangerous. It can, for example, result in us being less expectant of the resources of the Spirit in the present than may be appropriate. It can become too easy to assume that it is in the future that our relationship with God takes on a more significant reality than in the present. Although there is truth in this, there is value in imagining the future as drawing us into it. Some of our inheritance which we have been destined to enjoy in the future is actually available now, accessible as a result of the Spirit's involvement in our lives. Rather than 'now and not yet', the maxim 'now and still yet' identifies the fact that although the future holds the key to a comprehensive experience of salvation, the present offers the possibility for enjoying it to a greater degree than we may have anticipated.

3. The Holy Spirit empathizes with believers (Rom. 8:26–27)

a. Introduction

The most common illness treated by doctors in the UK is depression. It is the fourth most common problem in the world after bronchitis, diarrhoea and HIV/AIDS. It has been estimated that up to 10% of all women and 5% of all men suffer from clinical depression. The figure in the US is about 9% of the total population. Many more people, however, suffer bouts of depression sometime in their lives. Although it is a more common problem in the industrialized nations than in the Majority World, even here the numbers of people who are struggling to cope with life is increasing significantly. The rates for suicide are at an all time high. This is a phenomenon that affects rich urbanites and rural peasants. It has been estimated that more than a million commit suicide every year – more deaths than in all the wars that are currently being waged on the planet.

As believers, we are not immune to depression. Often, we may carry huge burdens which are too heavy for us on our own. We also may experience dark times when there seems no way out. However, the Spirit assures us that he is with us through our journey, at our side, in our corner. No corner into which we may have run for fear of what may be outside is too small for him not to be there with us. He who raised Jesus from the dead has the potential and desire to raise us up in our pain and to enable us to view it through his eyes.

After referring to the Spirit in a number of significant ways in Romans 8, Paul now, in verses 26-27, introduces a radically new concept in which the Spirit identifies himself with believers in what is possibly the most intimate fashion. The Spirit not only provides freedom in the next life for creation and the created (8:19–23), but he also provides a friendship in this life which is of a uniquely divine quality. Furthermore, not only does the Spirit provide wisdom in times of uncertainty and doubt, but he also prays when we cannot. Paul describes the Spirit as doing something for believers, not they for him. On this occasion, the Spirit is not being portrayed as working through believers, but on their behalf. He is not with them to facilitate their ministry for him; rather, he is ministering to them. The Spirit is praying for them.

b. The Spirit helps weak believers (Rom. 8:26)

Paul refers to the fact that the Spirit *helps* (8:26) believers, using a somewhat unusual word (*synantilambanō*) that is only used once elsewhere in the NT (Luke 10:40), and only three times in the LXX. There it refers to help offered to make it easier for people to bear a burden. In Numbers 11:17, the Spirit separates seventy of the elders to the role of assisting Moses to make it easier for him to carry the responsibility of leading the people. It is significant that in Romans 8:26, it is neither a judge (Exod. 18:22) nor an elder who is engaged in a supportive role, but the Spirit.

Furthermore, the help is offered to every believer. It is understandable that such a privilege should be granted to Moses, the great deliverer of the Hebrews from Egypt, who saw God miraculously redeem the nation and guide it for decades in the wilderness, who received the Ten Commandments, and who was a hero to Israel. Similarly, David, the one who was described as 'a man after my own heart' (Acts 13:22), is clearly an appropriate beneficiary of such supportive attention from God (Ps. 89:21). The startling revelation of Paul, however, is that such support is granted to every believer. It is not provided because of their strength, but their weakness; not because they are powerful leaders, like Moses or David, who were given substantially important roles that needed divine sustenance, but because they are fragile people who have been given divine commissions. It is precisely because they are delicate and brittle people, who feel the effect of the storms of life keenly, that the Spirit takes it upon himself to help believers who, even at their strongest, are still easily broken.

The weakness (*astheneia*, 8:26a) experienced by the believers is not identified by Paul, though it appears to result in an uncertainty as to how and what to pray (8:26b). The term is used in Jewish and secular Greek writings of that era to refer to a variety of conditions including spiritual as well as physical weakness and sickness. It is significant to note that it is derived from its opposite (*sthenēs*), which means 'strength', and an interpretation of strengthlessness underlies most of its uses.

The term *astheneia* is used to describe various aspects of weakness, including (in the Septuagint) emotional weakness (Job 4:4), economic weakness (Ps. 105:37), strengthlessness (2 Chron. 28:15;

173

Ps. 31:10) as well as sin (Jer. 18:23) and stumbling (with the consequence of death, Dan. 11:19, 41). In the NT, it refers to spiritual
weakness (Rom. 4:19; 8:3; 1 Cor. 8:9), illness (Matt. 10:8; 1 Cor.
11:30; Gal. 4:13), and also weakness of a general nature – economic
weakness (Acts 20:35), a sense of personal inadequacy (1 Cor. 2:3),
a sense of rejection (2 Cor. 11:30), powerlessness (Rom. 8:3) and
anxiety or demoralisation (1 Thess. 5:14).

Given that Paul does not clarify the cause of the weakness on
this occasion, it may be appropriate to envisage a context that could
include a range of circumstances, each of which may leave the individual believer destabilised and worried, uncertain how to pray and
what to say, and, most particularly, unsure what the will of God is
in the situation. They may long to feel whole again but they may
fear that this is a forlorn dream. The revelation offered by Paul is
that they have been entrusted to the Spirit who is dedicated to their
destiny. He is the one who takes over where they can do no more,
who prays when they cannot, who goes to God on their behalf
when they can only raise their eyes in the hope that a response may
come sometime.

Pain is not a sign that the Spirit is absent, nor is suffering evidence
that his compassion is limited. On the contrary, such experiences are
opportunities to benefit and develop; they are not accidents of fate,
but opportunities for faith to be exercised and the future changed.
A story is told of a girl whose life was filled with what seemed to be
an endless catalogue of painful experiences, as a result of which she
began to doubt whether God cared for her. On one particular day,
her father filled three saucepans with boiling water. In one he placed
potatoes, in the other he placed eggs, and in the last he dropped
coffee beans. Thirty minutes later, he placed them on three plates
and asked his daughter to touch them. The potatoes were soft, the
egg was hard-boiled, while the water in which the coffee beans had
been placed tasted good.

The girl learned an important lesson. The heat of life's trials and
traumas is rarely easy to bear and there are a variety of responses.
One can become weak and soft like the potatoes, unable to cope; one
can become bitter and hard, protected by a shell like the egg; or one
can become stronger and richer, like the coffee beans. Often, painful
experiences do not have easy answers and it is unhelpful to attempt
to identify them. However, when life boils with a heat that hurts, it
is possible to reach heights unachieved before. When the hour is at
its darkest, fear most frightening, trials most terrifying, certain facts
remain that can result in a different perspective being offered. The
Spirit is not caught unawares by our challenging experiences, nor is
heaven surprised by our pain.

c. The Spirit prays for believers (Rom. 8:26)

The Spirit who encourages believers to own God as their Father (Rom. 8:15), who bears witness with them that they are his children (8:16), now personally presents their deepest prayers to God on their behalf. There is no evidence in Rabbinic literature of the Spirit's involvement with prayers offered by people to God. Indeed, the notion of such a well-placed mediator is missing from much of Jewish religious thought. Paul startles his readers by introducing them to an action of the Spirit that is unique to the Bible, relating to his praying on behalf of believers. Paul does not indicate that believers are actively involved in this procedure; indeed, it appears that they are simply present as observers, watching the Spirit as he personally places their prayers before God, instead of them doing so.

Elsewhere, Paul refers to prayer in or with the Spirit (1 Cor. 14:14–15; Eph. 6:18), in which the believer takes an active part. It is possible that the same is indicated here in Romans 8:26, and that he is affirming the importance of praying while depending on the Spirit to guide the prayer. The imagery used, however, is much more graphic than to indicate an interdependency in prayer; rather, it presents the Spirit as the one who is engaged in prayer to the exclusion of the believer. That is not to suggest that the former prayer is inappropriate; indeed, to pray with the Spirit should be the aim of every believer. However, what Paul describes here is much more magnificent, in that the Spirit (who, as God, receives prayer) is presented as the one who prays, and who does so on behalf of those he has created.

The term used by Paul for prayer (*hyperentynchanō*) occurs nowhere else in the Bible, though a similar verb (*entynchanō*) is used (Acts 25:24; Rom. 8:27, 34; 11:2), which means, 'obtain an audience with', 'petition' or 'appeal to'. The term Paul used, however, includes the prefix *hyper,* which serves to emphasize the intensity of the prayer offered by the Spirit. Not only does the Spirit pray, but he is keen to pray. This is not a detached, dispassionate prayer. It is the result of a concentrated commitment by the Spirit to the believer; he is not unemotionally involved, but passionately drawn to the believer. Paul does not clarify the form of this prayer and it is therefore better not to expend too much time exploring the options, since that was not his intention in mentioning it.[19] The issue which is of significance is that the Spirit stands with believers and prays for them. Most importantly, since he is God, there is the guarantee that

---

[19] K. Warrington, *Discovering the Spirit in the New Testament* (Hendrickson, 2005), p. 93; Fee, *God's Empowering Presence*, pp. 580–585.

such intercession will be appropriate and successful. Not only does he know what to pray for, but also his requests will be in complete harmony with the perfect will of God.

This was a powerfully encouraging message to first century readers, who were beset by a range of weaknesses due to their insecure and powerless place in society. As Christians, they were despised by people of power. However, the message is also relevant today to believers who exist in an alien environment that sometimes actively opposes them, and seeks to squeeze them into conformity with its values, and in ways that leave them feeling both uncomfortable and discomforted.

Paul defines the prayer of the Spirit as 'with sighs too deep for words' (Rom. 8:26, RSV), indicating a depth of feeling that is associated with those occasions when one is so moved that it is difficult to coherently articulate one's emotions. The most that can be offered in those situations is a deep sigh or groan; these may be the most accurate expressions of an inner sense of emptiness and barrenness. However, while human silence may be due to the fact that one is drained of hope and light, this is not the case with the Spirit. The Spirit does not need to express his request in words, for a deeper, more profound relationship exists between him and God that is beyond human understanding or imagination. Such an unfathomable, subliminal bond needs no words to ensure that effectual communication takes place.

Of course, this concept of the Spirit praying for believers is more helpfully understood as being metaphorical, rather than an oversimplistic indication that the Spirit prays to the Father in the same way that believers do. Since the Spirit is God, it is difficult to imagine how he can pray when prayer is, by definition, to God; he does not pray to himself. The fact is that believers are in direct relationship with the Father, Son and the Spirit. There is no hierarchy in prayer that would indicate that to pray to the Father, one must use the services of the Spirit or the Son. Nor is Paul suggesting that the Spirit is more keen to help the believer than is the Father or Jesus. Indeed, in Romans 8:34, he reveals that Jesus prays for us also (Luke 22:31–32; Rom. 11:2; Heb. 7:25). Rather, he is building on the imagery of the Spirit being present in the life of the believer (Rom. 8:9, 11, 15), and encouraging his readers to realize that that same Spirit who dwells in them is actively engaged on their behalf throughout their lives – not just when they are severely struggling, but in all aspects of their lives, which are, at best, subject to weakness and powerlessness.

The message that is beyond words is that the Spirit, who is God, is so committed to believers that it is as if, for a moment, he is closer to them than he is to God, thus enabling him to pray with them to

God. It paints a picture more remarkable than words will allow. It also beautifully demonstrates the depth of majesty and humility of the Spirit, and his astonishing allegiance and daily dedication to believers. Such commitment results in Paul concluding the section with an anthem dedicated to the security of the believer. It climaxes with the recognition that the believer and the love of God are inseparable. The reason for this is that the Spirit of love is resident in the believer and is there to stay.

Although the Spirit is often viewed as being present to create the cataclysmic and the dynamic, he is also (and more often) recorded in the NT as being present in difficult times, acting as a supportive helper and friend. He can deliver the sensational but he also knows when we are struggling. On those occasions, he not only chooses to walk with us, but also reminds us that he is sharing our story with our Father. He engages in an ongoing heavenly dialogue on our behalf with the Father, who already knows all about us. Smail writes, 'We carry prayer within us, because the praying Spirit is within us.'[20] The challenge to believers is to try to listen to what the Spirit is praying, catch his heart and then join in.

[20] T. Smail, *The Giving Gift. The Holy Spirit in Person* (Darton, Longman and Todd, 1994), p. 210.

177

1 Corinthians 12:4–31;
Romans 12:6–8
14. The Holy Spirit provides gifts

1. Introduction

The gifts of the Spirit are mainly discussed by Paul in 1 Corinthians, a letter that was written to believers who, though charismatic, were verging on the chaotic, their basic problem being due to relationship issues. As a result of selfishness and a false view of their importance as individuals, the interests of others had been ignored. Consequently, Paul speaks to the issue of unity from the start (1 Cor. 1:10–17; 3:1–17). Thereafter, problems arising from their disunity are explored, including serious immorality (5:1–13; 6:12–20), a readiness to take one another to court (6:1–8), marital issues (7:1–40), lack of care over younger Christians (8:1–13), idolatry (10:1–22), gender issues (11:1–16), ignorance over the Lord's Supper and of the importance of internal harmony in celebrating it (11:17–34) and, finally, disorganized and selfish manifestation of gifts of the Spirit (12:1–31; 14:1–40).

Paul reacts to these problems by establishing principles of Christian conduct that celebrate the importance of variety not uniformity, love not selfishness, liberty not license – unison and harmony, unity and diversity, privilege and responsibility, and sensitivity to the Spirit and to each other. In particular, he demonstrates how these values should and could be attained through a correct use of the gifts that the Spirit gives to the church.

Paul does not engage in a systematic discussion concerning gifts of the Spirit, choosing not to explain their identity, offer guidelines for their use (other than for tongues and prophecy), or identify any precursors for their being received. He is interested in the broader (and more important) issues that reflect the person of the Spirit who functions in unity within the Godhead, expressing interdependency and constancy, love and grace. Paul desires that such principles be manifested in the church at Corinth and elsewhere.

2. Gifts of the Spirit are gifts of grace (1 Cor. 12:4)

One of Paul's emphases is that not only is the Spirit a gift to the church and every believer, but he also provides a variety of gifts for the benefit of all believers. Such gifts from the Spirit are often referred to as *charismata* (1 Cor. 12:4, 31), a helpful term because of the inclusion of the Greek word *charis* (grace) within it.[1] Thus, a helpful and popular translation is a '(free) gift' or 'gift of grace', given to the undeserving, to be freely and graciously distributed for the benefit of others.[2] Other than 1 Peter 4:10, Paul is the only NT writer who refers to them as *charismata*.[3] It may therefore be a term that he particularly chose to employ, probably because of its association with grace.

Although the notion of a gift is that it belongs to the recipient and not to the one who has given it, it is more accurate to accept that the *charismata* are on loan from the Spirit. They are manifestations of the Spirit through believers that are expected to be used in ways that are appropriate to his character and will. Even when individual believers may frequently manifest a particular gift, it is still preferable to understand these occasions as manifestations of the Spirit through those people, and not that they are using the gift of their own volition. It is difficult to be completely clear in the formulation of a precise practical framework for the use of the *charismata*; some (miracles, healings) are manifested more intermittently than others (administration, teaching), which are more permanent. Flexible, rather than rigid, contexts of use need to be embraced.

---

[1] Other words used for gifts of the Spirit include *dōrea* (Eph. 3:7; 4:7), *domata* (Eph. 4:8), *energēmata* (1 Cor. 12:6, 11) and *diakonioi* (Rom. 12:7; 1 Cor. 12:5).
[2] Some believe that such gifts were specifically given for the early development of the church but that they ceased when their purpose had been achieved (Cessationism). 1 Corinthians 13:8–10 has been interpreted as undermining a belief in the ongoing nature of some spiritual gifts. Paul, however, makes no such distinction between some apparently temporary gifts (including healing, tongues and prophecy) and permanent ones (teaching, administration). The timing of the demise of these gifts (13: 10) is believed by many to be the return of Jesus, though others prefer to assign it to the closing of the canon of Scripture. However, to suggest that the word 'perfect' (13:10, ESV) refers to the closure of the NT canon is improbable, since the readers of the letter had no concept that there was a NT, let alone a canon.
[3] Rom. 1:11; 5:15–16; 6:23; 11:29; 12:6; 1 Cor. 1:7; 7:7; 12:4, 9, 28, 30, 31; 2 Cor. 1:11; 1 Tim. 4:14; 2 Tim. 1:6.

3. Spiritual gifts are given by the Spirit (1 Cor. 12:7)

The term *pneumatikoi* (1 Cor. 12:1) is also used to refer to gifts of the Spirit; its value is that it emphasizes their relationship with the Spirit (*pneuma*).[4] Rather than such gifts being requested of the Spirit by believers, it is more appropriate to recognize that the manifestation of such gifts is the responsibility of the Spirit (1 Cor. 12:11). He is in charge of their dispersal (Heb. 2:4), each of the gifts in 1 Corinthians 12:8–9 being identified as given by the Spirit. Indeed, in just eight verses (12:4–11), the concept of the gifts being given by the Spirit is mentioned no less than seven times. Similarly, the Spirit is identified in the OT as enabling, among others, Elijah and Elisha to function charismatically.[5] Furthermore, the manifestation of 'spiritual gifts' does not indicate a superior spirituality on the part of the one who manifests them; they are 'spiritual gifts' because their source is the Spirit (12:7). Thus, to refer to them as 'gifts of the Spirit' instead of 'spiritual gifts' is helpful as it emphasizes the important fact that they are derived from the Spirit.

Although they are often specifically associated with the Spirit, Paul informs his readers that each member of the Godhead is involved in their being given to the church (1 Cor. 12:4–6). Any attempt to divide the gifts between the members of the Godhead is counterproductive to Paul's theme, namely diversity of gifts with unity of purpose and sensitivity in operation. Thus, to conclude that the Spirit provides the gifts, the Son administers them and the Father provides the power to manifest them would be too nuanced a perspective, and would inappropriately compartmentalize the functions within the Godhead. Paul is not offering a discussion of unity within the Godhead but in the church.

Given the regular references to the presence of the Spirit in the life of the church, it is logical that, in his letters, Paul should focus on the Spirit as functioning representatively as the distributor of the gifts. Not only are they bestowed by the Spirit but also the Spirit manifests himself through those gifts. Therefore, his character should be displayed when they are exhibited. The fact that the gifts are given by the Spirit should increase the sense of responsibility felt by those who administer them and, in particular, encourage them to do so appropriately, as indicated by the nature of the giver of the gifts. It is to be remembered that they are not derived remotely from a distance as a result of divine initiation from heaven, so much as resulting from his being present in believers. As a loving friend,

---

[4] Rom. 15:27; 1 Cor. 2:13; 9:11; 12:1; 14:1; Eph. 1:3; 5:19; Col. 3:16.
[5] Exod. 31:1–3; Judg. 3:10; 6:34; 11:29; 14:19; 2 Kgs 2:9–14.

he is happiest when his choice gifts to us are being used to benefit and bless others.

4. Gifts of the Spirit are for the benefit of others (1 Cor. 12:7)

Paul writes about the diversity of the gifts given as expressions of God's grace (1 Cor. 12:4–8), but with one specific purpose of benefiting others. Paul asserts that spiritual gifts should be operated harmoniously in diversity, not discordantly, but as a consequence of a dynamic relationship with the Spirit, resulting in beneficial relationships with each other (12:4–31). Paul associates the gifts with service to others (12:7), working for their benefit (12:6). They are described as being given for the corporate group (12:7; Eph. 4:12). Thus, they are not to be administered selfishly but selflessly, not for personal gain but to the advantage of others.

When the manifestation of a gift ceases to exalt the person of Jesus (1 Cor. 12:3) or to edify or develop other believers (Rom. 1:11), it ceases to be divinely inspired. When there is an absence of a manifestation of love, there is an absence of a manifestation of God through the gift (1 Cor. 13:1–3). It is no accident that joining up chapters 12 and 14 is the clearly defined presentation of love and its vital importance to the believing community. It is of significant importance in determining when someone is authentically manifesting a gift of the Spirit. Without it, the exercise of such gifts can be counterproductive, demeaning to the purposes of the Spirit and destabilising to believers.

The manifestation of the gifts must therefore be subject to careful assessment. Sanctified common sense, the shared wisdom of the Christian community, a comparison with biblical teachings and personal receptivity to the Spirit will help to confirm or reject the validity of a manifestation.

5. Gifts of the Spirit are varied (1 Cor. 12:8–10)

Paul provides four major lists of gifts (Rom. 12:6–8; 1 Cor. 12:8–10, 28–30; Eph. 4:11, cf. 1 Cor. 13:1–3; 14:6, 26), none of which is intended to be comprehensive but representative (1 Cor. 7:7 refers to the gifts of celibacy and singleness, or of being married). One of the main purposes of these lists is to demonstrate the diversity of gifts available to believers.

Some question the distinction between 'natural' and 'supernatural'

181

1 Cor. 12:8–10	1 Cor. 12:28–30	Eph. 4:11	Rom. 12:6–8
Wisdom	Apostles	Apostle	Prophecy
Knowledge	Prophets	Prophet	Service
Faith	Teachers	Evangelist	Teaching
Healing	Miracles	Pastor/	Exhortation
Miracles	Healings	Teacher	Giving
Prophecy	Helps		Mercy
Discernment	Administration		
Tongues	Tongues		
Interpretation	Interpretation		

gifts, preferring to identify a gift of the Spirit on the basis of its value to the Christian community. Hollenweger deduces that 'a charism is a natural gift that is given for the common good'.[6] Others, however, have refused to identify natural talents as spiritual gifts. A mediating position may be offered that allows for the possibility that, as well as those that are clearly supernatural, a gift of the Spirit may be a natural gift that has been invested with supernatural energy by God.

Thus, before Paul became a follower of Jesus, he was a scholar and activist on behalf of Judaism. After his conversion, the Spirit empowered his natural (God-given) abilities for the benefit of the Christian community. Often times, the Spirit chooses to use sensitivities, passions, strengths and gifts that were originally part of our created characters and personalities. He does not always do this but it should be no surprise when he does. Although sin has marred the image of God in us, the Creator made us in his image and he is perfectly able to redeem our characters for his service. After salvation, these gifts and sensitivities may be enhanced and supernaturally energised so as to achieve a higher potential of benefit for others. At the same time, the Spirit is capable of empowering believers to function in ways that are beyond their normal powers.

6. A Sampling of Gifts (1 Cor. 12:8–10)

Here Paul provides a list of gifts of the Spirit, a number of which are mentioned in other lists. They function as a sample of gifts that are worthy of brief consideration.

[6] W. J. Hollenweger, 'Gifts of the Spirit: Natural and Supernatural', in S. M. Burgess, E. M. Van der Maas (eds.), *The New International Dictionary of Pentecostal and Charismatic Movements* (Zondervan, 2002), pp. 667–668.

The word of *wisdom* is best understood as a Spirit-inspired revelation for a particular occasion rather than a natural propensity towards wisdom. The identity of the wisdom is not clear. It could relate to the spiritual development of the one to whom it is given, and be active in preaching and teaching. The fact that the word 'wisdom' is used elsewhere with reference to the wisdom available from Christ (1 Cor. 1:23–24, 30; Col. 2:3) may indicate that this refers to knowledge concerning the person and mission of Jesus. There appears to be little reason to be restrictive in this regard, however, and it is probably safest, in the absence of Pauline guidance, to keep the definition of the anticipated wisdom wider rather than narrower.

The word of *knowledge* may refer to a supernatural awareness of facts that would be otherwise unknown to the recipient (Acts 5:1–2; 9:10–12). Because the word *gnōsis* (knowledge) is used elsewhere in contexts that relate to the knowledge of God (2 Cor. 2:14; 4:6; Eph. 1:17), it is possible that this gift reflects those occasions when some aspect of God is being revealed. However, there is evidence of supernaturally inspired knowledge being recorded in other settings (John 1:48; 4:17–18; Acts 5:1–6; 27:10), and this suggests that a broader base of knowledge may also be appropriate.

The discernment of *spirits* probably describes the supernatural ability to identify the presence of an evil spirit (Acts 8:9–23; 16:16–17), the Spirit, or to identify the source of power motivating an act or word. The gift of *faith* is to be distinguished from the fruit of faithfulness, and saving faith. The faith referred to is best identified as the facility to trust God in a particular situation; thus, the gift of faith refers to a God-given assurance to undertake a particular action or offer a specific prayer (often in the absence of a biblical promise). The gift of faith is identified as a readiness to believe what God has promised or stated will occur. In those settings, the Spirit may choose to support a believer in following a particular course of action by providing a 'burst' of supernatural assurance or faith that their proposed action is the correct one. Thus, even though there may be no biblical mandate, the Spirit grants confirmation prior to the action being undertaken. It is this that protects the believer from functioning precipitously, precociously or presumptuously (Rom. 10:17; Eph. 2:8). The confidence provided by the Spirit to support one's actions or words is to be understood as a gift of faith. Paul is referring to a particular affirmation by the Spirit that the prayer, act or word to be offered is in keeping with his will and, therefore, he provides encouragement to act accordingly.

The phrase, *gifts of healing* (or literally 'healings'), has been the subject of a range of explanations.[7] It is possible that Paul believed that each individual healing is to be identified as a gift of healing; thus, the person who is healed receives a gift of healing. It may be that he is demonstrating the comprehensive power of the Spirit to provide restoration for all kinds of illnesses, or that some believers are enabled by the Spirit to facilitate the healing of particular illnesses. Although some have claimed the latter to be a true reflection of their own healing ministries, it begs the question as to what one should do if the particular restorative capacity is not available to those wishing to minister to someone in need of specific restoration. It is probable that the term *gifts of healings* best explains the purpose of the Spirit to provide a variety of healings through a diversity of believers, the gift being given when the Spirit wills it.

Although it need not be assumed that such ability resides permanently in a believer, Paul assumes the presence of healers in the church (1 Cor. 12:28). Such a definition may be applied to those who function in this gift more than other people, though the ministry of healing is more generally understood as being available to anyone, and effected through many believers (1 Cor. 12:7, 14). Gifts of healing are most appropriately manifested in conjunction with the gift of *faith* (1 Cor. 12:9), and words of *wisdom* and *knowledge*, or *prophecy* (1 Cor. 12:8–10). The reference to miracles refers to the ability to perform miracles other than healings.

The gift of prophecy is presented as being different from that offered by the OT prophets in a number of ways. Thus, for example, in the NT, prophecy is not restricted to a group of prophets; all are potential prophets (Acts 2:18). Also, the death penalty for a false prophet (Deut. 13:1–5, 18) is not applied to NT prophets who speak in error. Similarly, in contrast to OT prophecy, prophecies recorded in the NT are mainly intended for believers. The ecstatic prophecies and somewhat bizarre behaviour or incidents sometimes associated with certain OT prophets (Isa. 20:3–5; Jer. 9:1; Ezek. 3:24-26; 4:1 – 5:4) are much less prominent in the NT church (Acts 21:10–11; 1 Cor. 14:32) where sensitivity, care and good order are important elements of the manifestations (1 Cor. 14:40).

Since Paul anticipates that prophecies may be offered by a variety of believers, it is to be expected that the Spirit will speak in diverse ways to the community. Prophecies and other verbal utterances of a similarly charismatic nature are often associated with or preceded by mental pictures, images, words or physical sensations, the person who receives them then describing or explaining them to the congregation.

---

[7] K. Warrington, *Healing and Suffering. Biblical and Pastoral Reflections* (Paternoster Press, 2005), pp. 128-134.

This variety of presentation is mirrored, to a degree, in the Bible, including visions,[8] words,[9] symbolic actions[10] and inner direction.[11]

Prophecies are less related to foretelling the future, though that may sometimes occur, as it did in the NT (Acts 11:28; 21:10–11). Fundamentally, prophecy is an occasion when an individual, inspired by God (2 Pet. 1:21), speaks (sometimes spontaneously and extemporarily) with an emphasis on edification or exhortation, or both, thus reflecting the NT norm (1 Cor. 14:3–5). Increasingly, the expectation and practice is for prophecies to be offered by a variety of believers in a congregation rather than a set few, although some denominations prefer to identify prophets through whom it is expected the Spirit will speak to the community. The fallibility of prophecy is generally assumed to be due to its impermanent nature (1 Cor. 13:8). It is generally left to believers to decide concerning the authenticity of the information delivered, the prophecy rather than the prophet being the subject of scrutiny, though the lifestyle or the way in which the prophecy is offered may count towards its legitimacy. It is unclear from 1 Corinthians 14:29 whether the prophecy should be scrutinized by other prophets or by the wider congregation, though, in general practice, the latter is assumed.

The means whereby a prophecy is to be examined are manifold. A basic premise is that it should not contradict what is contained in the Bible. Where the prophecy is foretelling or unrelated to the Bible, other tests are needed. These may relate to the confidence that people have in the one prophesying, including their demeanour and attitude (1 Cor. 14:32–33, 40), one's common sense and experience, whether the prophecy is edifying (1 Cor. 14:3–5, 12, 26), the perception of the community of believers, and personal discernment as manifested by the Spirit (1 Cor. 14:24–25).

Some have identified prophecy with preaching, though Paul seems to indicate that it is a complement to preaching. On occasions, however, a person may preach prophetically, even without their knowledge that they are so operating. Indeed, many would aspire to preach in a way that demonstrates that the Spirit is inspiring their words and infusing the message with a supernatural dimension reflective of the Spirit, and not merely defined by the speaker. Prophecies are best offered in ways that encourage the hearers to engage in the task of discerning their value, as anticipated

---

[8] Acts 10:10–17; Rev. 1:1 – 4:1.

[9] Isa. 1:1; 2:1; Jer. 1:11; Ezek. 1:1–3; Amos 1:1; Obad. 1:1; Hab. 1:1; Zech. 1:7; Mal. 1:1.

[10] Ezek. 4:1–3, 4–8, 9–17; 5:1–4; Acts 21:11.

[11] Acts 15:28.

in 1 Corinthians 14:29–32. Prophecy of a personal nature should be offered with great care, and tested in conjunction with a range of guidelines (including discussion with other mature believers who are known and trusted, a personal sense of peace, and whether the message fits the current direction and focus of one's life).

Such messages need not be presented in archaic or religious language. Prophesying in the first personal singular, that assumes the words are directly spoken by God, is not helpful, as it implies that it may not be assessed by the listeners. Nor is it anticipated that such messages will only be in the form of sermons or spontaneous, unprepared exhortations. The Spirit is capable of speaking through a range of verbal communication including songs, poems, conversations, as well as actions, visions and dreams. His therapeutic touch is manifested variously – the beauty is that believers can participate in these opportunities for offering wholeness to others.

The gifts of *tongues* and *interpretation* have been one of the most problematic in the history of the church, and much has been written for and against their significance for believers today. The gift of tongues is best understood as an extemporaneous or spontaneous manifestation in a form that is a quasi-language. The speaker is in control of her or his speech and the forming of the sounds; the Spirit does not manipulate or coerce the speaker into a particular speech pattern. Whereas once only associated with Pentecostal believers, now many other believers also speak in tongues.

Although it is often, with the gift of interpretation, placed at the end of the Pauline lists of *charismata* (1 Cor. 12:10, 30), Paul valued speaking in tongues (1 Cor. 14:18). It may be defined as having a number of purposes. The book of Acts demonstrates that it was often (but not always, Acts 8:17; 9:17) associated with those occasions when people received the Spirit (Acts 2:4; 10:46; 19:6). Paul identifies its value in personal and public worship, in particular in praise and prayer (1 Cor. 14:2, 4, 15, 28). The manifestation of the gift of tongues also functions as a symbol of the presence of God, his closeness and his mystery, his immanence and his transcendence, in the Christian community.

The NT, other than Acts 2:6, does not indicate that an earthly language is being assumed by the writers when they refer to speaking in tongues. Although it is a common perception among many that tongues and interpretation are equivalent to prophecy, in that both result in information being presented to the hearers, the evidence of the NT is not clearly supportive of this view. Instead, those speaking in tongues are identified as speaking to God[12] (even in Acts 2:6,

---

[12] 1 Cor. 14:2, 14–16, 28.

the believers glorify God in tongues, the contents simply being understood by the hearers) in prayer or praise.[13] There is neither biblical support for the suggestion that the gift of tongues was intended to be a means whereby God communicated with believers, nor is there any indication that when a tongue is interpreted, it becomes equivalent to prophecy.

7. Every Christian receives a manifestation of the Spirit (1 Cor. 12:11)

By definition, all believers are people of the Spirit and thus are eligible to function as channels through whom he can minister to others.[14] With the privilege, however, comes the responsibility of maintaining a close relationship with the Spirit. The concentration by Paul in 1 Corinthians 12 is not on the gifts to which he refers or even on their diversity. Rather, it is on the diversity of their distribution to all believers. Indeed, he stresses this point no less than eleven times in five verses (12:7–11), beginning and ending the section by stating that *each* believer has been gifted. This does not mean that believers should necessarily expect to exercise all the gifts of the Spirit. Indeed, when Paul asked his readers if certain gifts were received by every believer, the implied answer was, 'no' (1 Cor. 12:29–30).

Thus, no believer should feel deficient because they may not have exercised one of the gifts in particular. The donation of gifts is dependent on the Spirit. Similarly, no one should assume that Paul is suggesting that every believer has his or her 'own gift' as an exclusive possession. The gifts of the Spirit belong to the Spirit, as does the power needed to manifest them appropriately. It is important to recognize that Paul encourages believers to realize their potential to be used by the Spirit (1 Cor. 1:7) and to use the gifts he grants to them (Rom. 12:6–8).

The concept of every believer actively functioning in the church is clearly biblical, but sometimes the leadership of local churches inappropriately functions as the depository of most of the gifts, especially the audible ones. This is not necessarily because of a desire of leaders to monopolize. It is often because of the lack of a framework for identifying how believers may be used by the Spirit, and thus limited provisions for such opportunities are created. In the context of the Christian community, there is value in believers

---

[13] Acts 2:11; 10:46; 1 Cor. 14:2, 14–16.
[14] 1 Cor. 12:6, 11; Rom. 12:4–6; Eph. 4:7, 15–16; 2 Tim. 1:7; 1 Pet. 4:10.

helping to identify gifts that have already been granted by the Spirit to others. Although this could unhelpfully result in a mechanistic procedure, it could, with care and sensitivity, enable believers to recognise that they are manifesting gifts of the Spirit in their lives more than they may have realised. At the same time, with mature guidance on the part of supportive believers, others could be helped to develop those gifts.

A number of years ago, I was conducting a weekend retreat for about fifty young Christians who were undertaking studies at the same university. On the Friday evening, we conducted an experiment. I asked them to spend time identifying strengths that they had observed in their colleagues. Having spent some time doing this, they shared their findings. It was interesting. As a result of them identifying gifts in their colleagues, they were able to encourage others with the recognition that they were valuable to the group because of who they were. The next part of the evening was also illuminating.

A female student was affirmed as having highly-attuned organizational skills, while another was confirmed by his friends as having the capacity to teach and explain facts enthusiastically and cogently. Such assessments they accepted as resonating with their own perceptions of themselves, but were encouraged that others had also identified them. To demonstrate their faith in this corporate judgment, the group requested that the first become their secretary when they returned to their university, and engage in planning for future events. She had been released to function in an ability that had been confirmed by her peers, and thus found fulfilment in exercising a gift that she believed that God had given to her.

The one who had been affirmed as having a capability to teach undertook his degree, then completed another degree, this time in theology, in a Bible College, stayed on and gained a Masters degree in applied theology and now functions as an Anglican priest. He is now putting into practice every week that ability which was affirmed by his friends all those years ago. We can help others to achieve their God-given destinies by taking time to help them identify the gifts that God has given them, and then seeking to enable them to find opportunities to exercise them.

There is little biblical justification for the notion that one may transmit a gift to another.[15] But this does not undermine the value of

---

[15] Paul writes that he wishes to impart a 'spiritual gift' (*charisma* and *pneumatikos* are used uniquely in this combination in Rom. 1:11), though the meaning is unclear. It is possible that the nature of the gift relates to his desire to preach the gospel to them (Rom. 1:15; 15:16), the gospel being God's greatest gift to

recognising and affirming gifts that have been bestowed on others and encouraging their use. It is in this regard that Paul encourages Timothy to develop his gift (2 Tim. 1:6), and that Barnabas and Paul were entrusted to fulfil the mission delegated to them by God (Acts 13:3), both occasions incorporating the laying on of hands. Similarly, the purpose behind the presentation of the gifts in Romans 12:6–8 is to encourage the readers to use those gifts that God has given to them, and to do it in ways that are appropriate.

8. Gifts of the Spirit should be sought (1 Cor. 12:31)

In 1 Corinthians 12:31 (ESV), Paul encourages his readers to 'earnestly desire the higher gifts'.[16] Much discussion has taken place over the identity of these particular gifts. Before this issue is explored, it is valid to pause and recognize that believers are recommended to manifest the gifts of the Spirit, whatever they may be. Although he is sovereignly in charge of their distribution, it pleases him when believers are prepared to partner him in their manifestation. This is an enormous privilege for believers. The one who has all power to do anything he chooses, and to achieve his objectives easily and successfully with no outside help, chooses to involve human, weak, imperfect believers in the process. At the same time, he enjoys

---

humanity, and the most definite sign of his grace. Indeed, *charisma* is used of the gospel in Rom. 5:15–16 and 6:23, as well as with other meanings not related to gifts of the Spirit (Rom. 11:29). It is also possible that he anticipates that they will benefit from that which he will share with them, the identity of which is uncertain (Rom. 1:13). Where he does use the word *charismata* to refer to gifts, such as prophecy and teaching (Rom. 12:6), he identifies them as being imparted by God, not people (Rom. 12:3). G. D. Fee, in *God's Empowering Presence* (Hendrickson, 1994), pp.488–489, argues that the preaching of the gospel to Jews and Gentiles is appropriately identified as a 'Spirit-inspired gift of grace'. To believe that they are devoid of gifts of the Spirit because Paul cannot get to them is ludicrous, and would indicate that the Spirit needs Paul to enable him to support the believers in Rome. This statement is more to do with Paul's desire to be with them to do good for them than it is to suggest that, without him, they are powerless. He is reflecting his frustration due to the fact that he cannot fulfill his plans to be with them. He is not referring to his helping the Spirit, but to helping them. Similarly, it would be inappropriate to interpret 2 Tim. 1:6 to mean that one may grant a gift to another via the laying on of hands.

[16] Although some have proffered the view that this may be translated better, 'You are earnestly desiring the higher gifts,' there is no evidence of this in the letter. It is possible he is speaking ironically of their desire to manifest the 'higher gifts', whereupon he shows them an even higher way – the path of love. However, in 14:1, 39, a similar exhortation and verbal combination is recorded. Since there, they have to be translated in the imperatival form, 'earnestly desire . . .' (ESV), it is more natural that this be repeated in the first reference also.

collaborating with them as co-workers in the fulfillment of his agenda.

When our children, Luke and Anna Marie were younger, we engaged in an activity at Christmas that soon became a tradition in our home. A few days before Christmas, we would decorate the Christmas tree. Christmas carols would be playing in the background and together, as a family, we would hang all the baubles on the tree. It took a long time; decisions were carefully made by the children as to which decoration should go where, and where the Christmas lights should be placed. It was a time of fun and family, and from our perspective as parents, the best part of the occasion was not the decoration of the tree but the enjoyment of being with our children, and seeing their pleasure at participating in the joint activity. Whether they did it perfectly or not was not the issue. Whether all the baubles matched was unimportant. What was important was that their participation had resulted in their presence with us. It didn't even matter, when they went to bed, if we had to make some amendments. Being together was of central importance.

Although it may sound too marvellous to be true, the Spirit enjoys us being co-partners with him in projects that he has prepared. Even though he could achieve his purposes without our involvement, he still chooses to use us. Even though our best efforts are not always as fruitful as they could be, he still prefers to incorporate us in the task. The reason is simple. He prefers to work with us, and for us to work with him, than to exist in a relationship where there is passivity on our part, and separation between us.

In encouraging his readers to seek for the higher gifts, it is possible that Paul may be suggesting that they demonstrate love as the highest principle in their lives, given that he develops it as his next topic (1 Cor. 13:1–13). Nowhere, however, does Paul refer to love as a gift of the Spirit. Alternatively, if he has ranked the gifts with an apostle being the most important and tongues as the least, it may be deduced that he is encouraging that they look to those that are most significant according to such a hierarchical grid. However, he does not clearly provide a hierarchy in his lists though passages such as 1 Corinthians 12:28 indicate that some gifts are more prominent than others in the development of the church.[17] As the lists demonstrate, however, the gifts identified vary from one list to the other, and often are placed in a different order to their reference elsewhere.

---

[17] It is possible that apostles, prophets and teachers are itemised as first, second and third due to their important formational role in the establishing of local churches. It is not necessary to believe that Paul was seeking to identify a hierarchy of roles; this is about gifts, ministries and function, not offices.

There is little reason to indicate why one gift should be more (or less) valuable than another since they are each given by the Spirit, and each has an important function in certain settings.

The grading of gifts by Paul would be irrelevant to a most important theme for him – which is diversity and variety, not a ladder of importance. Indeed, he emphasizes his disregard for the latter (1 Cor. 12:29–30) since he acknowledges that not all will be apostles, prophets or teachers. The theme of the chapter thus far has been to stress the importance of interdependency, giving equal recognition to all members of the body, however they function, including those deemed to be less important (12:12–26).

When Paul speaks of *greater gifts*, it is likely that he is referring to those gifts that are of a more beneficial nature at any given time; intelligibility and mutual benefit is high on Paul's agenda for determining the acceptability of when it is appropriate to exercise a gift of the Spirit. After setting the gifts in the context of love, he illustrates this point by contrasting tongues (without interpretation) and prophecy (14:1–25). Whereas the former benefits no one positively, other than the speaker, prophecy benefits everyone who hears it. In that equation, prophecy would be deemed to be the higher gift because it benefits the community, while the gift of tongues, without an interpretation, does not. If love is the channel for the deliverance of any of the gifts, it will ensure that each gift is presented in the most edifying way possible. Gifts of the Spirit are intrinsically equal to each other. The value of a manifestation of the Spirit is directly related to the need that has warranted the gift being exercised.

9. Gifts of the Spirit are given to be used (Rom. 12:6–8)

Paul is anxious that believers use all that the Spirit has given to them. Thus, the one who has been gifted with teaching should teach, the prophet should prophesy, the encourager should encourage (Rom. 12:6–8). They are not for personal or selfish use but for service to others, and for their benefit, the context of their use being love (12:9). Gifts from the Spirit are not to be worn as badges of achievement, or to be put on the shelf and admired, but are to be daily laid before the Spirit for him to use. More appropriately, believers should view themselves as living sacrifices to be presented in order to fulfil the will of God (12:1–2), exercising any and all of the gifts that may be given by the Spirit.

When writing to Timothy, Paul encourages him not to 'neglect your gift' (1 Tim. 4:14). Indeed, he instructs him 'to fan into flame the gift of God, which is in you' (2 Tim. 1:6). The identity of the gift

191

is not clarified.[18] The reader does not need to identify it; Timothy knows what it is. The message to him is to use what he has received from God. Whatever God has planted in our lives needs also to be given opportunities to bear fruit by being cultivated.

The significance of the information is to encourage Timothy not to neglect what has been given to him. What matters is that Timothy must not be restricted by his timidity and instead should use his gift and not be indolent. In association with the exhortation to use the gift given to him, the description of the Spirit may be instructive, for the aspects of the Spirit referred to are integral to the use of any gift. It must be manifested with love, power, and in a controlled way, all of which are possible under the influence of the Spirit (2 Tim. 1:7). The spiritual nature of these characteristics ensures that any gift of the Spirit to the believer will not be used in an insensitive or undisciplined manner. He functions in the believer not in weakness or cowardice, but in authority and integrity.

The Spirit who commissioned Jesus also commissions believers to undertake responsibilities on his behalf for the benefit of others. When Paul refers to *charismata* in Romans 12:6–8, it is for a central purpose – to remind his readers that the reason why they are given to believers is so that they should be used. Thus, he refers to a selection, each of which is followed either by the instruction that it should be used or by how it should occur. It is one thing to identify a gift that God has given but another thing to operate it appropriately and effectively. Dr Martin Luther King Jr. said, 'If a man is called to be a streetsweeper, he should sweep streets even as Michelangelo painted, or Beethoven played music, or Shakespeare wrote poetry. He should sweep streets so well that all the hosts of heaven and earth will pause to say, here lived a great streetsweeper who did his job well.' The Spirit expects no less dedication to the implementation of the gifts that he gives to us.

[18] It is possible that Paul is referring to Timothy's salvation (though the reference to the laying on of hands in 2 Tim. 1:6 is not supportive of this), his commissioning to ministry, or a gift of the Spirit that enabled him to function in ministry. Since verse 7 identifies this gift as having been given by God to Timothy, and because of its association with fire (fanning into flame), it is possible that he is referring to the Spirit himself, who is associated with power, love and self-discipline.

Galatians 5:16 – 6:2
15. The Holy Spirit and transformation

1. Introduction

In the OT, it was the Lord (Yahweh) who spoke to the corporate community (1 Kgs 22:14; Jer. 42:7; Amos 7:15-16); in the Gospels, it was Jesus who spoke (Matt. 11:15; Mark 4:9; Luke 8:8). Now, and since the day of Pentecost, it is the Spirit who has taken the initiative and discharged this prophetic responsibility. The responsibility of believers is to listen to the words of the Spirit and also to take action to obey or apply them; he speaks in order that believers should follow. The fact that one is able to listen to the Spirit is a privilege only available to believers (John 3:8) (other than to convict unbelievers of their need of Jesus, John 16:8–10). Such a benefit must not be treated as unimportant. The one who spoke and the universe obeyed and came into being is the one who deigns to speak words of advice to believers, choosing to express it in human language and in ways that are understandable to fragile people. Such a personable friend is to be honoured by a sensitive attentiveness and an alertness to act by those he seeks to influence.

Believers always run the risk of presuming on the privilege granted to them to have the Spirit as their personal friend and guide. The Israelites got used to the presence of the cloud that led them by day and the fire that joined it at night (Exod. 40:36–38; Num: 10:11; 14:14) and began to complain (Num. 11:1), disobey (Num. 11:33), oppose Moses (Num. 12:1) and rebel against God (Num. 14:1–4, 11). Ultimately, their presumptuousness led to their defeat (Num. 14:39–45). The tragedy that they experienced acts as a lesson to believers, who should not take for granted what the Spirit has given to them in choosing to be their intimate and personal teacher, mentor and friend.

The Israelites were commended if they listened to the law and obeyed its injunctions and were condemned if they did not. The Spirit, who is a superior advisor, also expects believers to listen to his careful counsel with a high level of concentration. They are not to treat the Spirit disrespectfully or dishonourably. Just because his touch may be lighter than the law does not mean that he is a light-weight. He demands complete loyalty from those he loves. He does not offer an easier code of conduct; one may not easily make excuses as to why one does not obey him. Whereas the law was contained in books that were too large to be carried and consulted when-ever needed, the Spirit is the constant companion of the believer. Whenever guidance is needed as to how to act or speak, his whisper is closer than one's own.

To ignore the internal promptings of the one who has chosen to walk with us, in order to guide us, would be a foolish and ungrateful action. Walking with the Spirit is demonstrated by a willingness to follow his direction, a readiness to listen to his guidance, and a keen-ness to comply with him, the managing director of our lives. The 'Spirit of the Lord', who was to 'rest on' the Messiah – 'the Spirit of wisdom and of understanding' (Isa. 11:2) – has chosen to reside in us. Ponder the privilege.

Paul writes to the Galatians, encouraging them to recognize that the Spirit is to be their guide with regard to developing their Christian lives. He recommends that they take advantage of his influence (Gal. 5:16), rather than look, in particular, to the law for guidance (5:18). In 5:16, Paul anticipates that if believers continu-ously walk with the Spirit,[1] they will naturally develop a lifestyle that is not dominated by sinful activities – not only is the Spirit their mentor, but also he empowers them. He enables them to achieve high standards of behaviour and in that regard, is fundamentally superior to the law. As a result of the benevolent presence of the Spirit, Paul anticipates that there will be beneficent progress in their lives.

2. Walking with the Spirit (Gal. 5:16)

Paul uses a concept that is derived from his Jewish heritage, that of walking (Gal. 5:16, ESV, RSV) as a description of an ethical lifestyle (Exod. 18:20; Deut. 13:4–5). This is a popular term for Paul else-where to describe one's conduct (Rom. 6:4; 8:4; Eph. 2:2), derived

---

[1] Paul may be indicating that the believer grows as a Christian 'with the help of the Spirit' or 'in the presence of the Spirit' or both.

from the Hebrew *halak*.[2] Although the RSV offers, *Walk by the Spirit, and do not gratify the desires of the flesh* (5:16), it is more appropriate to follow the majority of translations which present an imperative followed by a promise, *Walk by the Spirit, and you will not gratify the desires of the flesh*.[3] Indeed, Paul confirms the authority of the Spirit in positively mentoring believers by including a double negative, that could result in the translation, 'you will definitely not gratify the desires of the flesh'. The more believers listen to the Spirit, the less likely they will be to make mistakes and to listen to the wrong advice. In effect, if they walk with the Spirit, they will be protected from listening to inappropriate and unhelpful advice from other sources, be they human or diabolic, internal or external, isolated or insistent.

This is another remarkable ministry of the Spirit in that he guides believers individually, offering them personal guidance, responding to their life settings and enabling them to progress through life in active partnership with him. He is not just a powerful force but also a personal friend, mentoring them as well as ministering through them. If they take advantage of his personal touch, they will see it affecting their lives positively, for his character will increasingly be traced on their personalities.

The Spirit is capable of speaking to believers in ways that are appropriate to them as individuals, catering for their personalities and sensibilities. The Spirit speaks through them, sometimes supernaturally and sometimes without them realizing that they have been a channel of the Spirit to minister to another. Sometimes, the Spirit speaks through the Bible, sometimes in ways that are surprising by their immediacy and relevance, sometimes in ways that may not have been apparent to the original readers. The Spirit speaks through circumstances as well as conscience, through music and word, through scenery and sacrament, through silence and sound, or through an inner sense or feeling that one should or should not take a particular action. Leaders, in particular, are to be encouraged to explore these issues and to offer guidelines for implementing them appropriately.

It is grammatically possible that the assertion, 'walk by the Spirit' (Gal. 5:16, ESV, RSV) refers to the notion of believers walking in the presence of the Spirit. However, it as likely that he expects his readers to walk as people who are empowered by the Spirit. The concepts are not mutually exclusive; indeed, it

---

[2] The *Halakah* is the term used to describe Jewish rabbinic ethical and social guidelines.
[3] ESV, see KJV, NASV, NIV; R. N. Longenecker, *Galatians* (Word, 1990), p. 244.

may help to recognize that because believers are in the sphere of the Spirit, and because of his commitment to them, his power is not distant from them; on the contrary, he is present to empower them.

The term 'flesh' (*sarx*) (*. . . you will not gratify the desires of the flesh*, ESV) is used by Paul to refer to an opposite motivational and directional force to that of the Spirit (Gal. 5:16, 17, 19). On occasions, as we have seen, 'the flesh' is used to describe natural human life that is not malevolent, sinful or in opposition to God (Rom. 3:20; 1 Cor. 1:29). In this respect, such a lifestyle is to be pitied because it has not taken advantage of the superior guidance available as a result of the Spirit's involvement in one's life. It is an egocentric lifestyle, though not necessarily or always antagonistic to God; rather, it is often indifferent to or ignorant of God. However, on other occasions, the term is used of malignant attitudes and sinful actions that have negative consequences for the perpetrators and others (Gal. 5:19–21). It is in this respect that Paul uses the term here (5:16–19). He is concerned that his readers realize the danger awaiting them if they do not walk with the Spirit. Such a lifestyle will result in painful actions, harmful habits and sad, disappointed and cruelly disfigured lives. A different outlook is available for the believer, however, which will result in a completely different destination. This will result in a positive existence, exuding constructive and beneficial actions and attitudes, because the Spirit takes centre stage in the life of the believer. It is a life in which the believer walks with the Spirit.

3. Walking with the Spirit is superior to walking under the law (Gal 5:18)

One of the major reasons Paul wrote the letter to the Galatians was because its readers had been unhelpfully influenced by others with reference to the law.[4] The law is best understood as the contract or covenant established by God with the Israelites, which provided them with a standard of behaviour to abide by, and guidelines to enable them to fulfil it. Paul dedicates chapters 3 and 4 to exploring the issue and, in particular the purpose of the law, while in chapters 5 and 6, he offers an alternative route to God via the Spirit. His message is so radical to many that he spends the first two chapters

---

[4] The term 'law' (*nomos*) is capable of referring to the Ten Commandments, the Torah (and, in particular, the sacrificial system, and all that related to it, as well rites of passage, including circumcision) or the whole of the OT.

establishing his authority and thus his right to present his case before them. Consequently, he stresses the direct revelation that he received from God (Gal. 1:11–15), emphasizing that no one had inappropriately convinced him of this, nor did they amend or contradict him (1:16–23); on the contrary, the other apostles affirmed what he said (2:5–10).

This radical message has serious implications. The important basis of the relationship of the Israelites with God, providing them with a sense of their identity and an authoritative rule-book and guidelines for life and worship, was the law. However, that had not been given to the Gentiles, nor had it been part of their history. The question to be answered now by the Gentile believers was, 'Should the law be our guide, as it is for the Jews?' Paul's answer was clear and startling. The law that God had miraculously provided to the Israelites had now been superseded and a superior guide had been made available for Jewish and Gentile believers – the Spirit. Paul was not saying that the law was evil; on the contrary, as a gift from God, it was good and gracious. However, it was only ever intended to be a temporary influence until a superior guide should be given (Gal. 3:19–24). Now, instead of a one-size-fits-all guidebook, the Spirit comes as a personal mentor who prepares a strategy for development, carefully tailored to individual believers. The Spirit is a guide, not a guidebook; a friend, not simply a formula to be followed; a mentor, not a modus operandi. Believers are improved by the involvement of the Spirit in their lives, resulting in their destinies, as set by the Spirit, being achieved. Care must be maintained to ensure that such an emphasis is not assumed to be the basis for a life with no rules or absolutes, where rules are deemed to be illegitimate and self-discipline inappropriate. The Spirit is not blasé about sin; he is neither an easygoing guide nor an overly tolerant mentor. Although he is our friend he can be firm, for he is faithful to truth and a life of integrity. Thus, it is clear why Paul is insistent that the believers recognize the limited value of the law in contrast to the limitless value of the Spirit. Inevitably, although the law was the personal gift of God to his people, it was unable to effect a personal commitment to them since it is an inanimate legal system; however, the Spirit is passionately energized to make a dynamic difference to those he partners. In surrendering to the Spirit, we release ourselves into the arms of someone who loves those whom he leads. He takes care of those in whom he will create a mirror image of himself, gently tracing his design in their lives. After all, he is the Holy Spirit – different in all he does, unique in his ministry, the believer being the object of his careful attention.

4. The Spirit offers guidance for personal transformation (Gal. 5:22–24)

Believers who are walking with the Spirit are identified by Paul on the evidence and quality of their lifestyles. Although elsewhere, he relates the Spirit in the believer to charismatic gifts, here the emphasis is on sacrificial service, and caring for the needs of others – restoring them (Gal. 6:1), bearing their burdens (6:2) and doing good to them (6:9–10). The believer who walks with the Spirit is one who walks in harmony with others, who respects and supports them, partnering and sustaining them, thereby reflecting the Spirit.

Whereas the law points people in the right direction, identifying the rules for good behaviour, the Spirit enables believers to reach their destination. He empowers the believer to overcome sin, whilst at the same time identifying it. It is no surprise therefore that Paul uses an imperative 'walk in the Spirit' (a unique occasion in Paul – Gal. 5:16). The fact that it is in the present continuous tense emphasizes Paul's expectation that personal ethical development in society should be an ongoing characteristic of believers, a way of life, motivated and empowered by the Spirit. The Spirit heralds a new era, enabling believers to enter that era and empowering them to be improved throughout their lives.

It is probable that some of Paul's opponents accused him of advocating an undisciplined lifestyle that had no code of conduct, because he did not emphasize the law. As Fee asserts, however, 'To be "Law-less" does not mean to be lawless';[5] in reality, the standard of conduct Paul advocates is a higher one than any that the law could set. The Spirit, who reflects God more accurately than the law, is more keenly cognizant of the shortcomings of believers, and more capable of astutely pinpointing areas where improvement is needed. Whereas the law identifies a collection of wrongdoings, the Spirit introduces the believer to the full horror of sin. He has the ability to make believers feel much more unrighteous than the law ever could. However (and in contrast to the law), he is also the key to righteous living, and has determined to partner believers and to protect them from slipping their way to perdition. The Spirit sensitizes believers to the full range of sin, but in order to guard them from it.

Paul is not suggesting here that the Spirit enables the believer to keep the law better than the person who does not have the Spirit. Rather, he wants his readers to realize that the law has served its purpose; now, a better guide has come in the person of the Spirit (Gal. 4:1–6). This is not because the law was inaccurate or a mistake

---

[5] G. D. Fee, *God's Empowering Presence* (Hendrickson, 1994), p. 437.

that the Spirit has now come to remedy. Rather, Paul affirms that the Spirit in the believer achieves what the law could not do, or was ever intended to do – to affirm people as children of God and to enable them to reflect that calling through improved lifestyles.

Using a different set of metaphors in 2 Corinthians 3:16–18, Paul quotes from and adapts Exodus 34:34 to prove the supremacy of the Spirit-directed life.[6] Whereas, Exodus 34:34 describes Moses entering the Lord's presence and temporarily and personally removing his own veil, Paul describes believers as having the 'veil' removed from them permanently (2 Cor. 3:18), indicating that they are constantly in the presence of God (as a result of the Spirit). Paul then identifies the ability of believers, in contrast to Moses, to reflect God, or to radiate God with the help of the Spirit, or both. Thereafter, Paul reaches the apex of his presentation by exploring the transforming process of the Spirit, which highlights the final supremacy of the Spirit over the law.

The Spirit has the capacity, the desire and the determination to transform believers into the likeness of the Lord. On this occasion, Paul is not describing the activity of the believer to be transformed, but noting that it is the action of the Spirit that effects that transformation. Furthermore, it is anticipated as being fulfilled in the context of glory (2 Cor. 3:18). The concept of 'glory' (*doxa*) is used as a superlative when attempting to describe something or someone superior to all others. In the LXX, it is often used to translate the Hebrew word *kābôd*, and describes someone who has influence (Gen. 45:13), riches (Gen. 31:1; see also Eph. 1:18) or power (Isa. 8:7; see also Col. 1:11). It describes someone who makes an impression, who has a sense of presence and authority. In this regard, the word 'glory' is best used of God. He is superior to all and the best word that may be used to represent his deity (*Godness*) is 'glory'. It is the role of the Spirit to transform the believer within a life that is circumscribed by and filled with God. Such a life may be defined as 'glorious'. Life on earth for the believer is to be the changing room in preparation for the final whistle for time on this earth and the commencement of eternity, when the full expression of God's glory will be manifested.

5. The Spirit enables believers to be fruitful (Gal. 5:22–23)

A great deal of discussion has taken place over the meaning of Galatians 5:16–21 as to whether these verses refer to a believer or

[6] K. Warrington, *Discovering the Spirit in the New Testament* (Hendrickson, 2005), pp. 124–127.

unbeliever. However one understands these verses, Paul's major purpose is to identify the significant role of the Spirit in the life of the individual believer. It is this fact that must not be overlooked in any debate concerning the exact context of this experience. It is possible that Paul is describing the tension felt by believers to do right but who are tempted to do otherwise.[7] For them, the message of Paul would be that the Spirit is available to help them in the challenge and that they should take advantage of such a powerful and personal ally.

It is more likely, however, that Paul is contrasting unbelievers who have no one to help them, resulting in their lives being controlled by sin (Gal. 5:19–21), and believers who have the constant presence and power of the Spirit operating within them, their lives being dominated by love (5:22–23).[8] That is not to suggest that the believer does not feel the tension of living in a fallen world and being in a state of imperfection. However, whereas unbelievers are helpless to change direction, the Spirit is the helper of believers, enabling them to overcome the pull of the flesh. Paul is not suggesting sinless perfection but a perfect Spirit, who enables the believer to fight against sin and win. The emphasis is not on any helplessness felt by the believer (or unbeliever), but on the residential power of the Spirit in the lives of believers. The central thesis remains constant: the Spirit is committed and able to improve believers and enhance their potential for ministry.

Paul provides two lists of fifteen vices and nine virtues that define lifestyles of those following either their own agendas or the standard set by the Spirit. Paul is not intending to provide an exhaustive catalogue of sins or strengths, but sample lists. What is important for Paul is that his readers understand the sensational impact that the Spirit makes in the life of the believer. To ignore the work of the Spirit is therefore detrimental, for the Spirit is positively productive.

The Spirit produces fruit[9] in believers while sinful people, by their own efforts, produce harmful consequences. The latter is self-motivated; the former is Spirit-initiated. Furthermore, although believers work in partnership with the Spirit, and engage in personal discipline to achieve high standards of morality and spirituality,

---

[7] J. D. G. Dunn, *The Epistle to the Galatians* (A. & C. Black, 1993), pp. 298–300.

[8] Fee, *God's Empowering Presence*, p. 435.

[9] Although the word 'fruit' (*karpos*) is in the singular, it may be a collective term and thus as easily refer to a collection of individual fruits. Whether *karpos* is intended by Paul to be singular or plural is much less important than the fact that the source of the fruit is the Spirit.

the Spirit also produces fruit naturally in the believer. The Spirit is on their side, developing within them characteristics that naturally belong to him, bringing about his desires for their lives, radiating his personality in theirs. On their own, they are only capable of offering a pale reflection of God; with the Spirit, they have a personal trainer who creates a personal development plan just for them and then helps them to achieve it. As a result of his involvement, a metamorphosis takes place as the believer goes from being a pioneer with promise to being someone in whom the promise has been realized in practice.

The fruit listed by Paul relate to qualities associated with a life that is being controlled by the Spirit. They are not intended to be an exhaustive catalogue of such character traits but a sampling of those elements that facilitate the transformation of the temperament by the Spirit. Naturally, the list of fruit commences with *love*, for this motivates all the qualities that follow and best characterizes God (1 John 4:8). Interestingly, the noun used (*agapē*) is infrequently used in secular Greek; it is best understood when associated with the Spirit, who enables believers to love others in a way that is only possible because it reflects the love that belongs to the Spirit himself (Rom. 5:5). It is a love that is best described in superlatives, that has no upper limit, no depths to which it will not go for someone else; in short, it is the love of Jesus in the believer. The fruit of *joy* is elsewhere associated with the Spirit (Luke 10:21; 1 Thess. 1:6). Barclay defines it as 'the distinguishing atmosphere of the Christian life'.[10] It is not defined by its surroundings, but by the Spirit whose presence puts life into perspective, and who enables the believer to experience joy even when the journey is harsh, life is challenging, and one feels fragile.

Peace is not to be equated with the absence of noise or strife, but with the presence of God. Some years ago, a competition was held for artists to paint a picture that best celebrated the concept of peace. Many artists presented portraits of lakeside or country scenes, where tranquility and stillness captured the atmosphere of their paintings. The winner, however, painted a scene where a rushing waterfall poured over a cliff, spreading spray on the surrounding area. It signaled a cacophony of noise, restlessness, uncertainty and danger. It seemed to portray the opposite to peace. However, on a branch that hung perilously close to the torrential flow was a family of birds in a nest. They lived in the shadow of danger, the sound of the thunderous surge of water their constant companion. It did not control their lives, however; they experienced peace in their being together,

---

[10] W. Barclay, *Flesh and Spirit* (SCM, 1962), p. 77.

despite the danger. The peace provided by the Spirit is based on the establishment of the security of the believer as a result of the love of God for them. It is manifested in harmonious personal relationships and in the establishment of friendship with God. It seeks to overcome discord and establish friendship, to replace enmity with understanding, to hold hands instead of pointing fingers.

Patience is the ability to maintain one's focus and not to be discouraged, even when challenging pressures would suggest that the only response is to give in. It enables the person concerned to wait until the objective has been achieved, the storm has passed or the burden has been lifted. Indeed, the patience manifested by the Spirit enables the believer to function calmly and efficiently even when a situation may not have been resolved successfully. Patience in the face of pain and hope in the context of helplessness is the fruit that only the Spirit can infuse into the life of a believer.

The fruit described as *kindness* may also be understood as gentleness. It also is of central importance to one's relationships in that, like patience, it provides the ability to forgive, forbear and befriend in ways that result in the other person experiencing protection, security and lovingkindness. The fruit of *goodness* reflects that quality of generosity that ensures that personal relationships are maintained at the highest level of selfless commitment. Goodness is not equated with sinlessness but with liberality and munificence; it describes a person who is not satisfied simply to meet a need but to do so lavishly. Such a person may not have much to give but what they have, they bestow abundantly on others.

Faith (KJV) is to be equated with the activity of being faithful. It refers to the believer who is trustworthy, reliable and loyal. A number of Paul's friends received the highest accolade from him when he referred to their being faithful (Timothy – 1 Cor. 4:17; Epaphras – Col. 1:7; Onesimus – Col. 4:9). This characteristic is central to the maintenance of loving relationships and thus is manifested by the Spirit in believers.

The fruit of *gentleness* (meekness, KJV) describes the ability to soothe pain, to ease tension, to pacify trouble, to relieve anxiety and, to alleviate burdens. The meek person is someone who exudes care for others when they are laden with cares, providing solace when all they feel is stress. It is associated with the characteristic of being gracious and is also manifested in acts of kindness, politeness, courtesy and thoughtfulness.

The final characteristic referred to by Paul is that of *self-control*. Those in control of themselves manage their priorities resolutely, basing their actions on reason and love, not selfish desire. They are selfless and strong-minded, determined to do that which is right, whatever the cost. Consistency not compromise characterizes them. They are self-disciplined and ready to be challenged by adversity if good is the potential outcome. At the same time, they retain a sense of balance and fair-mindedness, and are ready to learn because they have a realistic assessment of themselves. They are not weak, prone to compromise or quick to give in. On the contrary, this virtue provides strength of character that knows when it is right to walk and when to pause, when to push forward and when to rest, when to talk and when to listen, when to follow and when to lead. Circumstances do not quickly influence their behaviour. They are not easily swayed or manipulated, but at all times are in control of their actions and reactions, their attitudes and their responses.

It is significant to note that the individual manifestations of the Spirit relate to virtues that are best manifested in corporate settings. They are not intended for the individual believer so much as for the individual in the context of a community. Others are to benefit from the radiation of the Spirit through believers. The law offers guidance for personal and corporate living; the Spirit enables the achievement of his objectives, which relate to lifestyle issues. The law objectively reminds people of the rules of community; the Spirit personally empowers people to obey him, and so enables them to fulfill Christ's guidance for his followers (Gal. 6:2).

6. The Spirit expects believers to bear fruit (Gal. 5:25 – 6:2)

Rather than look to the law for guidance, Paul encourages conformity to what the Spirit wants (Gal. 5:25 – 6:1) for the law cannot achieve what the Spirit can (5:23b). The logic of starting with the Spirit at salvation is that one should continue with the Spirit (5:25). It is also at this point (verse 25) that Paul introduces a new word 'follow' (stoicheō)[11] to identify how one should do this. Given that the basic meaning of this verb is 'to stand in line', as in a military context, it is possible that Paul is seeking to elaborate on the consequences of following the Spirit. Such followers are to be in line with his wishes; they should follow in his footsteps, march to his tune, keep to his standards.

Now, Paul describes how people of the Spirit should live, much of it relating to relational activities (Gal. 5:26; 6:1–2). As such, he clearly demonstrates that his advice that his readers should *keep in step with the Spirit* (5:25) is not intended to be merely understood metaphorically; nor is he content to simply contrast law and Spirit.

---

[11] This is translated in the RSV and ESV as 'walk' (Gal. 5:25).

He takes time to spell out in detail the consequences of partnering the Spirit. There is a personal cost that involves taking responsibility not only for one's own actions but also for those of other believers, caring for them and their welfare, as the Spirit does for them. He identifies such people as *spiritual* (6:1), which may refer to mature Christians[12] but more likely identifies all Christians who are, by definition, 'people of the Spirit'.[13] If the latter, this becomes a call to raise up themselves to the calling laid upon them by God, and to act accordingly as people in whom the Spirit dwells, and through whom he wishes to minister to others.

Paul anticipates that believers should exhibit lifestyles that reflect the Spirit; only then can they appropriately define themselves as *spiritual* – people who follow a code of conduct that was also resident in Jesus (Gal. 6:2). Thus, although Paul may have been accused of being antinomian,[14] the reality was that he was setting a much higher standard of behaviour than the law could ever set. Believers are not being encouraged to live to a high moral standard as a result of listening to a limited and external rule book, the law; they are to listen to an immediate and comprehensive guide to righteousness, the Spirit. When the Spirit takes over and imparts his wisdom and power, love, not lawlessness, results and the active role of the believer is to follow him.

It is not to be assumed that Paul teaches that believers should simply submit themselves to the Spirit and expect him to achieve his will automatically in them; holiness is not routinely inevitable for believers. One does not become more righteous simply by remaining a Christian; one has to participate in the process of holiness. Paul is not advocating a passive waiting for the Spirit to move the believer; rather, he is suggesting that the believer should keep up with the Spirit, walk to his pace and keep in step with him. There are two imperatives for Paul. Firstly, believers are to walk and, thus, make a conscious effort to move forward. Believers are not carried into the next life by angels; rather, they conscientiously and robustly are to make their own way there. Secondly, believers are to keep the Spirit in focus on their journey, for although they have a responsibility to progress, the process is under-girded by the Spirit. Central to Paul's message is that the Spirit is anxious for this partnership, encourages movement in this direction on the part of the believer, and imparts his power to develop his fruit in their lives.

[12] Dunn, *Galatians*, p. 319.
[13] Fee, *God's Empowering Presence*, p. 461.
[14] This technical term describes someone who does not abide by rules or conventions (Greek, *anti* [against] *nomos* [law]).

Tension caused by submission to a superior force was a familiar theme in Galatia. Although the province was under the dominating force of Rome, it was never completely controlled. Their ancient languages were maintained, in a culture when Greek was the common language, and Graeco-Roman polytheism made only limited inroads into their lives. The often intransigent attitudes and lifestyles of these people made them difficult to govern, resulting in frequent military interventions. Consequently, the emperor Augustus installed two legions of soldiers in the south and settled veterans throughout the area to help pacify the region. There was thus a constant pressure between the superior forces and the Galatian people, with the former seeking to bring about change and force their will on those who regularly resisted it. Now, Paul introduces his readers to a supreme force, the Spirit, whose power is awesome. His desire is also to effect changes in people but his motives are wholesome and benevolent.

The challenge for us relates to whether we willingly work with the Spirit, taking advantage of his wisdom and power, or whether we try to get by without his influence – or worse, rebel against it. Given the readiness of the Spirit to develop fruit in our lives, it is vital that we undertake the responsibility of ensuring that we do everything we can to listen for his guidance – and thus demonstrate that we are walking with him, and appreciating the value of his personal partnership. Often, we fail to realise the commitment of the Spirit to us, and thus assume that he is less willing to mentor us. On some occasions, we do not spend enough time looking in his direction for guidance or patiently listening for his voice. On other occasions, despite his speaking, we fail to obey. This responsibility demands discipline and effort. Our challenge is that we do not slip into exclusively using the Bible as our guide, forgetting that the Spirit who inspired and preceded it also speaks outside it as well as through it.

Ephesians 1:3–14
16. The Holy Spirit seals and guarantees believers

1. Introduction

Paul commences the letter to the Ephesians by metaphorically showering his readers with the blessings of salvation (Eph. 1:3–14).[1] In effect, he offers a Christian version of a Jewish poem of praise to God (*berakah*),[2] which concentrates on the benefits that are available to believers. It functions as a spiral staircase that takes the readers upwards to superlative expressions concerning the spiritual status of believers. They have been chosen from before time (1:4), destined to holiness and blamelessness (1:4), loved as sons of God (1:5–6), redeemed and forgiven as a result of lavish love (1:7–8), and centrally placed in the plan of God for the eschatological future (1:9–10). Before the readers have the opportunity to catch their breath, this extraordinarily long sentence, at least in Greek, concludes with Paul declaring that all that he has said is certain, for the Spirit is his witness, his seal and guarantor. At the commencement of this catalogue of God's gifts, he declares to his readers that they are beneficiaries of the Spirit.

2. The Spirit blesses believers (Eph. 1:3)

Many Bible translations offer the phrase *every spiritual blessing* in 1:3, thus indicating that the blessings given to believers by God are

---

[1] The identity of the specific community addressed in this letter is not certain since the name 'Ephesus' (Eph. 1:1) is missing from some important textual witnesses, though the predominant view of the early church was that it was sent to the city of Ephesus.

[2] Zechariah offers a similar peon of praise, also commencing with the same word 'blessed' (Eph. 1:3, ESV; Luke 1:68–75, ESV); see also Pss 41:1, 13; 66:20; 68:19.

spiritual not material, sacred not secular, timeless not temporary. It is probable, however, that Paul is less desirous to identify God's gifts as *spiritual* and more interested in identifying their source, the Spirit. The phrase translated *every spiritual blessing* may as easily (and more appropriately) be translated 'Spirit blessings' or 'blessings of the Spirit'.[3] It is not that the blessings are 'spiritual' and not 'material', but that all blessings granted to believers are from none other than the Spirit himself. He is the warden of God's treasure house of blessings for believers. Such a translation allows for the possibility of Paul stressing the spring from which the blessings flow, the Spirit, and their place of origin as *the heavenly realms*.

Although the verses that follow clearly identify the benefits of salvation as central to this particular revelation, the Spirit also provides materially and economically. This does not mean that he provides resources on demand, or that health and wealth are guaranteed to believers unconditionally before they die. His sovereign will ensures that his bestowals are always beneficial to us; in everything, he knows best and blesses accordingly with gifts that are appropriate. Believers benefit from God's provision of direction and wisdom, his caring for all aspects of their lives, including their spiritual wellbeing.[4] His resource of good gifts is varied and endless. Most of the readers would have been used to the belief that the gods cursed people, but the notion that they were blessed by God, and in such a magnanimous way, would have been a marvel, especially given that they did not have to coerce God to act thus.

Therefore, the blessings granted to believers by the Spirit may be physical as well as spiritual. His desire is for wholeness, in all areas of life, for those who are his. Wholeness, as defined by God, does not necessarily indicate physical or financial wellbeing; it does not necessarily equate with a trouble-free life. However, it does mean that in whatever circumstances we find ourselves, the Spirit is present to reflect his character through us and to achieve his will for the benefit of others. Sometimes he achieves this in unusual ways; it is the privilege of believers to look for these evidences of his love for them.

David was driving home one evening on a dark and lonely country road; it was to be his final trip as the factory at which he worked was closing down. Winter was coming and a chill had settled around his heart. That morning, their family Bible reading had been Ephesians

---

[3] G. D. Fee, *God's Empowering Presence* (Hendrickson, 1994), p. 666.

[4] H.W. Hoehner, in *Ephesians. An Exegetical Commentary* (Baker, 2002), p. 166, notes that in the OT, the concept of blessings referred to 'benefits from God in the sense of possessions, prosperity, or power'.

1, and the comment in the Bible study notes offered the statement, 'the Spirit is interested in blessing his people'. He saw a lady standing by a Mercedes; clearly she had a problem and he stopped his car to help. He was the first person she had seen for an hour and she was desperate, cold and frightened as the snow and darkness crept over the road. Within an hour, he had resolved the problem and she was able to be on her way. Before she left, she asked what she could pay him. He suggested that she should bless someone as he had blessed her. She accepted this and drove on, stopping at a small restaurant some miles further on. A waitress who was clearly pregnant served her and smiled as she did. When she finished her meal, the woman left payment for the meal on the table, leaving the restaurant before she had been given her change. Picking up the money, which included an unusually substantial tip, the waitress noticed a napkin on which the lady had written, 'Someone blessed me today and I want to bless you too.' The waitress was David's wife. It was a small gesture that David recognized as a sign of the presence of the Spirit who supervised his day and that of his wife.

3. The Spirit dwells in heavenly places (Eph. 1:3)

Such a supply of blessings is associated by Paul with *heavenly realms*, a phrase not used elsewhere by Paul other than in this letter (Eph. 1:20; 2:6; 3:10; 6:12). It was understood by many ancient people to refer to the sphere of existence of spirit beings (3:10; 6:12). This was particularly so in Ephesus, which had a strong tradition of magical practices that relied on the spirits to empower such magic.[5] One of the most popular magical customs related to 'Ephesian letters'. These were spells that were believed to have power to protect the bearer, fulfil one's desires, ensure success and generally achieve what was beyond one's natural capacity. The spirits that were believed to grant authority to such written and verbal incantations were assumed to live above the skies *in the heavenly realms*. Also, the term was used as a synonym for God in non-Jewish and Jewish writings. The Spirit of whom Paul speaks lives where deities were assumed to live and is himself divine. Thus, Paul uses the phrase, for it was especially relevant for his readers (Acts 19:13–19).[6] It is a

---

[5] See further C. E. Arnold, *Ephesians: Power and Magic* (Cambridge University Press, 1989), pp. 5–40.

[6] The common magical practices in Ephesus provide a useful context to the assertion by Luke that the miracles of Paul were 'extraordinary' (Acts 19:11); to people who were used to the supernatural, the miracles (by definition, supranormal) of God through Paul were identified as being of a very different order.

familiar term and Paul uses it to express a helpful concept relating to the authority of the Spirit who is intimately related to believers.

The blessings referred to by Paul are not waiting for the believer in heaven but are derived from heaven, where the Spirit and Jesus are (Eph. 1:20; 2:6). The blessings entrusted to believers are not manufactured on earth, or created by people, or contrived by chance. A heavenly deity, the Spirit, has processed them and provided them for believers. The one who lives there reigns supreme, having subjugated all other powers that were assumed to dwell there (2:21–22) and out of his riches, he grants blessings. Believers are thus characterized and contextualized by heaven and the Spirit who dwells there.

Ancient people believed in gods who were often arbitrarily malevolent. To protect themselves from these and demons, they often resorted to magic. People longed to be redeemed from the instability of human existence, especially the painful experiences caused by those malicious and powerful beings which lived in the heavenly places (Eph. 1:21; 2:2; 3:10; 6:12). Paul informs the readers that they are safe from such concerns for the one who dwells in *heavenly realms* is on their side, his many blessings to them being evidence of that fact. They are not tantalizingly packaged for a future occasion but placed in the lives of believers to be unwrapped and enjoyed in the present.

However, it is also possible that Paul is not just asserting that the blessings granted to believers come from one who is seated in the realm of the divine but that he has elevated believers to be there also. Paul is determined to enlighten believers concerning the proximity of the Spirit to them (Eph. 1:13; 2:18, 22; 3:20; 4:3; 5:18). Given this determination, it is likely that he also here introduces his readers to the notion that not only does the Spirit bestow blessings on believers, but that the greatest and most fundamental is his bestowal of himself. He welcomes believers into relationship with himself so that wherever he is, so are they; wherever they are, so is he.

4. The Spirit seals believers (Eph. 1:13)

Paul climaxes his prose of praise with a reference to the Spirit sealing believers. The Spirit is given to all believers before they have a chance to merit him. Although not specifically mentioned, the reference to sealing is a description of that event which takes place at salvation,[7] though some assume that it may refer to a subsequent experience,

---

[7] A. T. Lincoln, *Ephesians* (Word, 1990), pp. 38–40; Fee, *God's Empowering Presence*, p. 670.

often associated with water baptism,[8] or a later experience with the Spirit.[9] In Ephesians 1:13, Paul specifies that it is because of faith in Christ that the believer is sealed with the Spirit. It is important to remember that the Spirit who provides this sealing is described as holy (*hagios*). He is holy and thus different from all other deities; in fact, he is unique – he is not to be feared, for all he has to give is good.

Paul identifies the Spirit as being a seal of the believer (2 Cor. 1:22; Eph. 1:13; 4:30). The concept of 'sealing' provides Paul with an opportunity to explore the radical role of the Spirit in the granting of salvation to believers. The practice of sealing letters, objects (Rom. 15:28; Rev. 6:1, 3, 5, 7) and even people (Rom. 4:11; 1 Cor. 9:2; Rev. 7:4–8) was common in the ancient world, and symbolized a number of features. Any of these may have stimulated Paul to use the practice in order to explore the comprehensive nature of the Spirit's involvement in the life of a believer. Seals were generally generated by impressions in wax of a name or design that represented the owner, similar to the way farmers still brand or mark their livestock to identify to whom they belong.

Fundamentally, the seal signified ownership; it identified the sealed object as being genuine or authentic – the sealed item (livestock, slaves or objects) was owned by someone. The fact that the believer is sealed with the Holy Spirit indicates that the one who arranged for the sealing to occur, namely Christ, owns him. What would have been a surprise to the Jews and a shock to Gentiles is that the latter were included in this process (Eph. 2:11–22; 3:6). In a

---

[8] However, there is little evidence in the NT that water baptism is the occasion for this event (see Fee, *God's Empowering Presence*, p. 670, Lincoln, *Ephesians*, p. 40.

[9] See Fee (*God's Empowering Presence*, pp. 294–296; 670) and Hoehner (*Ephesians*, p. 237) for a discussion of the options. Some (H. Ervin, *Conversion-Initiation and the Baptism in the Holy Spirit: An Engaging Critique of James D. G. Dunn's Baptism in the Holy Spirit* [Hendrickson, 1984]) point to the aorist tense of the word, 'believing', suggesting that it implies a prior conversion experience followed by an experience of sealing, often associated with an infusion of supernatural power. However, the aorist tense is not always used to describe a past event but, as here, to refer to a distinct event. The occurrences are separate, but not in time. D. M. Lloyd-Jones (*God's Ultimate Purpose. An Exposition of Ephesians One* [Banner of Truth Trust, 1978], pp. 248–300) also argues for a experience of sealing that follows the act of salvation and associates it with an assurance of salvation. However, Paul relates the act of sealing to the event itself and not to any assurance that it occurred. Both Ervin and Lloyd-Jones indicate that this is an experience that should be sought. There is little evidence in this passage, however, that indicates that the sealing referred to by Paul should be sought by believers. This is an active work of the Spirit, believers being passive recipients of it. However, there is no doubt that power for service, and assurance of salvation, are both integrally related to the work of the Spirit in the lives of believers.

society which was increasingly becoming inhospitable to Christians – where persecution was to soon replace peace, where suffering and pain were to drown out songs of praise – it was a timely reminder by Paul that, although they were increasingly disowned, God had specifically chosen to own them. The Spirit is the guarantee of that fact.

A seal also signified safety and security (Deut. 32:34; Isa. 8:16). Matthew records that the stone that was rolled in front of Jesus' tomb was sealed (27:66). Even though that was achieved by a length of easily breakable material stretched across the stone, it represented the authority of Rome, and thus remained intact because of the consequences of someone tampering with it. Seals represented security. Items that had been sealed by a signature or imprint of a purchaser in the marketplace or harbour were deemed to be no longer for sale. The seal protected them even from being removed. Not only does God own believers but he ensures their safety by the presence of the seal, the Spirit. He is God's marker, God's message, warning off any potential aggressors – 'Hands off; touch them and you answer to me' (Ezek. 9:4–6; Rev. 7:1–8). Not only were the Ephesian believers a minority group in what was, at times, an antagonistic environment, but also society, as a whole, was unstable economically, socially and nationally because of regular upheavals in the Empire. Paul's message to the readers is clear – the Spirit is their seal to ensure that they realize that their security is set by none other than the one who owns all authority.

Seals were also used to signify that a transaction had been completed. When Jeremiah was instructed by God to buy a field (Jer. 32:7) he did so, sealing the deal in the presence of witnesses (32:10–14). At that point, neither he nor the vendor could change their mind. The purchase had been completed; the field now belonged to Jeremiah. Even though he was due to go away (into exile) for years, the field would always be his and redeemable when he returned (32:8). The moment the Spirit comes into the life of a believer, the process of salvation is not only commenced but, in a sense, it is also concluded. The seal ensures that the procedure initiated cannot now be stopped. It is possible that there was a lurking fear in the minds of the readers that something was lacking in their salvation. Paul emphatically states that they are saved, the seal of the Spirit being the present and certain confirmation of that fact.

Perhaps the most significant aspect of the process for Paul in his explication of the relationship between God and believers is that the sealed item was valuable to the owner. Ordinary objects were not sealed – they could easily be replaced. However, items that received a seal were thereby marked off as being special. To believers who had

211

already experienced mistreatment, rejection and even persecution, such a timeless lesson was priceless. Although others treated them as worthless, God had estimated them as being valuable, so much so that he had provided them with his inestimable Spirit to whisper constantly to them that they were treasured by God. Although it is not certain that the readers would have had each of these concepts in mind when they read of the seal in this passage, it does demonstrate that there was a wide range of potential reference points that would have been meaningful to them, and which enabled them to appreciate the significance of the action of the Spirit on their behalf.

5. The Spirit acts as a guarantee (Eph. 1:14)

In Ephesians 1:14 (also 2 Cor. 1:21–22; 5:5), Paul uses the word *arrabōn* (guarantee, down-payment) in relationship to the Spirit. He is God's first installment to the believer and as such, he acts as a guarantee for all that is to come, a promise for the future.

The Spirit, in particular, guarantees something that is yet to occur in the future – an inheritance, the identity of which is most significant. Although it may be assumed that the inheritance describes a legacy to be granted to believers throughout their lives, but especially after death, Paul has a much more startling revelation to impart. Paul identifies believers as being God's inheritance. In the OT, the nation of Israel is often referred to as God's inheritance.[10] Now however, the Spirit discloses that Christians are to be included among those who are to be redeemed as God's inheritance. It would be a gracious act of God to present gifts to believers after death, but for them to be presented to God as a gift for him to enjoy is remarkable; indeed, such a concept is so astonishing that if the Spirit did not affirm it, no one would believe it.

In the Bible, the concept of redemption, where it relates to people, is always an act initiated by God (Deut. 14:2; Isa. 43:1; Mal. 3:17; Acts 20:28; 1 Pet. 2:9). It is probable that the same perception is being addressed here. The remarkable fact which Paul articulates is that believers are to be God's possession and inheritance. The Spirit is the pledge that God will fully redeem believers as his own possession (Eph. 4:30). Little wonder that the author concludes the verse (and section) by offering praise to God for the quality of loving care and security that belongs to believers; they are loved beyond their understanding.

As a fire was constantly maintained in the centre of Ephesus as a

---

[10] Deut. 32:29; Pss 33:12; 74:2; Isa. 63:17; Mic. 7:18.

symbol of its security, so also the Spirit is an eternal flame, whose presence guarantees the everlasting nature of believers. Not only are they elevated to heavenly places, but heaven has come to dwell in them. For some, fear may have crept into their minds because Jesus had not returned despite his having promised that he would. Paul reminds them that the Spirit would guarantee them in the absence of Jesus' return and ensure that when he did, they would be what God had always intended, his special inheritance. The Spirit is the heavenly bodyguard who is entrusted with the responsibility of ensuring that we reach our eternal destination. It is a task he takes up willingly, pursues it faithfully and achieves it successfully, the hope of the future being as secure as is his personal seal in the present.

The experience of many of the readers with regard to the gods they served before they became believers was very mixed. Generally, people assumed that the gods were apathetic towards people, this also being a foundational precept in some of the major philosophical schools of the era. The suggestion that they might wish to develop a relationship with people was rarely entertained. For Paul, however, Christianity was not a distant religion in which God is remote; the fact that Jesus had ascended did not signal that he was absent. The remarkable aspect of Christianity is that the Spirit has taken up residence within the worshipper, functioning as a constant reminder of the superlative quality of their position as believers. If doubts creep in to their minds, they are encouraged to remember that the Spirit, and all that he is and does, has been promised (Eph. 1:13).

In 2 Corinthians 1:22, Paul adds that the Spirit has been given as a guarantee 'in our hearts'. Given the understanding by the ancient reader that the heart indicated the centre of the will and volition, its use by Paul demonstrates the centrality of the gift of the Spirit, in that he is presented as being the one who is able to affect the emotions, the mind and the will of the believer. Such commitment on the part of the Spirit is inestimable. Although Paul teaches that the Spirit has promised good gifts that are to come, he also reminds his readers that the Spirit himself is the promise. The Spirit is primary in importance and thus superior to all the good gifts he gives. The readers do not need to concern themselves with the possibility that they have presumptuously assumed these truths. The fact is that God has promised the Spirit to be their seal and guarantee. All they have is because of him and it is all centrally located in the sovereign plan of God.

The resident Spirit functions as evidence of the fact that God owns believers, assessing them as of significant value to keep safe until their eternal destiny has been reached. The powerful Spirit guards believers and embraces them in his care. The significance

213

of the truths in these verses is of paramount importance for us as believers. When we are overwhelmed, we need to remember that we are still overshadowed by the Spirit. When we are under pressure, we are simultaneously under the controlling influence of the Spirit. When we are in a crisis, we are still in the Spirit's care. When fear grips us, the Spirit grips us tighter. When we find ourselves struggling awhile, we are sealed in with the Spirit himself forever. He is the guarantee that our journey will reach its conclusion even though it is beyond time. He is the one who marks us out as special people, partners us in the adventure and also welcomes us home at the end.

Ephesians 2:11–22
17. The Holy Spirit provides access to God

1. Introduction

Dr Martyn Lloyd-Jones writes of Ephesians 2:18, 'There is nothing beyond this; this is the very top. The acme. This is the quintessence of the Christian faith and the Christian position . . . one of the most glorious statements that is to be found in the whole range of Scripture.'[1] The remarkable proximity of the Spirit to the believer is worthy of enquiry, in order that we be amazed by such a truth. At the same time, the more we appreciate the potential for change as a result of encountering the Spirit, the greater the possibility that we may be transformed. From Ephesians 2:1, Paul has explored the radical change that has occurred in the lives of his readers since their salvation. They have been transformed, Paul graphically illustrating the fundamental nature of this change by identifying their previous existence as death (Eph. 2:1, 5), whereas now they are alive with Christ (2:5). Once they followed the ways of the world, the prince of the power of the air (2:2), and their own sinful desires (2:3), but now they are seated with Christ (2:6), saved through faith (2:8), and given the opportunity to explore 'the incomparable riches of his grace' (2:7). All this has been achieved by the love, mercy and grace of God (2:4–5, 7–8).

From Ephesians 2:11–17, he reminds the Gentiles among his readers that they are no longer separated from Christ (Eph. 2:12); now, Jews and Gentiles have been reconciled to God through Jesus (2:16). As such, both nationalities are privileged to enter the presence of God, a process made possible by the Spirit.

[1] D. M. Lloyd-Jones, *God's Way of Reconciliation* (Banner of Truth, 1972), p. 310.

2. The Spirit provides a welcome (Eph. 2:18)

Believers are described by Paul as benefiting from being *in one Spirit* (2:18, ESV). The phrase 'in one Spirit' is probably intended to describe the sphere in which believers now live; they are spiritually alive because of the Spirit's sustaining care. They walk with the Spirit, they are empowered by the Spirit and the context of their life is the Spirit. Because they are so closely related to the Spirit, they have continuous access into God's presence. The supreme status of the Spirit, who wraps himself around every believer, makes it inevitable that wherever he is, they are also. Since he is God, that means they are constantly in the presence of God.

Paul wrote to people who lived in an era where huge inequalities existed; the same exist today, a feature that is even more pronounced in the Majority World. Many different doors are closed to people who do not possess the right credentials for entry. The same occurred in ancient Ephesus, at the heart of which was the agora (110 metres square), a place where many activities took place, relating to politics, entertainment, education, religion and commerce. It also housed the Advisory Council, where legal cases were heard and judicial decisions were pronounced. It was known as the *Ecclesia*, a term used elsewhere in the letter for the church (Eph. 1:22; 5:24–32). However, not everyone was allowed into this protected place; the marginalized were locked out.

The message of Paul to his readers confirms them as wholeheartedly welcomed into the *ecclesia* (church) of God and indeed, into his very presence, because they are constantly marked out as people of the Spirit – those who desire to walk with the Spirit, those with whom the Spirit has chosen to walk. No priests or priestesses are needed to introduce them to the deity, no calling cards have to be offered, no appointments pre-arranged. There is no fear of interrupting God with one's presence, no double booking, no anxiety as to the nature of his response. The Spirit has ensured a place in the centre of God's presence, for that is where he already resides.

Previous access to God was through the temple and that for only a very small, special selection of Israelites. Now, it is in association with the Spirit and anyone and everyone is welcome, at any time and anywhere. Church is not the place believers visit every week. It is the place where God chooses to stay permanently. It is not where believers go in order to hear from God; it is who and where believers are, as a result of which God can speak to them.

3. The Spirit provides access to God (Eph. 2:18)

It appears that Paul wishes to deepen the understanding of the readers with regard to the significance of the presence of the Spirit in their lives, with specific reference to their proximity to God. Thus, he uses the term, *access* (Eph. 2:18) to describe the entrée to God created by the Spirit for believers.[2] Even though the Spirit is God, Paul paints a literary picture that aims to create a more remarkable impression on his readers. Despite his divine status, the Spirit is presented as undertaking a service for believers, resulting in their being presented to God in a superlative fashion; they are located in the very presence of God himself.

The term 'access' (*prosagōgē*) was used in a variety of ways in the ancient world. It described the informal process undertaken when introducing people to one another, but also was used, in some ancient cultures, in a more technical sense, in which someone was designated to present a person to a more important dignitary. Such a presenter was identified as a *prosagogue*. Perhaps more significantly, however, the term is used to refer to unhindered entrance or open access. Rather than the Spirit being viewed as introducing believers to God, Paul encourages believers to realize that because of the Spirit's association with them, they have been provided with direct right of entry to God.

The *prosagogue* was employed on a number of occasions, each of which has value in identifying the close relationship established by the Spirit between the believer and God. However, before these are explored, it is important to remember that Paul's presentation must not be illegitimately applied. For example, it would be inaccurate to suggest that the Spirit is needed to introduce the believer to the Father as if the latter was unaware of the believer. Nor is it valid to assume that the Spirit is simply involved in a formal procedure of introducing believers to the Father.

Paul offers a metaphor to highlight certain truths but, as a metaphor, it cannot fully describe the depths of the reality. Nor should it be interpreted to mean what it was never intended to indicate. As a metaphor, it has boundaries: its main intention is to provide a picture that may help to shed light on a truth that is fundamentally

---

[2] In Eph. 3:12, Paul refers to access to God being provided for by Jesus. He is not contradicting himself here by referring to the Spirit as the one who provides access. Rather, he is demonstrating the integral role of Jesus and the Spirit in the process of integrating believers into relationship with God. Although there is a tendency for many Christians to distinguish the members of the Godhead so that they almost take up separate modes of existence, Paul is more at home with a dynamic Trinity where the persons function interdependently.

inexplicable. Where it may be difficult for some truths to be comprehensively unpacked, metaphors help to move in that direction and to enable the beauty of the truth to be enjoyed, at least in part. Some of the fundamental aspects of this portrait of the Spirit have significant practical applications.

Wherever believers are, for example, they cannot be closer to God, for they are where the Spirit is and he is God. The fact that Paul uses the present continuous tense, 'we have' (*echomen*), indicates that this access is available continuously. It is not that the Spirit constantly interrupts the Father by announcing our presence, but that it is impossible for the believer to exist outside God's presence. Access to the Father is the present privilege and possession of the believer. Such open access to God must not be taken for granted, overlooked or ignored. On the contrary, such a sensational concession should be enjoyed and explored, but respectfully and sensitively (Heb. 4:16).

The *prosagogue* was used to present people to their superiors in order to serve them. Similarly, believers are encouraged to recognize that God is desirous of using them to fulfil his purposes. Even though he could achieve his objectives more easily, completely, efficiently and perfectly himself, he chooses to use inadequate, weak, imperfect believers. The one who created the universe prefers to provide believers with opportunities to be with him, serving with him, being resourced by him, despite that fact that he could sovereignly and supremely complete his agenda with no outside help.

In the earlier verses of this chapter, Paul has emphasized the separation between God and Gentiles, designated as objects of his 'wrath' (Eph. 2:3), 'separate from Christ' (2:12), 'excluded . . . and foreigners' (2:12, 19), 'without God' (2:12), once 'far away' (2:13, 17), and in a state of hostility (2:14, 16). However, because of their faith in Jesus, there has been a radical transformation in their relationship with God. Now, they have been 'brought near' (2:13, 17), peace has been established between God and them (2:14, 15), barriers have been destroyed (2:14) and reconciliation has taken place (2:16), for now they are 'members of God's household' (2:19). Having established this remarkable reversal, Paul now inserts a graphic illustration of its significance by referring to the Spirit as the one who provides access to the most special place imaginable – the intimate presence of God, his private space.

4. The Spirit forms believers into a temple for God (Eph. 2:21)

Paul has not finished exploring the sensational nature of the relationship of the believer with God as facilitated by the Spirit. He now uses the metaphor of a temple to elucidate a further truth. Not only is God accessible to believers, but also the Spirit makes believers accessible to God (Eph. 2:22); not only does the Spirit bring the believer into the closest proximity to God but, also, he seeks to identify that God is centrally located in them. Thus, he describes the readers as being part of a 'holy temple' (2:21), a metaphor he has used elsewhere (1 Cor. 3:16–17; 2 Cor. 6:16; 2 Thess. 2:4). The term used for 'temple' (*naos*) is significant in that it is often used to describe the most important part of the temple, the Holy of Holies; the temple precincts are referred to as *hieron* (1 Cor. 9:13). The implication is that believers are being developed by the Spirit as a community in which God chooses to dwell as he did in the central location of the ancient temple. They are viewed by him as a special base for his dynamic presence, as was the tabernacle or the Holy of Holies in the Jerusalem temple.

Such a notion would have been startling to Jewish readers. For them, the Jerusalem temple was most significant as the place where God's glory was believed to dwell. For this privileged role to be transferred to the church would have been extraordinary. That Gentiles were to be included as part of that community would have provided an even more challenging message to them. The picture presented by Paul is of Jewish and Gentile believers in community with one another, a community in which God chooses to place himself. Of course, though a momentous privilege, this is a challenging responsibility. As Fee states, 'God not only dwells among his people, but is himself present, by the Spirit, within his people, sanctifying their present earthly existence and stamping it with his own eternity.'[3] Believers should conduct themselves not as if God lives at a distance in heaven but in recognition that he exists in immediate proximity to them. Furthermore, the bodies of the believers, as the individual habitations of the Spirit (1 Cor. 3:16–17; 6:19–20), are to be the channels of righteous lifestyles. The presence of God in believers accentuates the challenge for morality in their lives. The fact that they share this corporate body with other believers should be a motivation to holiness. Their actions make waves that can affect others, positively and negatively.

The significance of the temple imagery for Ephesian readers is astonishing. Many temples dominated Ephesus. Indeed, on two occasions, Ephesus was honoured by being named as 'temple warden' (*neokoros*) for emperor worship for the province. The most important deity venerated in Ephesus was Artemis (or Diana to the Romans) who was believed to be the ruler and mother of everything. Her fame spread beyond the Roman Empire, as far as Egypt to the South, Mesopotamia to the East and Scandinavia to the North. Her temple

---

[3] G. D. Fee, *God's Empowering Presence* (Hendrickson, 1994), p.136.

THE MESSAGE OF THE HOLY SPIRIT

in Ephesus was one of the seven wonders of the ancient world, measuring 70 by 130 metres, the roof resting on seventy columns, each
two metres wide and twenty metres tall. The image of Artemis was
believed to have fallen from the sky (Acts 19:35) and was kept in the
temple. Indeed, most ancient temples were created to act as a shrine
to the god, not as a place for worship or communal gatherings for
religious activities. Most religious activities, including sacrifices, actually took place outside the temple. Paul's message is thus appropriate
for he is stating that, in common with the main purpose of temples,
believers have been charged with the responsibility and privilege of
being the receptacle of God, destined to be the home in which he
chooses to live; the address of God on this earth is the church.

In contrast to the many Ephesian temples, God had only one temple
in pagan Ephesus – the believers. Theirs was a major responsibility,
for they were the ones who were to reflect God to the people. In 1
Corinthians 3:17, the readers are reminded that they are a 'holy' temple.
This refers to the need for them to exhibit righteous lives but, more
fundamentally, that they realize that God has set them apart – and
therefore that they are to manifest such distinctiveness in their lives.
The potential is that, as a result of their becoming more like him, others
will want to become more like them, and thus eventually like him.

Again, Paul astonishes his readers by revealing the surprising fact
that God entrusts himself to believers who are to act as the base of
his operations in the world. Ancient temples were used as banks to
store valuables but the church is identified as containing a treasure
of inestimable value – God himself. God is everywhere on this
planet, but he is particularly present in his people.

Too often believers treat their relationship with God as that which
becomes active on Sundays or when with other believers. However,
Paul's message is that, because of their relationship with the Spirit,
believers should daily immerse themselves in the most significant
benefit of that bond – access to God. They must walk carefully
therein but they can do so boldly: respectful but also rejoicing;
enthralled but also excited; impressed but also intrigued; challenged
but also changed; lost in wonder but also lost in love and praise.

5. The Spirit forms believers into a dwelling place for the Lord (Eph. 2:22)

This is the only time Paul uses the word *dwelling* (*katoikētērion*).[4]
He emphasizes the fact that believers are the habitation of God by

---

[4] Its only other reference is Rev. 18:2.

declaring that they have been *built together* (Eph. 2:22) to create a habitat for God. Furthermore, he describes this as being *in the Spirit* (2:22, RSV). This probably describes the fact that because of their life in the sphere of the Spirit, they now automatically become the dwelling place of God.[5] Thus, Paul continues to create metaphors to help them realize their proximity to God; they are in the Spirit, therefore, God is in them.[6] These statements are not intended to comprehensively explain or even define these facts but to move in the direction of portraying something which is fundamentally inexplicable – believers and God are inextricably linked to one another, because the former are immersed in the Spirit.

Paul identifies this united relationship also in 1 Corinthians 6:17, where he reminds the readers that as a result of the Spirit, believers have been joined to the Lord, resulting in them being spiritually united with him. The language cannot bear the weight of the inestimable truth that Paul is revealing, nor can one's intellect accommodate it. It is extraordinary and gracious, the result of the Creator arranging for his created beings to house him. He who inhabits eternity also inhabits humanity, weak and flawed at that. It is by an act of the divine will that the Spirit centralizes the believer into God's place of residence.[7] Such is the unique quality of salvation that, without believers doing anything, they become part of the dwelling place of God.

The responsibilities of engaging in such close proximity with the Spirit are not to be overlooked. When Ananias and Sapphira lied to Peter about the amount of money they had gained from the sale of some property, they had also, in effect, lied to the Spirit (Acts 5:3, 9). The Spirit is so inextricably joined to the church that sin takes on a different dimension. The Spirit takes it seriously; it is not committed by the believer and acknowledged from a distance by the Spirit. On the contrary, his immediate presence in the church means that sin is registered quickly, and believers need to recognise that his response is not necessarily only to offer forgiveness. Sometimes, the future usefulness of individual believers may demand being more rigorously refined by the Spirit.

But the potential of such a relationship is immense. Russell

[5] Fee, *God's Empowering Presence*, pp. 684–685; H.W. Hoehner, *Ephesians. An Exegetical Commentary* (Baker, 2002), p. 389.

[6] He has already identified them as being 'in Christ' (Eph. 2:7, 10, 13).

[7] It is also possible that in using the phrase 'in the Spirit', Paul is also seeking to identify the Spirit as the one who dynamically and deliberately creates this immediacy between God and the believer. However, the metaphor must not be pushed too far; the miracle of grace must not be lost in spending too much time seeking for an explanation that will completely satisfy the intellect.

Herman Conwell was born in 1843 and became a lawyer and a minister. One day, a young man told him he would have loved to go to college but it was too expensive for him. Conwell, at that moment, decided to build a university for poor, but deserving, students. He was inspired in this quest by a story that he had heard earlier in his life. It involved a South African farmer who sold his farm to search for diamonds. Unfortunately, although he travelled hundreds of miles, he never found any. In his despair, he jumped into a river and drowned, a penniless failure whose dream had turned into desolation. A few years later, a man who had purchased the farmer's land found an unusual rock and took it home where it was noticed by a friend who later informed him that it was the biggest diamond that had ever been discovered. The farm was transformed into the Kimberly Diamond Mine – the richest in the world.

The story inspired Conwell to recognise that each person has the potential for great things if they but develop the ground on which they stand, the life which they have been given, and the dream to which they aspire. He established Temple University in Philadelphia, raising six million dollars in the process. Believers have been granted the privilege of being the recipients of a relationship with God who has resources that are made freely available in order that aspirations can be achieved, visions can be accomplished and destinies can be reached against the odds. Let us not be slow to chase the dreams God has given to us, in partnership with the resourceful Spirit.

Ephesians 4:1–16, 25–32
18. The Holy Spirit and unity

1. Introduction

When I was nineteen, I joined Operation Mobilization for a year's evangelism in Europe. As preparation, I was sent a collection of sermons to listen to. Although a number were dedicated to evangelistic issues, I was surprised that the first concentrated on the topic of unity. I could not understand the relevance of such a subject to young people who were dedicated to telling others about Jesus. I soon learned the wisdom of those who had indicated that we needed to actively consider the importance of unity. As I spent time in small groups of people engaging in mission in Belgium, Italy and England, differences and potentially divisive issues crept into our time together that could have caused dissension and spoiled our mission activities. Unity is a treasure for believers to seek with each other. Unity is targeted by the devil, to break up relationships and fellowship in the church today. Words that I learnt years ago still ring true today – 'To love the world, for me is no chore. My only real problem is my neighbour next door.' The tragedy is that this can too easily define our relationships with other believers.

The plea for unity and the plague of disunity is noted throughout the pages of the Bible. In writing his first letter to the church in Corinth, Paul spends the first four chapters dealing with these themes, and thereafter identifies a lack of harmony and cohesion amongst the believers as the cause of all their many problems. It is little wonder that Jesus prays for unity among his followers (John 17:11). The potential for harming the church by disunity is greater than for most other sins. Disunity distracts from the core mission of the church, which is to reflect God with integrity to other believers and unbelievers, the latter generally only seeing God through the former.

I was startled to read a sermon by a Muslim cleric who called for unity amongst Muslims in his community. He identified division as the greatest problem facing Islamic religious leaders today and pointed out the dangers of disunity, providing evidence from the Qur'an. However, the most troubling sentence of the sermon was his plea that unity should be encouraged because 'disunity and division are characteristics of the disbelievers' – those who worship a God other than Allah. When Christians poorly reflect the harmony so desired by Jesus and Paul, the results are tragic.

The intensive nature of Paul's exhortation to the Ephesians to live worthily (Eph. 4:1) is significant (*parakaleō*: I urge, exhort). That he also inserts an emphatic personal pronoun 'I' (*egō*), and reminds them of his captivity, further serves to remind the readers of the importance of this issue and the seriousness of his exhortation. He dedicates the first three chapters of his letter to a description of the remarkable commitment of the Spirit to them – blessing them (1:3), sealing them (1:13), acting as their guarantee (1:14), providing wisdom and revelation (1:17; 3:4, 5), initiating ongoing access to God (2:18), forming believers into a dwelling place for God (2:22), and empowering (3:16) and filling them (3:19). It is not surprising that the first word of this new section in Greek commences with the word, 'Therefore' (4:1). Because of their privileged position as believers, they are to take seriously the expectations anticipated of them. The climax of his hope and a central component of a worthy life is that they will experience unity (4:3).

2. The Spirit of unity (Eph. 4:1–6)

Unity is a precious commodity and Paul emphasizes this by providing a sevenfold list of 'ones', commencing with the reference to *one body*, concluding with *one God and Father of all*. The body of believers exists because the one God has chosen to be their father and to welcome them as children, whose privilege it is to share the common bond of being in a family. The *one hope* they have is an eternal one (4:4) where, in the absence of sin, perfect harmony is to characterize their existence. It is to this quality of unity that they have been called (4:4), a unity that has already been initiated (4:3) and is characterized by the Spirit (4:4).[1] They are to maintain and guard that unity consistently and continuously in their relationships

---

[1] The commencing words 'There is' (Eph. 4:4) are not in the original Greek; they have been included to provide a clearer reading of the text. For Paul, however, he presents the truth starkly – 'one body and one Spirit'.

with one another because of, and with the help of, the Spirit. The quality of this unity is characterized by the word *peace* (4:3). Paul is encouraging them to actively strive for unity while recognizing that, as a fruit of the Spirit (Gal. 5:22), walking with the Spirit will result in peace being expressed through them.

The unity expected by Paul is identified by the explanatory virtues located in Ephesians 4:2. It is a unity that is characterized by lowliness (or humility), meekness (or gentleness, courtesy), patience, forbearance (or a readiness to be faithful to others) and love, each identified as fruit of the Spirit (Gal. 5:22–23). It is not peace at any price or unity that is based on weak compromise. It is the kind of unity that is reflected in the inter-dependent relationship within the Godhead, which comprises *one Spirit . . . one Lord* and *one . . . Father* (4:4–6), a perfect trinitarian unity. It involves a dedication to maintaining honourable principles of behaviour and an unquestioning loyalty to each other. This is a high calling, a super-human task that needs the help of the Spirit.

Because of its importance to the destiny of the church and the heart of the Spirit, however, it also demands a careful and robust commitment on the part of every believer. Each one is to take responsibility for the development of others, edifying them and giving them a reason to believe that their presence in the church is vital. Increasing the self-confidence of other believers, as well as enabling them to advance from their potential into the reality of service to God and others, is a privilege and responsibility of every believer. Indeed, it is not surprising that Paul uses the word *oikodomeō* (build up) to conclude this section (4:16). He also uses it to identify the anticipated result of God's plan of providing gifts of leadership to his church to 'build up' believers (4:12). Such an activity will result in Paul's exhortation for unity to be practically realized (4:13). The only other time this word for 'unity' (*henotēs*) is used by Paul is in 4:3; it is no coincidence – it commences and concludes this section, its importance central to the whole. The unity that is characteristic of the Spirit and derived from the Spirit has the potential of being a reality in the church if believers follow him and those God has gifted to them.

Geese have much to teach believers about unity. The reason they fly in a vee-formation is of great significance for as each bird flaps its wings, it creates uplift for the bird that follows. It has been estimated that by flying in such a formation, they add at least 70% greater flying range when compared to one bird flying alone. Therefore, they aim to fly in concord with one another. When the leader becomes tired, another goose takes its place. Furthermore, it is thought that geese honk to encourage the leaders to keep going and when a goose gets sick, or becomes exhausted and falls out of the formation, others join it to help and protect it, staying with it until it is able to fly again or until it dies. Only then do they join the main group or another one. When believers recognise the importance of community, they will achieve higher standards of togetherness and a clearer sense of direction. The Spirit has a similar vision of interdependency and mutual support with reference to believers in the church. He is working to establish such a community and, therefore, so should we.

3. Aids to unity (Eph. 4:11–16)

Paul stresses that it is not the responsibility of the believer to initiate unity, for that has already been achieved by the Spirit; they are to maintain it (Eph. 4:3). Although he does not outline a framework for the maintenance and protection of this unity, the rest of the chapter offers ample guidelines. In Ephesians 4:2–3, he emphasizes the foundational need of love, meekness and a determination to excel in sustaining a strong commitment to unity. Thereafter, he identifies leaders who are placed in the church by God to develop mature believers who exist in a communal context of love (4:11–16). He follows these facts with clear suggestions for the development of harmony and inter-dependency (4:25 – 6:9), reminding the readers of their corporate enemy, the devil (6:10–12). They have a significant source to enable them to follow Paul's advice – the Spirit (5:18). If they rely on him and the resources he offers (6:13–18), they will be able to maintain the unity that has been initiated by the Spirit.

God has placed people in the church who have been gifted to facilitate its mission and development. They have a significant role in assisting believers to achieve their aim of experiencing unity. In Ephesians 4:11, Paul identifies apostles, prophets, evangelists, pastors and teachers (or pastor-teachers) as having foundational roles in the church. Their major responsibility is to release believers to minister on behalf of, and to, the church (4:12), in order to bring about unity and maturity (4:13–16). On other occasions, Paul identifies gifts of the Spirit that are manifested through believers but, here, he concentrates on the fact that there are individuals who are themselves gifts to the church, enabled to function in particular ways as a result of the empowering work of the Spirit. It is not *charismata* that are being defined here so much as the identification of Christ's gift of the Spirit to his church (4:7).[2] It is because of the

---

[2] The word used by Paul here for 'gift' (*dōrea*) is used of an unmerited, free gift (also 3:7). The fact that the feast of Pentecost was associated with Psalm 68, from

Spirit that believers can be facilitated to engage in ministry. He is the one who has initiated the plan that empowers leaders to enable believers to fulfil *works of service, so that the body of Christ may be built up* (4:12).

The gifts given to the church are identified by Paul as being to *equip the saints* (Eph. 4:12, ESV). The word used by Paul for 'equip' (*katartismos*) is only used here in its noun form in the NT, though it is used thirteen times as a verb where it refers to restoration (Gal. 6:1), mending (of nets, Matt. 4:21), preparing something for a purpose (Rom. 9:22; 1 Thess. 3:10), and teaching (Luke 6:40). Its meaning is, therefore, clearly anticipating the achievement of an objective as a result of an action. It was rarely used before the NT, though there, it described the repairing of bones, setting of limbs or restoration in surgery.[3] The value of Christian leaders is in ensuring that those in their Christian communities are prepared, taught and restored; the foundational responsibility is to mentor and make ready a people prepared to function in ministry, and to make a difference in the local church and in the wider constituency. The realization of such aims is to be in the context of unity; it is to be the framework which will enable the church to be built up.

Paul is not desirous of establishing an ecclesiastical model, or identifying ecclesiastical offices, or dividing clergy from laity. The purpose of verse 12 is to stress the functional nature of these roles; they are given to enable believers to fulfil an objective, to achieve a goal, to complete a task. They are not so much offices as they are opportunities for the Spirit to use individuals to enable other believers to continue in the footsteps of the Spirit, fulfilling what he instituted, achieving his objective – the unity and maturing of the church. Jesus who has been exalted (Eph. 4:8) is so committed to his church that he provides those gifts that are needed to ensure the maintenance of its integrity and completeness; his desire is for wholeness in its most comprehensive sense. Not only did he pray for unity among his followers when with them (John 17:11), but he also continues to initiate the means for the fulfillment of this aspiration.

Any movement in this direction of facilitating believers to function effectively in ministry is encapsulated by at least two major characteristics – truth (Eph. 4:15) and love (4:2, 15–16), the latter

---

which Paul quotes (Eph. 4:8), may indicate that he was thinking of the gift of the Spirit to the church when he wrote of 'Christ's gift' (4:7, ESV). As a result of this event, the ministry gifts, that he refers to in 4:11, are manifested.

[3] H.W. Hoehner, *Ephesians. An Exegetical Commentary* (Baker, 2002), p. 549.

being the final word in the section. Love is the finishing touch to the passage, and central to the quest for unity. In contrast to living deceitfully or dishonourably (4:14), believers are to live transparently, exhibiting a conduct that is characterized by authenticity and integrity. As part of this model, they are to take responsibility for others. Although Paul is not encouraging inappropriate intrusion into the lives of others, he is anticipating that where there is error, believers should be prepared to be the channel of the Spirit to provide correction (Gal. 6:1; Jas. 5:19–20). As long as truth is shared in love, it is always the right thing to do. Truth without love is less than valuable (1 Cor. 13:3).

4. The Spirit experiences pain (Eph. 4:25–32)

In Ephesians 4:30, Paul, after itemizing sins that should not be present in a believer's life, concludes that such activities not only create disunity and cause pain but they also grieve the Spirit. The suggestion that the Spirit can be grieved is only recorded in the NT here. The clearest OT reference to this feature is Isaiah 63:10, 'Yet they rebelled and grieved his Holy Spirit,' with reference to Israel's rejection of God. The emotion relates to 'being hurt, feeling pain or distress' rather than 'irritation or annoyance'. This is perhaps the most serious aspect of the significance of the presence of the Spirit in the lives of believers.

The implications of his presence with, and his gifts to, the believer are to be seriously considered. The fact that this is the only time where Paul describes the Spirit as *the Holy Spirit of God* (Eph. 4:30) is a graphic reminder of the one of whom he is speaking. Furthermore, it is instructive to note that Isaiah 63: 10 continues, 'So he turned and became their enemy and he himself fought against them.' The punishment for such an act by the Israelites was severe. The fact that Paul does not indicate that similar consequences are forthcoming for believers if they act similarly is worthy of careful consideration. In the OT, if a person lived inappropriately, the Spirit would leave them. For believers, however, the Spirit has committed himself never to leave them. Even when they sin and cause him pain, he will not leave them; he chooses to stay even though the experience causes him sorrow.

To sin against such love is an action that indicates a particular kind of ingratitude that cares more for sin that hurts the Spirit than for holiness that gives him joy. Paul is keen to warn his readers that they have the capacity of causing him embarrassment or hurt. He is the one who has taken it upon himself to vouch for them, to act as a permanent guarantor, representing them before God, affirming and protecting them.

Moses provided the Israelites with a similar challenge, a new start that involved loving God and walking in his ways, which would result in blessing (Deut. 30:15–20). However, there are two notable differences. Firstly, if they did not fulfil this responsibility, Moses told them, 'you will certainly be destroyed. You will not live long in the land you are crossing the Jordan to enter and possess.' No such threat hangs over the believer if they do not take up their challenge to live worthy lives. This is not a call to complacency, however, nor an indication that God now operates on the basis of softer rules. On the contrary, the new relationship with believers established by God has actually higher standards and more serious consequences. Secondly, the Israelites were expected to fulfil their responsibilities with regard to obeying the law, with little evidence of any of the supernatural enabling of the Spirit that is granted freely to believers. To ignore or overlook such support is an ungrateful act that results in significant costs being borne by believers, but also by the Spirit. The Israelites were in danger of losing their inheritance, but believers are in danger of bringing sadness to the Spirit who has sealed them.

The challenge is as relevant for believers in the present century as it was for those who lived in the first century. The Spirit has feelings and emotions; the one who preceded the creation of humanity is so intimately involved in the lives of his creation that they have the capacity to hurt the one who created them. They sin against love, not simply a law. It is as if they break the Spirit's heart – not just a commandment. Sin for the believer should be viewed as a relational action, not merely a rejection of a rule. Someone gets hurt, and that hurt includes the Spirit. When Pope John Paul II spoke on June 18, 1983 in Poland, he reminded his audience, 'Tell me what you love, and I will tell you who you are.' The challenge to believers then and now is to recognize the implications of their actions. If they allow the flesh to determine their practices instead of the Spirit, they demonstrate who or what is their true love.

It is as if Paul is recommending that the readers consider the humiliation of embarrassing someone who presents them positively – whom they let down and thereby bring his reputation as a guarantor into disrepute. It is the height of ingratitude for people to hurt the one who has authenticated them. Worse than that, Paul is concerned that his readers do not commit the kinds of sin that undermine the Spirit's agenda. The author of Hebrews 10:29 similarly speaks of his concern about people insulting the gracious Spirit. The one who has cleansed us, and is in the process of cleaning us, watches us as we wallow in the muddy waters of sin, knowing that there is the probability that we shall crawl out, realizing what we have done and asking for his forgiveness.

Even though we know we don't deserve it, and even wish that he would walk or look away from us, so that we could allow our sorrow to wash over us a little longer, he is closer than we realize. In the process of our coming to him in repentance for refreshing, he is already pouring his grace over us. Such inexplicable love must be the basis for passionately walking close to him and thereby looking away from sin. He is too good for us to give him grief, too sensitive for us selfishly to sin, too loving for us thoughtlessly to let him down.

The Spirit has brought believers to the start of the race, has given them the resources to reach the end, and has promised to be their coach. It is up to us to take advantage of our trainer and to win. We may take note of the words of Dr Martin Luther King, Jr, who said, 'If you can't fly, then run. If you can't run, then walk. If you can't walk, then crawl. But whatever you do, keep moving.'

When Winston Churchill was the Prime Minister of the United Kingdom, he visited his old school at Harrow, London, where he had studied in his youth. He was to speak to the pupils, as he had done nearly a year previously. It was 29 October 1941 and the country, with its allies, was engaged in the chaos and turmoil of the Second World War. Two years had already passed since the conflict had started and the people were weary of war; little did they know that four more years of fighting were to come. In this darkness, Churchill spoke these words, 'The ten months that have passed have seen very terrible catastrophic events in the world . . . But we must learn . . . and this is the lesson: never give in, never give in, never, never, never, never – in nothing, great or small, large or petty – never give in, never yield to the apparently overwhelming might of the enemy . . . persevere to conquer.' We do not know when Jesus will return and signal the end of life as we know it. But we do know that the Spirit is with us, empowering us and engaging the enemy alongside us and on our behalf. And our commission is never, never to give in.

5. Case studies in unity

a. A theological case study (Acts 15:1–29)

In Acts 15, the early believers faced a challenge relating to the issue of unity. The question was raised due to Gentiles coming to faith in Jesus. For many Jews, this was an unexpected event. However, having occurred, the issue of church boundaries was high on their agenda for discussion. The fundamental inquiry related to whether Gentiles could be part of the church; a consequence could have been separate Jewish and Gentile Christian communities. James, the leader of the Jerusalem church, sat in judgment (Acts 15:13–22), the witnesses, including Peter, Barnabas and Paul (15:12), were called to provide testimony, while all the apostles and elders considered the situation (15:6). It was a test case that would have significant consequences, so important that Luke provides most of a chapter rehearsing the event for his readers.

The conclusion of the council held in Jerusalem was that the mission to the Gentiles was God-ordained. The presence of the Spirit in the discussion was of significance (Acts 15:28), Bruce describing him as the 'chief Author of their decision'.[4] The Spirit who delights in unity had helped to guide the early believers to accept the unprecedented and unexpected – the community which owned Jesus as Saviour, God as Father and the Spirit as their director of mission was open to all peoples, irrespective of their nationality. It is little wonder that when Paul and Barnabas presented this news to the believers in Antioch in Galatia, there was a great deal of relief and joy (15:30–31). They were now officially welcomed as part of the larger group; they had been accepted, included and thus valued. Important in the decision was the willingness of the believers to listen to the Spirit and to those who had been entrusted with the leadership of the church, the apostles and elders. The debate was conducted in harmony and unity (15:25), incorporating a desire to reflect truthfulness (even though it may include rebuke [15:24]), and revealing a willingness to listen respectfully (15:12), and to respond in love (15:28). Each of these features are itemized in Ephesians 4, where Paul directs his readers' attention to the concept of unity, and reminds them of their responsibility to take advantage of what God has done to expedite it, namely the giving of the Spirit (Eph. 4:7) and leaders (Eph. 4:11).

The account in Acts 15 provides graphic evidence that unity and fellowship is not always easy to maintain. Just a few verses after the announcement of the affirmation that unity had been achieved between Jew and Gentile, a dissension developed between some of those who together had brought unity in the wider church, resulting in a disagreement that led to Paul and Barnabas separating from one another (Acts 15:37–40). It related to whether John Mark should accompany them on their next mission trip. A case may be made

[4] F. F. Bruce, *The Book of Acts* (Eerdmans, 1975), p. 315.

for the perspectives of both Paul and Barnabas. Paul's caution to take him may have been due to an understandable concern that his previous departure (13:13) may have signified a defect in determination, which needed time to be rectified before undertaking such an important and arduous mission. On the other hand, Barnabas' readiness to give John Mark another opportunity may have stemmed from a pastoral desire to provide the prospect of success to replace a perceived failure in the past. The characteristic that was missing was the capacity to accept each other's views as legitimate and thus to maintain fellowship; unfortunately, 'They had such a sharp disagreement that they parted company' (15:39). In maintaining unity, believers have to learn the important lesson of agreeing to disagree, but doing so, where legitimate, as a result of a willingness to accept the validity of the perspective of others.

b. A practical case study (Acts 11:19–30)

In Acts 11:28, in Antioch, Agabus offered a prophecy that foretold of a famine that would severely affect people throughout the Roman Empire. The response of the believers there was to send a gift (presumably monetary, since Paul and Barnabas take it on their behalf [11:30]) to the believers in Judea. The background to this gift is recorded in verse 11:20, where Luke states that some months earlier, many Greeks in Antioch became believers, so much so that the news spread to Jerusalem (11:21–22). Barnabas was dispatched to check on this strange phenomenon of Gentiles becoming believers, and he was pleased to affirm that the news was true, and that the faith of these new Christians was authentic (11:22). Indeed, it was in Antioch that the title 'Christian' was first used to identify believers in Jesus (11:26). Together, he and Paul established the church in Antioch, staying there for a year (11:25–26). There is no record of any animosity on the part of the believers in Antioch concerning the question of their being admitted into the church by Jewish believers in Jerusalem. Such uncertainty on the part of some Jewish Christians was reflected a few verses earlier (11:1–3). The evidence of the Antiochene believers, recognizing the importance of unity, is that they readily sent help to others in their Christian family, including those who were yet to be convinced of their admissibility. Yet again, younger Christians had something to teach their elders about the grace of God.

c. A social case study (Acts 8:4–8, 14–25)

In Acts 8:4–8, Luke records that many Samaritans came to faith in Jesus as a result of the preaching of Philip. However, what is significant for this present discussion relates to the willingness of the Jewish apostles to send Peter and John, to ensure that they were welcomed as authentic members of the church; consequently, they prayed that they would receive the Spirit (8:14–16). They did not seek to withhold this blessing from them but, on the contrary, took steps to make certain that it occurred.

To understand the significance of this action by the Jewish believers, it is necessary to remind oneself of the history of relations between Jews and Samaritans. If the Jews disliked Gentiles, the level of animosity towards the Samaritans was, if anything, worse. The divisions between the Samaritans and the Jews were centuries old, going back to the time when, as a mongrel race of people, they were drafted in to populate Israel after their exile. These foreigners caused a great deal of trouble to those returning to Judea, and who attempted to rebuild the walls of Jerusalem (Ezra 4:1–24; Neh. 2:19 – 6:19). The dissension increased to such an extent that the Samaritans established their own capital (Samaria) as a rival to Jerusalem, built their own temple on Mount Gerizim, and established their own priesthood and religious laws. The Samaritan temple was destroyed by the Jews, under the leadership of John Hyrcanus, in 128 BC as was Samaria, after surrendering through famine, the Jews honouring the memory with a festival.

After that, feelings between Jews and Samaritans became extraordinarily bitter and events were to exacerbate the situation. In AD 10, for example, some Samaritans entered the temple in Jerusalem at night during the feast of the Passover, scattering the courts with human bones, thus making them unclean. The Jews responded by excluding the Samaritans from the temple forever, even from the outer courts that had hitherto been open to them. They were publicly cursed in synagogues and were declared unable to participate in the Messianic kingdom.

In the era of the Spirit, however, Samaritans were welcomed into the Christian family which had been, until then, a Jewish community of believers. Remarkably, the Jews in Jerusalem send two of their most important leaders to guarantee the safe entry of Samaritans into the church. Indeed, on their way back to Jerusalem, Peter and John also preached in many Samaritan villages (Acts 8:25). A remarkable transformation has taken place. Areas that Jews were reticent to enter (for their safety as much as anything else) were now being visited in order for them to share the good news with outsiders. A new inclusive community had been established in which all were welcome. The chapter concludes with Luke identifying that even an Ethiopian, and a eunuch at that, was also to be included (8:26–38). The church at its most fundamental is a family.

233

If characteristics associated with family are not replicated in the lives of its members, they need to consider whether they are truly reflecting the family of believers as God intended it to be.

The day of Pentecost acted as a model of unity in the context of diversity. Believers need to be aware of the possibility that their questioning whether God should be working in other parts of the church is as inappropriate as the Jewish Christians in the early church, who doubted the possibility that God could be working among the Gentiles. Similarly Macchia writes, 'We have no right to criticise the ecumenical conversation taking place in a variety of contexts unless we are involved in the blood and sweat of labouring alongside it.'[5]

Similarly, believers should be wary of (unintentionally) creating a framework, outside of which it may be assumed that the Spirit does not, or should not, function. Indeed, it may be more appropriate to be prepared to widen our expectations with reference to the work of the Spirit, by considering how he has led others into new dimensions of spirituality (whose denominational or spiritual traditions may be different from our own). The tendency to elitism is a constant threat to any who espouse a particular spiritual experience. However, the dynamic and creative Spirit exists to create unity in diversity, rather than a monochrome community, and the NT often reflects this two-fold agenda.

In 1964, Nelson Mandela was sentenced to life imprisonment for plotting revolution in a context of apartheid. He made a speech on April 20, 1964 that was part of his defence, concluding with these words, 'I have fought against white domination, and I have fought against black domination. I have cherished the ideal of a democratic and free society in which all persons live together in harmony with equal opportunities. It is an ideal which I hope to live for and to achieve. But if needs be, it is an ideal for which I am prepared to die.' Similarly, unity among believers is not an optional extra, or an aspiration for which only a little energy should be expended. It is of central importance. On May 10 1994, Mandela celebrated the climax of that dream when he became President of South Africa.

Believers today need to take greater steps to realize a similar dream of unity in the church. Rather than concentrate on differences, areas of agreement should also be identified, strengths affirmed and weaknesses acknowledged. Patience and forgiveness is needed on the part of all, as well as a greater realisation of the universal nature of the church. The breaking down of barriers needs to

[5] F. D. Macchia, *Baptized in the Spirit. A Global Pentecostal Theology* (Zondervan, 2006), p. 221.

take place particularly among those in Christian leadership. Bridges may be built via dialogue, the sharing and exploration of differing doctrinal distinctives in seminaries, and in a readiness to learn from one another. There needs to be a willingness to engage in repentance on both sides for words, deeds, unfounded criticisms and prejudicial assumptions, as well as occasions provided for engaging in corporate prayer.

Pluess draws a parallel with the fairy story of the ugly frog, who turns into a handsome prince when the princess receives him as her companion. He concludes that this piece of fiction may provide a model for the emergence of a ready engagement in dialogue and companionship with those who may initially appear uncomfortably different from oneself, but who may yet become close companions of a type that had not been previously anticipated.[6]

I have been privileged to engage in dialogue with Christians from denominations different from my own. Although none of the parties felt any need to compromise or amend their respective traditions, the exercise has been immensely profitable, resulting in a much clearer level of appreciation of each other's spiritualities, beliefs and practices, as well providing opportunities for fellowship, mutual understanding and respect, and a readiness to engage in further dialogue and prayer. In these tentative steps towards each other, we have, I believe, been moving towards the aspiration of the Spirit, that the church he initiated should be united, experiencing harmony, though not necessarily without individual distinctives.

[6] J-D. Pluess, 'The Frog-King or the Coming of Age of Pentecostalism,' *Cyberjournal for Pentecostal-Charismatic Research* (2001), (www.pctii.org/cyberj/).

Ephesians 5:18 – 6:18
19. Be filled with the Spirit

1. Introduction

Paul encourages his readers to ensure that the Spirit is the dominating force in their lives (Eph. 5:18–20). Thereafter, from 5:21 – 6:9, he describes the consequences of such a Spirit-controlled life as being corporate worship and thanksgiving (5:19–20), and submission to one another (5:21 – 6:9). In the final few verses of the letter (6:17–18), he adds two elements that will be important in demonstrating that believers may benefit from the presence of the Spirit in their lives – prayer and speech.

2. Be filled with the Spirit (Eph. 5:18)

As with the command not to grieve the Spirit (Eph. 4:30), Paul employs another imperative here. Believers are to *be filled with the Spirit* (5:18), the present imperative form used indicating a continuing filling. He does not exhort them to be full of the Spirit, or to be filled as a one-off experience; rather they continuously are to be being filled with the Spirit. He is not anticipating that, as a result of this, someone comprehensively and for all-time will be Spirit-filled. Rather, he is referring to the process of being filled with the Spirit more than one was before. Indeed, although 'being filled with the Spirit' is a common term to describe various spiritual experiences, it is often used inappropriately. Nobody, other than Jesus, has been, or will be, filled completely with the Spirit in the way anticipated by Paul. Nevertheless, this should be an aspiration of every believer – continuously to be filled with the Spirit in a process that never ends. Paul is not exhorting them to be manifesting more and more gifts of the Spirit, but rather to manifest the life and character of the

236

Spirit. The church at Corinth exercised a multiplicity of gifts of the Spirit but, because of their selfishness and uncaring attitudes to one another, they clearly demonstrated that the Spirit was not filling them in the way anticipated here by Paul.

In view of the fact that the Spirit desires to fill believers, controlling them and enabling them to follow his agenda, it is incumbent on them that they take time to ensure that he is given opportunities so to do. Because of his creative genius, he is perfectly capable of providing opportunities to interact with us in ways that are appropriate to our personalities and characters. He is not a scary, intimidating Spirit but a sensitive Spirit who treats us with respect and care. His desire is not to control us in ways that are detrimental or destructive but to allow us to experience his love more, and to taste heaven before we get there. It is valuable, therefore, to provide flexible frameworks for personal encounters with the Spirit that will result in spiritual development. In this process, it is helpful if variety and creativity are foundational elements. It is also beneficial to set targets for change that can be assessed. These measures need not necessarily lead to guilt if the desired development has not occurred. However, they will provide opportunities to monitor change as one considers one's journey thus far.

Actions that could help in providing a greater sense of the Spirit's influence in our lives include reading a book about God, writing a poem or song about an aspect of his character, thinking about an element of his being that is particularly meaningful to oneself, studying a characteristic about his being that is intriguing, identifying some practical ways whereby one might recognize God in one's daily life, forming a programme whereby one spends a short time with God at certain times of the day, and setting some targets for personal change. In it all, we are creating opportunities for the future to manifest occasions of transformation. Such a practical mindset helps to focus our desire for change and to increase the possibilities for that change to occur. These targets, and others that may be devised, have the potential also of benefitting one's community as well as oneself.

Some years ago, a nationwide poll was conducted in the USA which sought to reflect the spiritual life of evangelical Christians. The overwhelming conclusion was that although the majority wanted to change and to be better, few had created frameworks for change to facilitate this aspiration in any practical way. If we are to grow spiritually, we need to erect some scaffolding in our lives that can provide opportunities to ensure that growth occurs. To reach a destination, targets need to be assigned – not too easy but also not too hard, not too many and for a measured time – whereupon one may assess the growth.

An exercise I conduct with my students commences with them taking time carefully to consider an area in their lives where they would like to see a change (maybe a habit to remove, or one to adopt). They then write each of their targets on a card and place it in an envelope, which is sealed with wax and kept by myself. At the end of the semester, each receives their envelope back and the contents are removed. If appropriate, they share with the rest of us how they have fared. It is a simple exercise but it carries with it a life-transforming routine that recognises that success generally only comes if it is worked on carefully, diligently and intentionally. The difference for believers is that we can benefit from the strategic involvement of the Spirit also.

Why does Paul speak of their being filled with the Spirit?

The verb 'to fill' is used elsewhere in Ephesians to refer to being filled with God or Christ (Eph. 1:23; 3:19; 4:10). The concept advanced by Paul is that those who are so filled should reflect the character of the one who fills them. The subject (God, Christ, the Spirit) who fills the believer is thus more important than the verb which describes the infusion. Luke describes a man as being 'full of leprosy' (Luke 5:12, ESV) and Elymas as being 'full of all kinds of deceit and trickery' (Acts 13:10). Such conditions controlled their lives. Stephen (Acts 7:55) and Barnabas (Acts 11:24), on the other hand, are described as being 'full of the Holy Spirit' – the Spirit controlled them.

Too much time has been expended on seeking to identify when and how such filling occurs, or whether it happens more than once, rather than on the significance of the presence of its subject in the believer's life. This is the central, important issue for Paul. Much has been written concerning the identification of this 'moment' of filling. For Paul, it is a moment in motion, a constant flow of the Spirit. The influence of the Spirit may be as a waterfall flooding through the life of the believer, though it could also be reflective of a gentle mist or light rain that saturates the one who is affected by it. The consequence of the experience is more important than the terminology used to describe it.

The metaphor, 'Do not get drunk on wine . . .. Instead, be filled with [or, by] the Spirit,' may be understood in a number of ways. However, it is unlikely that Paul is concerned about drunkenness in the church of Ephesus, as elsewhere he does not refer to it in the letter (though see Rom. 13:12–13). If this had been a problem in the Ephesian church, one would have anticipated that his advice would have been more directly related to it, even including a proposal to desist from drink. It is possible that he is simply contrasting a foolish action (getting drunk), which has negative consequences, with a wise one (being filled with the Spirit), which has positive consequences. It is most likely, however, that he is drawing a comparison between the actions of someone who is drunk and the life of someone who is filled and thus controlled by the Spirit. A major significance of being drunk is that one is no longer in control of oneself; the drink becomes the controlling force (Acts 2:4, 13, 15). Similarly, Paul teaches them that the Spirit is to be the dominating force in their lives,[1] identified as 'Spirit-inebriation' by Fee.[2] If believers are filled with the Spirit, the result will not be debauchery, but worship, thanksgiving and loving relationships. The potential consequences of such a Spirit-controlled life are thus radically important for the individual and corporate lives of the believers.

Paul is not suggesting that the Spirit is to be identified as a liquid, which may be ingested or leaked out. He does not associate being filled with the Spirit with an emotional experience or indicate that it is purely personal. On the contrary, the evidence that one is filled with the Spirit is that there will be a benefit to others, as well as a development in one's relationship with God, in terms of worship and thanksgiving. Such an aspiration to be filled with the Spirit is thus to be viewed as a regular occurrence in the life of the believer. Such occasions may well affect the emotions and the intellect, and should result in the ongoing transformation of one's character, relationships and spirituality. Rather than being rare, such times, when the Spirit identifies areas where his controlling influence is needed, should be anticipated as special, intermittent interactions with the Spirit. They may result in moments of quiet determination to follow the Spirit in a given area, or be accompanied with emotional experiences that leave us speechless but different. What matters is what follows the moment. According to Paul, there should be a positive consequence that will help develop the life of the believer concerned, with an outflow that blesses others also.

3. Evidence of being filled with the Spirit (Eph. 5:19 – 6:18)

From Ephesians 4:1, Paul has been identifying responsibilities of the believer. He concludes the third chapter with 'Amen' and begins the next chapter with 'Therefore' (in the Greek). In the first three chapters, he explores the remarkable privileges of believers because

[1] So also A. T. Lincoln, *Ephesians* (Word, 1990), p. 344.
[2] G. D. Fee, *God's Empowering Presence* (Hendrickson, 1994), p. 722.

239

of the commitment of the Spirit to their ongoing development from the moment of their salvation. Moving on, he then reminds them that such benefits have consequences. Having been blessed by the Spirit so much, they need to remember that there are responsibilities to be borne – they are to walk worthy of their calling (Eph. 4:1), in the unity initiated by the Spirit (4:3), using his gifts (4:11–13), being determined not to sadden him (4:30). The route to pleasing the Spirit is described by Paul in terms of adopting lifestyles that reflect high moral standards in personal and corporate spirituality (4:25 – 5:16), as a result of which, they will be 'imitators of God' (5:1), doing 'what pleases the Lord' (5:10).

Following on from these aspirations, it is logical that he should write about understanding 'what the Lord's will is' (Eph. 5:17). Very simply, Paul states that to achieve the latter, one needs to be filled with the Spirit (5:18) and notes that one of the ways that will be evidenced is in corporate worship (5:19–20). He then widens the concept of worship to include relational submission to one another, husband-wife (5:22–33), parents-children (6:1–4), masters-slaves (6:5–9), concluding with the conflict between the devil and the Spirit-empowered believer (6:10–20). Being filled with the Spirit is manifested when one's relationships with others, including God, are conducted authentically and with integrity.

Being filled with the Spirit, however, is not only associated with self-control, corporate responsibility and discipline. It is also manifested by joy (Eph. 5:18–20). He who has already achieved the most for us will not give up on us now. The Spirit is dedicated to believers, not simply to keep them on the straight and narrow. He is not a heavenly bouncer to keep them in line, a policeman from paradise, a matron with attitude, a headmaster with a stick, a chain around our legs or a supernatural straitjacket to keep us holy. Rather, he is our heavenly bodyguard, our tour guide to get us to our destination and to make sure that we enjoy the journey. His plan is that we be holy, but the route is lined with joy (Luke 10:21). It is a path of 'righteousness . . . and joy in the Holy Spirit' (Rom. 14:17).

When someone is filled with the Spirit, there is always a positive consequence that demonstrates the controlling influence of the Spirit. The references in Acts where Luke uses the term are instructive. In Acts 2:4, when the disciples were 'all filled with the Holy Spirit', they spoke in tongues and glorified God (Acts 2:4, 11). When Peter is described as being 'filled with the Holy Spirit' again, he demonstrates this by offering a powerful statement to the religious leaders who had arrested him. In Acts 4:31, when the believers are again described as being 'filled with the Holy Spirit', it results in their speaking 'the word of God boldly'. In Acts 9:17, after Ananias lays his hands on Saul in order that he 'be filled with the Holy Spirit', he is immediately healed of his blindness, followed by his preaching about Jesus in the synagogues of Damascus (Acts 9:20). In Acts 13:9, Luke records that Paul is 'filled with the Holy Spirit', followed by his pronouncing judgment on Elymas who opposed his preaching.

Finally, in Acts 13:52, Luke records that the disciples were 'filled with joy and with the Holy Spirit', despite experiencing persecution. This was followed by their preaching in the synagogue in Iconium, resulting in many believing their message (Acts 14:1). When people are filled with the Spirit, there is a transformation, though this is best reflected in their bearing testimony (by words and life) to their faith and the good news of Jesus. When somebody is filled with the Spirit, someone else benefits.

4. The Spirit's sword and prayer (Eph. 6:17–18)

Paul's two final references to the Spirit in Ephesians are included in his description of the armour with which believers are to clothe themselves (6:10–20). He encourages the readers to use *the sword of the Spirit* (6:17). The sword is given by the Spirit (identified as part of 'the full armour of God', 6:11) who also provides its effectiveness, 'its cutting edge'.[3] The sword is given, by the Spirit, to believers for them to use with his assistance. The sword is not to be equated with the Spirit, but with *the word* (see Isa. 49:2). The sword (*makaira*) refers to a short sword or dagger often used in offensive and close combat, probably less than sixty centimetres in length.

The imagery would thus lend itself to be understood as a powerful resource of the Spirit that is to be accessed, not particularly in defence but in attack. It is not for protection from being attacked but to be used in moving forward and taking new territory. The Spirit is interested in more than holding the line; he desires to advance.

Similarly, when Jesus responded to the devil in the wilderness, he was not simply parrying his attacks. He was making incisive movements forward, putting the devil on the back foot. Although the devil may have thought he was controlling the temptations cleverly, in reality, they were opportunities for Jesus to put him in his place and to remind him to whom he was speaking ('Do not put the Lord your God to the test,' Luke 4:12).

If Paul is reminded of Isaiah 11:4,[4] he is transferring to believers

---

[3] Lincoln, *Ephesians*, p. 451.
[4] Similarly, Eph. 6:14 is reliant on Isa. 11:5.

a privilege that was granted to the Messiah. As Messiah would be empowered by the Spirit (*pneuma*) with his word (*logos*), so now Paul states that believers will be granted a similar authority. The term used by Paul here for 'word' (*rhēma*) is sometimes used in ways that are different from the very common term *logos*, which is also translated as 'word'; on other occasions, they are interchangeable. The words *rhēma* (and *logos* [1 Thess. 1:8]) are sometimes used to describe the good news of the gospel (Eph. 5:26).[5] Paul may thus be reminding the readers that, though they may be unconfident or nervous in their sharing the gospel, the involvement of the Spirit ensures that its presentation will be supernaturally supported. This is a concept that has been offered elsewhere by Jesus (Matt. 10:20). In a similar way, the Spirit is offering to be a source of wisdom to believers when they speak, as a result of which they will advance the kingdom of God.

It is probable, however, that Paul is emphasizing the role of the Spirit to inspire speech at a given point in time, rather than only to refer to the Scriptures or even the gospel. The emphasis may thus be on the fact that the Spirit seeks to inspire believers to impart the message he wants to be revealed. They are thus enabled to function prophetically as messengers of the Spirit. Although it is not easy to tease these concepts apart, if there is any distinction in Paul's mind, he may be encouraging the believers to expect the Spirit to guide them in their communication. What they need to do is to be prepared for the impetus of the Spirit, to be ready to be spokespersons for the Spirit. Thus, while the Spirit is ready to impart wisdom, believers need to be sensitive to his guidance so that they may speak authoritatively when he leads them. The words of the message are of course crucially important, but the willingness of the messenger is vital. Believers are thus offered opportunities to be couriers for the Spirit, receiving messages from him then to present them to others – a fantastic privilege and an immense responsibility.

The second reference to the Spirit is in the context of praying *in the Spirit* (see also Jude 20). It is probable that Paul is here identifying the value of the power of the Spirit when it is incorporated in prayer. Although some have identified this with praying in tongues, it is more likely that it refers to the practice of praying in cooperation with the Spirit, when the Spirit assumes a significant or central role in the process. He is not suggesting that this is a higher form of prayer, but that this should reflect all prayer. Thus, Paul is probably reminding the readers that the role of the Spirit in prayer is to be the initiator of their prayers. Lincoln concludes, 'The writer is

---

[5] Lincoln, *Ephesians*, p. 451; Fee, *God's Empowering Presence*, pp. 728–729.

calling for prayer inspired, guided, and made effective through the Spirit.'[6] Prayer is not to be viewed as an opportunity to instruct or advise God as to the best outcome, but to listen to the Spirit who will advise the believer how best to pray. Again, such a prayer will demonstrate that the one praying has taken the time to be directed by the Spirit, who then guides the content of the prayer.

Prayer should be undertaken in the expectation that the Spirit will provide wisdom concerning how to pray. Prayer need not be equated with sending multiple, disparate petitions to God and then simply waiting for a response. On the contrary, the response from God actually is ready before the prayer is articulated. The role of the Spirit is to aid believers in knowing how to pray and what to pray for, as well as facilitating the process. Prayer is much less an isolated exercise of the individual believer than one might assume. Instead, it is intended to be the result of a dialogue between the believer and the Spirit. When praying for others, whilst one ear should be attuned to the person being prayed for, the other should be available to the wisdom and guidance offered by the Spirit. A developing aware-ness of the presence of the Spirit in one's life can lead to a greater expectation that his resources, made available to all believers, may be directly used in a given situation, in which one may be a channel of God's power for the benefit of others.

Praying in the Spirit demands that time be given to listening for the guidance offered by the Spirit as to how one should pray. On occasions where prayer is offered on the basis of a promise offered in the Bible, the petition may be confidently offered, since God does not break his promises (Num. 23:19). Where Scriptural guid-ance is unavailable, prayer should be offered in partnership with the Spirit, who may guide us through the community, inner conviction, prophecy or external circumstances. This is probably the kind of prayer consciousness that Paul has in mind when he encourages his readers to be constantly in prayer (Rom. 12:12). Prayer is not intended to be a monologue, but a dialogue. It is possible that we may be missing out on many times when the Spirit desires to be more actively involved in the conversation of prayer, but we have not heard his guidance because we weren't listening for him.

I remember reading of a book that offered many guidelines for getting God's attention. The truth is that we don't need to learn how to get God's attention; he's already perfectly attentive to our situations. What I am learning to do instead is to give him my atten-tion and to listen for him. You may have heard the story of a group of radio operators turning up for an interview and being shown to

[6] Lincoln, *Ephesians*, p. 452.

a rather crowded waiting room to wait their turn to be interviewed. However, the call never came. After some uncertainty as to the outcome of the situation, one man suddenly jumped out of his chair and ran to the door of the interview room, coming out again a few minutes later to announce that he had been offered the job. To the astonishment of those present, he told them to listen and, sure enough, a morse code was being tapped out, informing them that the first person who responded to this message and came into the interview room would be offered the job. But only one man was listening. In prayer, we have the opportunity to be guided by the fount of all wisdom in helping us to pray appropriately – our responsibility is actively to listen.

Conclusion

This has been an exploration of someone who desires relationship with believers and not a theological enquiry into a doctrine. Whilst recognizing that the Spirit is part of the Godhead and functions in relationship and harmony with the Father and Jesus, this book has concentrated on the Spirit. As such, I have sought to discover aspects of the Spirit that will result in our being impressed with him but also captivated by his desire to relate to us. It has been my intention for us to understand the Spirit a little better but, much more, to help us recognize his proximity. I have tried to stimulate your thinking but also to warm your emotions, to encourage you to be intrigued with the Spirit but also to edge you closer to him and to recognize how close he already is to you. He is an endless source of exploration and we shall never finally close the book on describing him completely. As children who are presented with a delightful treasure, however, he draws us to himself, to enjoy him forever. We may run towards him or tentatively tiptoe in his direction, looking over our shoulders as if we are still uncertain as to whether this is ground that is too holy for us. However we approach him, the one thing of which we can be certain is a welcome – a coming home to the one who already has us in his heart.

Reliance on a relationship with the creative, dynamic and personal Spirit is important. It demands trust, honesty, maturity and a determination to listen to the rarely silent Spirit. It is the pathway of Paul, who also encourages his readers to 'live by the Spirit' (Gal. 5:25), 'walk by the Spirit' (Gal. 5:16, 25, ESV), and 'be filled with the Spirit' (Eph. 5:18), as a result of which they will develop godly lifestyles. These factors, of course, offer challenges as well as privileges. It is sometimes easier to consult rules for behaviour, as contained in (or based on) the Bible, than to listen to an intimate and immediate friend. Both are needed, though the latter calls for a developing relationship with the Spirit that demands discipline and time, and a readiness to obey his commands.

Our challenge is that we do not assume that the Spirit rarely speaks. Too often, we may not expect the Spirit to lead us and to mentor us personally. Consequently, we do not anticipate that he might. He speaks but because we are not listening, we may be missing his voice. Walking with the Spirit is relational, and that demands dialoguing with our director.

Many of us live in a world which is filled with activity; the one element we lack most is silence. And because of that, we often fail to hear the Spirit speaking to us. Sometimes, he has to shout. Josh was a very successful executive who was driving through a deprived Chicago suburb in his sleek, new, expensive, powerful Jaguar XKE. Suddenly, a brick smacked into it. He ground the car to a halt and raced back, grabbing the young boy who had thrown it and began to shout at him, his anger tumbling out of him like a hot liquid. He yelled, 'Why did you do that?' The youngster, who looked about six, said, with tears dripping down his cheeks, 'I'm sorry but I didn't know what else to do. I had to get someone to stop. My brother has collapsed and I can't lift him. He's too heavy for me.' Josh's temper subsided as rapidly as it had risen as he helped this little child, whose problem was too big for him to handle. He walked slowly back to his glossy car and saw the dent in the door. At that moment, he decided not to get it repaired. It was his way of reminding himself not to travel so fast in life that a brick would be needed to get his attention to help someone in need. May we be ready to respond to the whisper of the Spirit, as well as to those occasions when he stands in front of us and blocks our way until we recognize he is there.

An exercise that I have often encouraged my students to engage in involves spending a little time every evening thinking back through the day, identifying occasions when the Spirit may have spoken, and writing them down in a journal. These may have occurred in a conversation, or a word that had been spoken to them; they may have been the result of spending time with others, reading the Bible or another piece of literature; they may have happened as a result of something that had been seen or heard. The value of the exercise is that it encourages the students to realize that the Spirit is speaking more often than they may have thought. These Spirit-encounters are opportunities for him to open a window into our world and to let us know that he is with us – for him to say hello. The Spirit is to be experienced and his presence to be enjoyed.

On a few occasions, I have needed guidance with my computer to rectify a fault or identify the way forward in a particular process. The guidance has often come as a result of clever technology. Even though my guide has been based thousands of miles away, the direction I needed was offered, often as a result of the person concerned taking over my computer and mouse, interacting with the programme on my behalf. As a result, all that I needed in order to continue with my work was achieved. My guide had known very little about me personally, nor was there a relationship established between us of any great significance. However, despite these facts and the distance that separated us, practical guidance was offered and gratefully accepted. The tragedy that waits in the shadows is that the ever-present Spirit, whose dedication to us is incomparable, may be ignored if we forget that his skill, care and love are directed towards us. The fundamental lesson to be learned is that the Spirit is dedicated to our development, and that his influence is motivated by love and personal commitment to us.

Study guide

The aim of this study guide is to help you get to the heart of what I have written and challenge you to apply what you learn to your own life. The guide provides material for each of the sections of the book.

These questions and suggestions are intended to help you think about the Spirit and his involvement in your life. Be thoughtful and creative in your responses. Don't rush to provide answers and don't necessarily try to answer all of them. Choose those that are most appropriate to you. If you are able to work through them with others, that may prove a valuable experience as you learn together from each other. The objective is to facilitate an opportunity for you to discover more about the Spirit, to explore his character and to encounter him as your friend and mentor.

'He, like his name "Spirit", is a mystery. The marvel is that he has invited us to explore him, to commence a journey that is to be our eternal destiny – the endless discovery of the Spirit' (p. 16–17).

1 Samuel 16:11–13; Matthew 3:11–16; Acts 2:2
1. Who is the Holy Spirit and what is he like? (pp. 15–32)

1. Which of the metaphors for the Spirit in this chapter are most meaningful to you? Why?
2. If you could choose a different metaphor for the Spirit, which would you choose? Why?
3. When you think of the Spirit, what picture, thought or emotion comes to your mind?
4. What is special to you about the Spirit?
5. To use in prayer, what would be an appropriate name for the Spirit?

6. How have you experienced the presence of the Spirit?
7. Write a poem or some prose exploring an aspect of the Spirit, as reflected in this chapter.
8. What can you do to appreciate the Spirit more?

'*Sufficient to say that the Spirit, the Father and Jesus are each independent and interdependent, separate but inseparable, distinctive but constantly engaged in reciprocal relationships with each other*' (p. 16).

PART ONE. THE HOLY SPIRIT IN THE OLD TESTAMENT

Genesis 1:1–3
2. The Holy Spirit is the energiser of all creation (pp. 35–41)

1. Take a leaf or stone, or gaze at the darkness or the moon or some other aspect of nature, and let it direct you to thoughts of the Spirit who was involved in its creation.
2. What aspect of your life needs transformation and renewal? Present it to God and ask the creative Spirit to make a difference to your situation.
3. What practical steps can you take to be more creative?
4. Develop a plan for the next three months, and determine targets to be achieved in order to complete it.
5. Can you identify any occasion in your life when the Spirit brought renewal or helped you to undertake a new initiative?
6. Ask the Spirit what he wants you to do today.
7. Ask him to energise you today; do it every hour, on the hour.

'*No one suggested the idea of creation to the Spirit nor did it meet a need within him. He chose to do it. His creation of the world was a remarkable act of gracious altruism. He created because he is God and his creation is crafted out of love*' (p. 36).

Judges 3:7–11; 6:24 – 8:28; 11:1–40; 13:25 – 15:15
3. The Holy Spirit works wonders through weak people (pp. 42–48)

1. In what ways do you feel fragile and weak? Remember the Spirit delights to empower those who feel powerless.
2. Do the stories of the people mentioned in this chapter encourage you or challenge you? Why?
3. In what areas would you benefit from the enabling power of the Spirit? Present them to him, and ask for his involvement in your life today.
4. Can you think of a time when you noticed the Spirit helping you when you felt weak? Describe it.
5. How can you ensure that you do not lose sight of the remarkable support the Spirit gives to you?
6. Is there an area in your life that you feel may be hindering the Spirit from using you as much as he may wish? If so, ask his forgiveness, then make a strategy to ensure that it is removed, and ask for his support in the process.

'Words have been spoken, gestures offered, smiles given, deeds done, prayers uttered and unbeknown to those engaging in the action, the Spirit has supernaturally worked a miracle on their behalf for the benefit of others' (p. 44).

PART TWO. THE HOLY SPIRIT IN THE GOSPELS

Luke 1:41–79; 2:25–35
4. The Holy Spirit is associated with proclamation (pp. 51–56)

1. What has encouraged you in this chapter?
2. What can you do to ensure that you are doing your best to be an appropriate channel through whom the Spirit can speak?
3. Ask the Spirit to give you the courage to speak when you feel that he is inspiring you.
4. Ask the Spirit to speak through you today. Put a sticker on your watch, or wear an elastic band on your wrist, as a means of reminding yourself to be open to the Spirit and to act as his messenger today.

Luke 1:35; 3:22; 4:1–15
5. The Holy Spirit authenticates Jesus (pp. 57–69)

1. What do you feel about the Spirit as a result of considering him in this chapter?
2. Who authenticates and affirms you? How does it make you feel when this happens?
3. In what ways does the Spirit affirm you?
4. Think of a current situation where you feel marginalised, insecure or afraid. Now, imagine the Spirit is with you and consider the difference that this makes, knowing that he is always there.
5. In what ways does it help to know that the Spirit is so completely different from any other being in his support for you?
6. Consider areas in your life where you need his supervision and attention. Offer them to him in prayer and ask for a greater appreciation of his presence with you.
7. Thank him for the fact that he accompanies you in your life and strengthens you, even though, sometimes, you may forget that he's there.
8. How can you emulate the Spirit and affirm someone this week?

'The Spirit is associated with the creation and completion of commissions, with powerful proclamations, and with being a constant presence for those he chooses to partner. Such provision is also available to believers who need supernatural support to achieve the agenda that God has set for them' (p. 65).

Luke 4:16–30; 12:8–12
6. The Holy Spirit commissions Jesus (pp. 70–84)

1. Read Jesus' sermon recorded by Luke (4:15–19) slowly and aloud. Stop after each sentence and ask yourself, 'What does this reveal to me about the Spirit and the message he inspired through Jesus?'
2. In what ways would you benefit from the therapeutic touch of the Spirit now? Offer your need to him in prayer and ask for his support.
3. Write a prayer or some prose to God concerning an aspect of suffering in your life. Then, allow the Spirit to speak to you as a response, and write it down.
4. What does the Spirit's involvement in situations dominated by suffering teach you about him?

5. Consider some believers who are suffering now. How do they reflect the Spirit in their lives? Thank God for them and pray that they will know the sustaining energy and radiating presence of the Spirit.
6. How can you prepare yourself to ensure that you remember the supportive presence of the Spirit for future suffering that might come into your life?
7. Are you ready to ask the Spirit to transform your view of suffering so that you can experience it as a place of blessing and fruitfulness?

John 3:1–10; 4:7–26; 7:37–39
7. The Holy Spirit and salvation (pp. 85–96)

1. Do you sometimes doubt your salvation? Why?
2. What difference does it make to know that the Father, Jesus and the Spirit participated in your salvation?
3. Do you relate more to Nicodemus and his path to faith or to the woman from Samaria? Why?
4. How do you see the significance of the imagery of the believers being 'baptised' into the church?
5. What meaning does being 'born of the Spirit' have for you? What does it indicate to you about your future spiritual development and potential?
6. What for you is the most important reason that the Spirit is described as 'living water'?
7. What can you do to ensure that you increasingly benefit from the refreshing nature of the Spirit?

John 14:12–17; 15:26 – 16:7, 13–15
8. The Holy Spirit is the Paraclete (pp. 97–108)

1. Try to imagine what the disciples felt like when Jesus said that he would be leaving them.
2. Now imagine some of their thoughts and feelings when he spoke about the Spirit replacing him.
3. How do you think they anticipated the Spirit being part of their lives, in comparison to the personal presence of Jesus with them?
4. Which of the possible meanings of 'Paraclete' (pp. 101–102), as a description of the Spirit, is most meaningful to you? Why?
5. How can you practically benefit from the work of the Spirit as Paraclete?

253

6. What difference does it make to you to realise the varied aspects of the Spirit's commitment to you?
7. Ask the Spirit at the beginning of the day to help you remember that, as a result of his presence, you have the potential of functioning supernaturally on his behalf.

'The life-giving Spirit provides refreshing life, incisive guidance, personal cleansing and individual refining in this life as a foretaste of the life to come. The Spirit inspires hope in the hearts of believers in that he promises to be with them throughout their lives. This was graphically experienced by the disciples, who were afraid that in losing Jesus they were losing everything. In reality, fear was replaced by hope' (p. 98).

John 16:1–11
9. The Holy Spirit convicts unbelievers (pp. 109–118)

1. What have you learned about the Spirit from this chapter?
2. Identify some of the challenges facing you as a believer in this largely non-Christian society. How do they make you feel?
3. Offer some of these situations in prayer and ask for the sustaining power of the Spirit to help you to face them.
4. Identify one unbeliever who is close to you and ask the Spirit to convict that person of his or her sin and need of Jesus. Then, be ready for opportunities to share the gospel with him or her this week.
5. What difference does it make to you knowing that the Spirit is involved in mission with you?
6. Thank God that when the Spirit convinced you of your need for Jesus, you placed your faith in him.

PART THREE. THE HOLY SPIRIT IN THE BOOK OF ACTS

Acts 1:8; 4:1–31; 6:8 – 7:60; 13:4–12
10. The Holy Spirit and evangelism (pp. 121–130)

1. In what ways does telling others about Jesus make you feel nervous?
2. Why is it difficult to speak concerning your faith to unbelievers?

3. What have you learnt through your life that has helped you share your faith with others?
4. Can you think of an occasion when you sensed supernatural help in speaking about Jesus to an unbeliever?
5. Ask the Spirit to provide you with opportunities to speak about Jesus this week.

Acts 2: 1–12
11. The Holy Spirit at Pentecost (pp. 131-141)

1. Identify important consequences of the Spirit coming on the day of Pentecost. Which is the most important for you?
2. What can you do practically to ensure that some of these consequences are realised in your life and in Christian community?
3. What does the manner of his coming on the day of Pentecost reveal to you about the Spirit? Which aspect is most significant for you?
4. How have you encountered or experienced the presence of the Spirit in your life?
5. Do you think all the wind, fire, speaking in tongues and speaking to the crowds would have been surprising to the early believers who participated in the event? Why/why not?
6. Why did the Spirit come fifty days after Jesus died? Why did he not come earlier?
7. In what ways did the transformed lives of the believers affect unbelievers?

'Once, the Spirit had been rarely experienced; now he has franchised all believers to manifest him in their lives personally and for the benefit of others. Little wonder that the Spirit's coming was so exciting to the early believers, whose lives took on a dynamic character that was often accompanied by miraculous phenomena' (p. 132).

Acts 5:3–9; 8:29–40; 10:19–23; 11:12–15; 13:2–4; 16:6–10
12. The Holy Spirit guides believers (pp. 142–150)

1. How does it make you feel knowing that the Spirit wishes to guide you in your life?
2. How can you let him increasingly and practically guide you?
3. In what ways has the Spirit used the Bible to guide you in the past?

4. How can you be sure that it is the Spirit who is guiding you? What tests can you use to ensure that you are hearing from the Spirit?
5. How can you ensure that you do not take for granted the willingness of the Spirit to guide you?

'Paul explores probably the most fundamental issue relating to people then and now, including believers. It is a perennial problem of life for everyone, and it relates to moral and ethical aspects of life. It relates to how one can know what is the proper action to take, the correct decision to make, the right word to say, the appropriate thought to think – and then to determine how one can do what is the best. In short, this defines the battle between good and evil, a conflict that was present in the Garden of Eden and which continues to create havoc in the lives of individuals and communities' (p. 153).

PART FOUR. THE HOLY SPIRIT IN THE EPISTLES

Romans 8:1–13, 14–23, 26–27
13. The Holy Spirit opposes the flesh and affirms believers (pp. 153–177)

1. When do you know that you are living according to the principles of the flesh and not of the Spirit?
2. Offer a paraphrase of the concept of being 'in the Spirit' (pp. 158–160). What does it mean to you?
3. In what ways does the Spirit make us free (Rom. 8:2)?
4. What does it mean to 'put to death the misdeeds of the body' (Rom. 6:11; 8:13)?
5. What aspect of the concept of adoption is special to you? Why?
6. Which aspect of God being your Father is most important to you? Why?
7. What do you look forward to most about heaven?
8. What can you do to ensure that some of your heavenly inheritance also becomes a reality now?
9. What differences are made to you when you consider the picture of the Spirit praying for you?
10. Read the following prayer aloud and make it your own . . .

Can it be that
my sins of yesterday are forgiven,

my sins of today have been forgiven,
my sins of tomorrow will be forgiven?

Can it be that God has welcomed me as his child?

Can it be that
I am forgivable,
I am acceptable,
I am accepted,
I am forgiven?
Yes even me?

But my sin looms like a wall before my eyes.
It blocks my sight of God;
it blots my life;
it bruises my best intentions;
it breezes its way into my life
again
*   and again*
*   and again;*
it breaks my heart.

Before my burning bush,
I bow my head.

Words drift into my mind.
'Your sins of yesterday are forgiven;
your sins of today have been forgiven;
your sins of tomorrow will be forgiven.
It is certain; it has been decided by me, your God.
I have welcomed you as my child.

'Therefore,
you are forgivable,
you are acceptable,
you are accepted,
you are forgiven.

'Yes,
especially you.'[1]

---

[1] K. Warrington, *God and Us. A Life-Changing Adventure* (Scripture Union, 2004), pp. 53-54. Used by permission of the publishers.

1 Corinthians 12:4–31; Romans 12:6–8
14. The Holy Spirit provides gifts (pp. 178–192)

1. What gifts do you feel the Spirit may have presented to you for the benefit of others?
2. How are you developing your potential in this area?
3. Are you encouraging other believers by affirming their strengths and gifts?
4. Provide ways whereby one may be able to identify gifts that God has given to believers.
5. Do you think believers may be granted a gift that may reside with them indefinitely? Why/why not?
6. What tests are valid to determine if a gift is being manifested appropriately?
7. How can we be certain that a gift of prophecy is authentic?
8. Which gifts of the Spirit need greater exposure today?

Galatians 5:16 – 6:2
15. The Holy Spirit and transformation (pp. 193–205)

1. How have you changed in the past twelve months in your relationship with God?
2. Ask others to comment on positive changes that they have seen in you. Offer your comments on the development of others.
3. What can you do personally to ensure that you are taking advantage of the resources of the Spirit to enable you to improve?
4. Take an apple and cut it open. Take out a seed, stick it to a small card and place it somewhere prominent. It will help to remind you that you have the potential of bearing fruit.

Ephesians 1:3–14
16. The Holy Spirit seals and guarantees believers (pp. 206–214)

1. Why is the issue of security important to you?
2. How do you feel knowing that God wants you in heaven with him – so much so that he has given the Spirit to ensure that you get there?
3. What can you do to demonstrate your gratitude to the Spirit for his commitment to you?
4. Write a paragraph expressing the commitment of the Spirit to

you and the pleasure you feel, as a result. Place it somewhere prominent for you to read from time to time.

'People longed to be redeemed from the instability of human existence, especially the painful experiences caused by those malicious and powerful beings which lived in the heavenly places . . . Paul informs the readers that they are safe from such concerns for the one who dwells in "heavenly realms" is on their side, his many blessings to them being evidence of that fact' (p. 209).

Ephesians 2:11–22
17. The Holy Spirit provides access to God (pp. 215–222)

1. Do you sometimes think that you are not good enough to be able to enter the presence of God? Why/why not?
2. What one aspect of the Spirit's involvement in your life causes you to feel a sense of wonder?
3. What are some of the consequences of the Spirit making you part of God's temple, in which he now resides?
4. Imagine being presented to the Father by the Spirit. What difference does such a thought make to you?
5. Thank the Spirit for his proximity to you and for the potential consequences of such closeness.
6. Write a poem or some prose exploring your special place with God as a result of the Spirit.

Ephesians 4:1–16, 25–32
18. The Holy Spirit and unity (pp. 223–235)

1. Can you think of some good examples of unity being expressed?
2. What are some consequences of disunity?
3. What can you do to reflect the Spirit in his desire to bring unity in your relationships with unbelievers?
4. Provide five different words for 'grieve' that help to clarify how the Spirit feels.
5. How does it make you feel when you know that your sin grieves the Spirit (Eph. 4:30)?
6. Why does he choose to stay with us despite our sinfulness?
7. Tell the Spirit you are sorry for those times you have brought sadness to him. Thank him for loving you.

8. Write the words of Churchill – 'never give in' – on a card and place it somewhere prominent.

'When believers recognise the importance of community, they will achieve higher standards of togetherness and a clearer sense of direction. The Spirit has a similar vision of interdependency and mutual support with reference to believers in the church. He is working to establish such a community and, therefore, so should we' (p. 226).

Ephesians 5:18 – 6:18
19. Be filled with the Spirit (pp. 236–244)

1. How can you tell if someone is filled with the Spirit?
2. When have you felt that you reflected the Spirit in your life?
3. How can you learn to listen to the Spirit when you pray?
4. Follow the example I suggested concerning the targets and the envelope (p. 238).
5. How can you develop a sense of expectation of the Spirit's practical influence in your life?
6. What can you do to ensure that life is not so busy that you miss the voice of the Spirit?

The Bible Speaks Today: Old Testament series

The Message of Genesis 1 – 11
The dawn of creation
David Atkinson

The Message of Genesis 12 – 50
From Abraham to Joseph
Joyce G. Baldwin

The Message of Exodus
The days of our pilgrimage
Alec Motyer

The Message of Leviticus
Free to be holy
Derek Tidball

The Message of Numbers
Journey to the promised land
Raymond Brown

The Message of Deuteronomy
Not by bread alone
Raymond Brown

The Message of Judges
Grace abounding
Michael Wilcock

The Message of Ruth
The wings of refuge
David Atkinson

The Message of Samuel
Personalities, potential, politics and power
Mary Evans

The Message of Chronicles
One church, one faith, one Lord
Michael Wilcock

The Message of Nehemiah
God's servant in a time of change
Raymond Brown

The Message of Job
Suffering and grace
David Atkinson

The Message of Psalms 1 – 72
Songs for the people of God
Michael Wilcock

The Message of Psalms 73 – 150
Songs for the people of God
Michael Wilcock

The Message of Proverbs
Wisdom for life
David Atkinson

The Message of Ecclesiastes
A time to mourn, and a time to dance
Derek Kidner

The Message of the Song of Songs
The lyrics of love
Tom Gledhill

The Message of Isaiah
On eagles' wings
Barry Webb

The Message of Jeremiah
Against wind and tide
Derek Kidner

The Message of Ezekiel
A new heart and a new spirit
Christopher J. H. Wright

The Message of Daniel
The Lord is King
Ronald S. Wallace

The Message of Hosea
Love to the loveless
Derek Kidner

The Message of Joel, Micah and Habakkuk
Listening to the voice of God
David Prior

The Message of Amos
The day of the lion
Alec Motyer

The Message of Jonah
Presence in the storm
Rosemary Nixon

The Message of Zechariah
Your kingdom come
Barry Webb

Other titles in The Bible Speaks Today series

New Testament

The Message of the Sermon on the Mount (Matthew 5 – 7)
Christian counter-culture
John Stott

The Message of Matthew
The kingdom of heaven
Michael Green

The Message of Mark
The mystery of faith
Donald English

The Message of Luke
The Saviour of the world
Michael Wilcock

The Message of John
Here is your King!
Bruce Milne

The Message of Acts
To the ends of the earth
John Stott

The Message of Romans
God's good news for the world
John Stott

The Message of 1 Corinthians
Life in the local church
David Prior

The Message of 2 Corinthians
Power in weakness
Paul Barnett

The Message of Galatians
Only one way
John Stott

The Message of Ephesians
God's new society
John Stott

The Message of Philippians
Jesus our Joy
Alec Motyer

The Message of Colossians and Philemon
Fullness and freedom
Dick Lucas

The Message of Thessalonians
Preparing for the coming King
John Stott

The Message of 1 Timothy and Titus
The life of the local church
John Stott

The Message of 2 Timothy
Guard the gospel
John Stott

The Message of Hebrews
Christ above all
Raymond Brown

The Message of James
The tests of faith
Alec Motyer

The Message of 1 Peter
The way of the cross
Edmund Clowney

The Message of 2 Peter and Jude
The promise of his coming
Dick Lucas and Christopher Green

The Message of John's Letters
Living in the love of God
David Jackman

The Message of Revelation
I saw heaven opened
Michael Wilcock

www.ivpbooks.com

For more details of books published by IVP, visit our website where you will find all the latest information, including:

Book extracts	Downloads
Author interviews	Online bookshop
Reviews	Christian bookshop finder

You can also sign up for our regular email newsletters, which are tailored to your particular interests, and tell others what you think about this book by posting a review.

We publish a wide range of books on various subjects including:

Christian living	Small-group resources
Key reference works	Topical issues
Bible commentary series	Theological studies